Women, marriage and property in wealthy landed families in Ireland, 1750–1850

MANCHESTER
1824

Manchester University Press

Women, marriage and property in wealthy landed families in Ireland, 1750–1850

DEBORAH WILSON

Manchester
University Press

Manchester and New York

distributed in the United States exclusively by Palgrave Macmillan

The right of Deborah Wilson to be identified as the author of this work has been asserted by her in accordance with the Copyright, Designs and Patents Act 1988.

Published by Manchester University Press
Oxford Road, Manchester M13 9NR, UK
and Room 400, 175 Fifth Avenue, New York, NY 10010, USA
www.manchesteruniversitypress.co.uk

Distributed in the United States exclusively by
Palgrave Macmillan, 175 Fifth Avenue, New York,
NY 10010, USA

Distributed in Canada exclusively by
UBC Press, University of British Columbia, 2029 West Mall,
Vancouver, BC, Canada V6T 1Z2

British Library Cataloguing-in-Publication Data
A catalogue record for this book is available from the British Library

Library of Congress Cataloging-in-Publication Data applied for

ISBN   978 07190 7798 2   *hardback*

First published 2009

18 17 16 15 14 13 12 11 10 09   10 9 8 7 6 5 4 3 2 1

Typeset in Sabon
by Servis Filmsetting Ltd, Stockport, Cheshire
Printed in Great Britain
by CPI Antony Rowe, Chippenham, Wiltshire

Contents

Acknowledgements

This book is based on a Ph.D. thesis completed at Queen's University Belfast. I owe a great deal of thanks to my supervisor, Professor Mary O'Dowd, for her continuous guidance, encouragement and patience throughout the long research process. I would also like to thank the staff of the following libraries and archives: the Public Record Office of Northern Ireland, the National Library of Ireland, the National Archives of Ireland, the Public Record Office, London, and Queen's University Library.

I have benefited enormously from the generous comments and valuable feedback of many people. In particular, I wish to acknowledge the following: Dr Heloise Brown, Catriona Crowe, Professor David Dickson, Dr Anthony Malcomson and the staff and students from History seminar groups at Queen's University Belfast and Trinity College Dublin. The late Professor Peter Jupp gave me great encouragement and advice on turning my thesis into this book, for which I will always be grateful.

I wish to express my gratitude to my parents, Linda and Robert Wilson, and my sister, Christine Scott, for their love and faith that I would actually finish my research. Thanks also to my friends, Julie Magill and Heloise Brown, for their constant support, wit and inspiring discussions. The completion of this book coincided with the birth of my wonderful son Joseph, a new home and a new job. Therefore my biggest debt is to my partner, Kieran Sherlock. I am eternally grateful to him for his good humour, help and endurance as I juggled the pleasures and challenges of home and work life while wrestling with an unfinished manuscript.

Tables

Abbreviations

NAI	National Archives of Ireland, Dublin
NLI	National Library of Ireland, Dublin
PRO	Public Record Office, (National Archives), London
PRONI	Public Record Office of Northern Ireland, Belfast

Glossary of legal terminology

Chattels: Items of property other than land.

Chattels real: Leasehold property.

Common law: Body of English law derived from custom and judicial precedent.

Criminal conversation: Often abbreviated to Crim. Con., this was a civil suit against the lover of an adulterous wife, and was an essential prelude to a private divorce bill.

Separation from bed and board: Divorce *a mensa et thoro*, literally 'divorce from bed and board'. A legal separation granted by church courts on the grounds of adultery and/or cruelty.

Dower: A widow's common law entitlement to a life interest in one-third of her deceased husband's landed property.

Entail: Method of settling property over several generations by deed to ensure it passed intact to future heirs.

Equity: A branch of English law that developed to counter perceived imbalances in common law.

Fee simple: Tenure of land not subject to entail.

Fee tail (or fee entail): Tenure of land which is entailed.

Feme covert: Literally 'a woman covered'. A married women whose legal identity was absorbed, or 'covered', by that of her husband.

Feme sole: Literally 'a woman alone'. A woman without a husband who therefore retained her own legal identity.

Heir/heiress: A person legally entitled to ownership of a property upon the death of another.

Jointure: A twice-yearly, or quarterly, payment arranged for a woman at the time of her marriage, to take effect upon the death of her husband. This was a life interest and was either charged upon the husband's estate or paid from investments.

Marriage settlement: Private deed drawn up by solicitors at the time of marriage to arrange provision for the wife and children of the marriage.

Pin money: An amount of money arranged for the personal use of a woman during her marriage. This was a life interest and was not payable in arrears.

Separate estate: Either land or investments held in trust for a married woman, for her own use during marriage, not subject to the control of her husband.

Statute law: Legal rules and principles established by statute.

Strict settlement: Type of marriage settlement that arranged the transmission of land to future generations and arranged provision for the wife and children of a marriage.

Trustee: A person holding property on behalf of another as specified in a deed of settlement.

Introduction

Aims and sources

As Marylynn Salmon has noted, women's ownership and management of property is 'an important baseline for learning how men and women share power in the family'.[1] Until the 1990s, women featured in the historiography of the landed class in Ireland either as bearers of assets to advantageous matches or as potential drains on family estates as a result of long widowhoods.[2] When the lives of women from this class have been examined by biographers, these tend to be uncritical narratives of exceptional women from prominent families. The interests of these women have been regarded as inseparable from the interests of their family, and there is little consideration of the impact of gender on women's lives in this class.[3] Two exceptions examine the position of women in more detail: Stella Tillyard's biography of the Lennox sisters, which explores women's lives in the Fitzgerald and Conolly families, and Sean Connolly's consideration of the life of eighteenth-century single women in his study of the life of Letitia Bushe.[4] Furthermore, by 2008 there has not been any comparative work on the lives of well-known women from landed families, or a consideration of how women's experience of property and family in this section of society may have differed. This book seeks to contribute to existing historiography by looking beyond the dynastic and economic concerns that dominate the current history of the Irish elite.

This book explores the legal, familial and social factors that influenced women in Ireland in their experience of property in the period 1750–1850. The evidence is drawn from the personal and legal documents of twenty landed families, an approach which facilitated legitimate comparisons and made possible the use of a wider range of sources than a study that focused exclusively on landed records. Each family received an annual rental of at least £10,000 at some stage in this period. To place this figure in perspective, the equivalent purchasing power of £10,000 in 1850 was £720,000 in 1998.[5] These families were therefore amongst the wealthiest in Ireland, which restricted the field of research to those who were more likely to have shared financial backgrounds, rather than including the wider landed class, which contained greater variations in wealth and lifestyle. The wealthy landed class were more likely to have shared financial backgrounds and to have used similar methods to provide for family members. It was also necessary to choose a date range that would make possible a survey of the practices employed by this class in making provision for women. The date range 1750–1850 was selected as, by the beginning of this period, methods of settling estates and of arranging pin money and jointure for women were in place in the wealthy landed class; after 1850, the impact of the Great Famine on landed estates changed the economic context within which landed families existed.

The limited sample facilitated a wide use of sources, making it possible to compare the legal and theoretical position of women and property in different families with their actual experience. In common with many of their class, these families left vast archives of sources, composed of personal letters, estate correspondence and diaries as well as the legal documentation of a large landed estate: marriage settlements, last wills and testaments, mortgage bonds and account books. Consultation of such sources is essential as it reveals the types of property women had access to and what they had the power to bequeath, as well as offering some insight into the impact of these property arrangements in the daily lives of women.

Because of the primacy of land as a source of income and status in the period 1750–1850, it is impossible to consider the experience of women and property in landed families without considering the income from landed property. This is particularly important for the purpose of comparing amounts of jointure received in comparison with the one-third life interest in their husband's property which women would have been entitled to had they been able to claim dower. Late nineteenth-century landed estate rentals compiled by John Bateman, for example, are available in published form.[6] However, rental in the period before 1850 raises problems for the historian as it was not uniform practice for landowners to record gross rental in this period, at least not in a form that has survived in family papers.

When gross rental is recorded, a further problem of ascertaining net rental, the actual income of landowners, arises. It has been argued by David Large that the period 1790–1815 was one of 'greatest affluence' for Irish landowners owing to rising rents, while the period after 1815, following the Napoleonic wars, was one of comparative hardship. Rent rises were small and were 'much more difficult to get in than they had been in the previous twenty-five years'.[7] Furthermore, as Anthony

Malcomson notes, 'the financial situations of great landed families were constantly shifting, in the light of births and deaths, marriages and mortgages, inheritances and bequests'.[8] Therefore, there could be a significant difference between the gross rental from a landed estate and the actual income of a landowner. If we also consider changing rent levels throughout this period and contemporary disparities between acreage values on different estates, establishing correct figures for rental income appears to be impossible.[9]

For the purpose of this study, I have estimated rental based on a variety of sources when gross rental figures are not available in family and estate papers. One method, used by A. T. Harrison as a means to estimate the rentals of the estates of the Marquess of Downshire, the Marquess of Londonderry and Lord Dufferin, was to take figures published by Bateman and reduce the late nineteenth-century figures by one-third, in order to estimate early nineteenth-century rental.[10] Therefore, although the figures used are in some cases estimates, in the absence of reliable figures they provide an impression of family rental and facilitate comparative study of provision for women from the families in this study.

The Irish landed class, 1750–1850

By the beginning of the eighteenth century the majority of wealthy landowners in Ireland were English or Scottish settlers, their land acquired during plantations or as royal grants for services to the English Crown. These families, an Anglo-Irish protestant elite, comprised a small proportion of the population which owned a vast proportion of land in Ireland. A survey of the Irish peerage, published in 1799, listed thirty of the wealthiest landowners in Ireland, all of whom took at least £14,000 from their estates in rental income.[11] Throughout this period the greatest number of large estates were in Ulster: by 1876 these numbered nineteen out of the forty-one landed estates in the whole of Ireland that were valued at £20,000 or more.[12] It is therefore fitting that out of the twenty families surveyed here, the estates and family houses of fourteen families were located in the nine Ulster counties. The remaining six families were dispersed throughout counties Dublin, Cork, Wicklow, Kerry and Kildare.[13]

These families settled in Ireland at different times. Of the fourteen Ulster families, nine acquired land in the seventeenth century. These were mainly acquisitions derived from the grants of Charles II or James I, or plantation grants. The two exceptions were the Donegalls, whose land was based on the dealings of the family adventurer Chichester, and the Ernes, who purchased land later in the seventeenth century. Three families, the Wards, Lords Bangor, the Alexanders, Lords Caledon, and the Blackwood family, Lords Dufferin, all amassed sufficient wealth through marriage and other dealings to purchase their estates after settling in Ireland in the eighteenth century. The wealth of the Caledons was based on the first Lord Caledon's fortune, made by his work for the East India Company. The connections of the remaining two Ulster families, the Meades, Earls of Clanwilliam, and the Hill family, Marquesses of Downshire, predated the seventeenth century. The Meades were of Gaelic descent and can be traced to fourteenth-century Cork. The family's estates were in County Tipperary and County Down. The Hill family arrived in Ireland some time in the sixteenth century and acquired land through grants and purchases.

The six families located in the counties south of Ulster included the Fitzgeralds, Dukes of Leinster, the oldest Irish family in this study, whose Irish connection dates from the Anglo-Norman settlements in the twelfth and thirteen centuries. The Wingfield family, Viscounts Powerscourt, derived their land in the sixteenth century as payment for acting as marshals. The Boyle family, Earls Shannon, received their estates as grants from Charles II in the seventeenth century and the Westenras, Lords Rossmore, acquired their estate through marriage in the eighteenth century. Out of the remaining two families, the Conollys of Castletown in County Kildare were the only non-peerage family. They arrived in Ireland at least as early as the seventeenth century and their vast estates were based on purchases made by William Speaker Conolly in the late seventeenth century. The Browne family, Earls Kenmare, of County Kerry are the only Catholic family in this study. They arrived in Ireland in the sixteenth century and were an active Jacobite family. Their title was, in a limited way, recognised by the eighteenth-century Irish parliament. With two exceptions, the Conollys and the Earls of Kenmare, all the families in this study were protestant peers. All the remaining peerages were Irish, except for the Duke of Abercorn, who held a Scottish title.

As the wealthiest section of society, these families were also the most powerful. In 1852, 68 per cent of Ireland's 104 MPs were from landed families, and in all elections up to 1880 landlord influence played an important role in returning candidates.[14] In County Down, Arthur Hill, the second Marquess of Downshire, has been regarded as 'the most powerful political magnate in late eighteenth-century Ireland' as well as one of the wealthiest men in Ireland.[15] Politics in County Down was dominated by the Hill family, and the only serious opposition to this power came from another wealthy landed family, their neighbours, the Stewart family, Lords Londonderry.[16] Yet there were great differences between families. In County Down, the wealth and power of the Hills and

Stewarts was on a greater scale than that of their neighbours. Although the Blackwoods, Lords Dufferin, were the sixth richest family in County Down, their wealth was significantly less than that of the Hills and Stewarts.[17] On the marriage of Mary Sandys to Arthur Hill in 1786 the Downshire rental was £17,104.[18] In 1818, on the marriage of Frances Anne Vane-Tempest to Charles Stewart, the future Marquess of Londonderry, the Londonderry estate was £31,500.[19] The rental of the Dufferin estate by 1800 has been estimated at £10,000, and by the 1840s, during the minority of the fifth Lord Dufferin, this had risen to an annual rental of £18,000.[20]

The Irish wealthy landed class shared a similar lifestyle with their English contemporaries, and this set them apart from other Irish landed families as a distinct social group. Ireland was more expensive to live in than England.[21] Eight out of the twenty families held additional land in England, and all would have lived at least part of the year in England. Many made marriage alliances in England, sent their sons to English schools and universities and participated in the round of social engagements that was the 'Season', residing for part of the year in Dublin and increasingly, after the Union, in London. They travelled abroad, wore the latest fashions and read the latest books. They bestowed patronage on their estates and entertained the local gentry when at home.[22] The Londonderrys are the one example here of a family with connections to industry: they had a lucrative mining interest in County Durham, England. Another factor that led to residence in England was the reality of pursuing a career in British politics. It has been argued that the British policy of excluding Irishmen from top jobs meant that 'they had no alternative but to quit Ireland if they were to rise in the world'. The Lord Lieutenancy, for example, was held only five times in the eighteenth century by an Irish landlord, each of whom was an absentee landlord with good English connections.[23]

Although the connection with English life was a crucial element of Irish elite culture, there were also important differences between Ireland and England. The Irish peerage, for instance, which by 1810 numbered 129 Irish peers, was distinct from the United Kingdom and Scottish peerages. It has been noted by one historian that 'common estimation . . . set Irish peers on a lower rung of the social ladder than English peers'.[24] An Irish peer could not sit in the British House of Lords without an additional English, Scottish, United Kingdom or Great Britain peerage, a distinction that was regarded as 'degrading' by some commentators.[25] To acquire an English peerage, even at a lower level, was a mark of social advancement, and Irish peers have been characterised as having feelings of provincial inferiority.

This complex group of people lived a lavish lifestyle that was not sustainable and the period 1750–1850 was one of increasing indebtedness for Irish landed families. There were many reasons for this. The wealth of Irish landowners derived almost exclusively from rents. Unlike their English contemporaries, they had little opportunity in the period covered here to supplement rental income with industry or mining.[26] The sole exception was the Londonderrys, who derived a significant proportion of their wealth from the Durham coalfields brought to her marriage by Frances Anne Vane-Tempest Stewart, Lady Londonderry. The Irish practice of leasing land for lives renewable has also been cited as one reason for the lack of investment and control exercised by landlords over their estates.[27] However, while some landlords did not invest in their estates, it has been noted that after 1830 a small number of landlords took increasing interest in estate improvements. Lord Dufferin, for example, was one of a number of landowners awarded a medal by the Royal Agricultural Society in Dublin for his work in encouraging his tenants to drain their land.[28] Such interest in estate improvement was due to the decline in leasing and the desire of landlords to reverse the trend towards subdivision on their estates. It also was influenced by developments on English estates, where drainage was regarded as an investment which would benefit the landowner.[29] Existing problems on Irish estates peaked in the 1840s when the Great Famine devastated parts of Ireland and led to a widespread reorganisation of landed estates, as landlords sold off land through the encumbered estates courts to pay debts. However, the long-term the impact of the Encumbered Estates Acts was limited: by 1876, 20 per cent of Ireland was owned by landlords with estates ranging from 2,000 to 5,000 acres, while over 50 per cent was owned by less than 1,000 landlords.[30]

Women in the wealthy Irish landed class

The comparison of legal theory and family settlements with the actual experience of women is an approach favoured in histories of women and property in England published in the 1990s. In her study of the ideology that informed the legal development of married women's separate property in England, Susan Staves uses equity cases concerning women's property issues alongside printed legal treatises. Staves's aim is to compare the theoretical position of women with what actually occurred in the Court of Chancery in practice.[31] A similar concern with theory and practice is central to Amy Erickson's study of women and property in early modern England. Erickson's main sources are probate records and marriage settlements as well as printed legal treatises.[32]

The legal position of women and property in eighteenth- and nineteenth-century Ireland was the same as that of their English contemporaries: it was based on the English common law doctrine of coverture, by which a woman lost her legal identity and the right to own property upon marriage. However, although English common law was established in Ireland by the sixteenth century, Irish statute law on marriage and property developed along different lines. One of the problems of coverture, from the perspective of the Irish political elite, was the impact it had on the protection of protestant property interests. This is illustrated by the problem of the abduction of heiresses in Ireland.[33] In the history of abduction, women feature as victims of their gender and legal status. The reputations, and sometimes the lives, of propertied women were endangered by the opportunism of socially and economically marginalised lower gentry, who regarded abduction, although illegal and often violent, as 'strategies through which property could be gained'.[34] Clandestine marriages presented a similar problem for the Irish elite, and, in a bid to protect their property interests, this led the Irish parliament to introduce statutory measures to intervene in the previously private act of marriage. This unprecedented intervention in the marriage contract, which declared some marriages legally invalid, is explored in chapter 1 within the context of the development of statute law on marriage in the seventeenth century in Ireland. Statute law also intervened in the structure of the family, increasing the power of fathers over the marriage choices of their children. There were therefore two concurrent ideologies at work, as the authority of a father over his children was strengthened, while at the same time the patriarchal family structure could be overturned in the case of catholic–protestant intermarriage in order to protect protestant property interests.[35]

Women's status in law was, however, only one facet of their experience of property. An important feature of recent histories of women and property is the acknowledgement that there may be 'vast differences between the official rules under which women are supposed to live and the actual conditions of their lives.'[36] English law was made up of four separate systems, the most prominent being common law and equity. While common law enshrined the dependence of a married woman on her husband, equity enabled the same woman to have access to separate property during her marriage, for her own use and free from the control of her husband. Women from wealthy families were therefore spared some of the financial disadvantages inherent in the subordinate position accorded to women by law. This situation has led to an assumption among some historians that rank and wealth were the defining features of upper-class women's experience of property, and that upper-class

women were defined by their class, rather than by their gender.[37] There
has been an assumption that women from this class 'had always been
protected by elaborate family and marriage settlements'.[38] As one historian has noted, '[e]ven if the dominant discourses of femininity were
belittling, the reverence for rank, wealth and position remained over-
whelming'.[39]

Similar assumptions are evident in existing studies that include women
in the Irish elite, where there has been a predominant focus on wealthy
heiresses.[40] However, the experience of women in these families was
more complex.[41] Not all women who married into landed families were
heiresses, and not all had access to large incomes settled as separate
estate. Also, the assumption that all women from wealthy families were
well provided for by separate property arrangements, and therefore
escaped the gender constraints experienced by their lower-class contemporaries, is problematic and has been questioned by other historians. For
example, the ideological basis for the development of family settlements
has been investigated in recent histories of women and property in
England, and it has been concluded that while upper-class women were
often economically independent, their actual place in the family property
hierarchy diminished as common law right to dower was replaced by
jointure.[42] In order to explore the relationship of women to the family
estate, chapter 2 outlines provisions made for women in marriage settlements and last wills and testaments. In Ireland, as in England, the most
important aspect of family property arrangements in this period was
inheritance, the procedure by which both landed and moveable property
is transmitted between generations.[43] Irish elite women, like their English
contemporaries, were placed firmly within the family, and the basis of
their experience of property was determined by the nature of provision
made in family settlements.

Having established the boundaries within which women's experience
of property operated, the remaining chapters consider the property experience of women in relation to the family estate, how women related to
the concept of the family interest and in what contexts their interests differed. The third chapter will consider instances, in this class, when the
traditional structure of the family was suspended, such as when the heir
to the estate was a minor, or insane. The consequent reorganisation of
family affairs resulted in a broader scope for the involvement of women
in financial business.

The guardianship of a minor or of a mentally incapacitated family
member was an acceptable role available to women. If the ward was heir
to the family estate this was also a potentially powerful role. The remit
of guardianship depended on arrangements made within the family. After

the death of Price Blackwood, Lord Dufferin, in 1841, his widow, Helen, Lady Dufferin, was appointed only as guardian of the person of the only child of the marriage, Frederick Blackwood, the future fifth Lord Dufferin, while other family members managed the Dufferin estate. However, Mary Hill, Marchioness of Downshire, was guardian of her eldest son's persons and estates after her husband's death, as also was Jane Brownlow, Lady Lurgan, from Brownlow House, County Armagh.

Another type of guardianship which had the potential to elevate the importance of informal property relations began when the head of a family was declared legally insane. This occurred in the Ward family, Lords Bangor, of Castle Ward, County Down. When the second Lord Bangor was declared legally insane in 1781, years of bitter feuding within the family followed, and Arabella Ward, widow of Lord Bangor's younger brother, Edward, entered into disputes with Lord Bangor's brother, Robert, and sister, Ann Catherine, over her role as committee of the estate and person of Lord Bangor.

Chapters 4 to 6 consider the roles taken by single, married and widowed women. The family property relations illustrated in these chapters are indicative of the types of formal and informal power available to elite women. Individual women feature as landowners, prominent in estate management and local politics, either in their own right or as deputies for under-age sons. The income that resulted from the rent of a landed property was not the only benefit of landownership in this period. The social and economic power that resulted from the interconnectedness of the franchise with property benefited disenfranchised landed women as well as men. In addition, political power and patronage were to a large degree facilitated by family connections.[44]

The interconnectedness of family and politics in this period provided elite women with opportunities to exert their social and family influence for political ends. Elite women acted as political hostesses, and balls, dinners and private correspondence could provide useful political gossip, as well as opportunities to lobby for political patronage and promote their family's interests.[45] Some women, thanks to their personal wealth and influence within the family, exercised significant power in their locality. In the Ulster Museum in Belfast there are two portraits on display of Theodosia Meade, Countess of Clanwilliam, painted in 1765, the year of her marriage, by Joshua Reynolds and Thomas Gainsborough. As two portraits by such eminent society painters suggest, the Countess of Clanwilliam occupied an elite social and economic position in County Down society. She was the daughter and heiress of Robert Hawkins-Magill and his wife, Lady Anne Bligh. In 1765 she married John Meade of Gill Hall, County Down, the future Earl of Clanwillian and heir to estates in counties Tipperary and Down. The Countess's economic position, and therefore her social and political position in County Down, was assured by a settlement made during her marriage by which she arranged, despite her coverture, for the property she had brought to her marriage as portion to be transferred into her ownership.[46]

Another exceptionally wealthy woman was Mary Hill, Marchioness of Downshire, the only daughter and heiress of Martin Sandys and Mary Blundell. As the heiress of her mother, her father and her uncle, Edwin Sandys, Baron Oombersley, Mary Sandys brought a large portion to her marriage and also owned a substantial landed estate in England as separate property. In 1786 she married Arthur Hill, Lord Fairford, the future second Marquess of Downshire. The Downshire estates included land in counties Down and Antrim, as well as land outside Ulster in counties Kildare and Wicklow. On her husband's death in 1801, the Marchioness of Downshire managed the Downshire estates, and she played a prominent role in County Down politics during the minority of her eldest son, Arthur Blundell Sandys Hill, the third Marquess of Downshire.

Women in the MacDonnell family, Lords Antrim, were similarly wealthy and were also prominent in local politics. The Antrim estate was located in counties Antrim and Londonderry. Anne Katherine MacDonnell, Countess of Antrim, was the eldest surviving daughter of Randall MacDonnell, Marquess of Antrim, and inherited a portion of the Antrim estate, and title, on her father's death in 1791. Her sister, Charlotte Kerr, inherited the title Countess of Antrim, as well as an additional portion of the Antrim estate, on Anne Katherine's death. Frances Anne was the only daughter, and heiress, of Henry Vane-Tempest and Anne Katherine. In 1819 Frances Anne married Charles Stewart, Lord Stewart and the future third Marquess of Londonderry, as his second wife. In addition to the valuable mines in County Durham that Lady Londonderry brought to her marriage, she owned an estate in County Antrim. She was prominent in the management of her estate as well as local politics and was also regarded as a leading Tory hostess in London.[47]

In 1747, aged fifteen, Emily Lennox, the third daughter of Charles, second Duke of Richmond, and his wife Sarah, married James Fitzgerald, twentieth Earl of Kildare, and moved to live in Ireland at Carton House, County Kildare, and Leinster House in Dublin. After her husband's death in 1774, Emily scandalised Irish society, and the Fitzgerald family, when she married William Ogilvie, the tutor of her children. In 1758, Emily's sister Louisa Lennox married Thomas Conolly and moved to Ireland to live at the Castletown estate in County Kildare. Conolly was the nephew of Speaker Conolly and heir to vast estates that included land in counties Kildare, Donegal and Londonderry. The Duchess of Leinster and Louisa Conolly managed the households of two of the wealthiest and most powerful families in Ireland at this time, and their social influence was such that they continually received petitions requesting patronage and political intervention in parliamentary matters.[48]

Despite the undoubted wealth and influence of some women in the landed class in this period, their experience was diverse, and this is apparent within families as well as between families. One example is the Blackwoods, Lords Dufferin, from Clandeboye, County Down. Dorcas Stevenson Blackwood, Baroness Dufferin and Clandeboye, was the eldest daughter and the heiress of James Stevenson of County Down. In 1751 she married John Blackwood. In 1800 Dorcas was created Baroness Dufferin and Clandeboye and was succeeded by her eldest son, James Stevenson Blackwood, Lord Dufferin. In 1801 James, the future Lord Dufferin, married Anna Foster, the daughter of Margaretta, Viscountess Ferrard, and John Foster, Baron Oriel of Ferrard. James was succeeded by his brother Hans Blackwood, whose eldest son, Price Blackwood, became the fourth Lord Dufferin in 1839. In 1825 Price Blackwood married Helen Sheridan, the daughter of Thomas Sheridan and his wife Caroline Henrietta Callendar. Helen was also the granddaughter of Richard Brinsley Sheridan, playwright and politician, and the sister of Caroline Norton and Georgiana Seymour, Duchess of Somerset.

The title conferred upon Dorcas, Baroness Dufferin and Clandeboye, which then passed to her eldest son, indicates her powerful status within the Blackwood family. She was a very wealthy widow, retaining a life interest in her father's estate that had been brought as portion, after her husband's death. Helen, Lady Dufferin, was in a much less powerful position within the family, as she had no income settled as separate estate, and appears not to have brought a portion to her marriage. Of the three Blackwood women, Helen is the most well-known figure in local history. She was the author of songs such as 'The Irish emigrant', and Helen's Bay and Helen's Tower, both in County Down, and the latter of which was built during famine relief works on the Clandeboye estate in 1847, were named after her.[49] However, less powerful women in this class also had access to the informal power inherent in family connections and the nature of appointments in institutions such as the navy that made knowing the right people an advantage. Helen, Lady Dufferin, who in other ways was one of the least powerful women in this study, was instrumental in furthering the Blackwood family interests by promoting the careers of her son and other Blackwood men through her uncle Sir James Graham, First Lord of the Admiralty.

Informal roles available to women included those in advice and loan networks, household and family financial management and charitable benevolence, and these applied to single, married and widowed women. Lending and borrowing between families was an acceptable practice at least from the seventeenth century, and there was a good market for moneylenders in this period in Ireland as indebtedness was part of life for Irish landowners. One of the most dramatic examples was the second Marquess of Donegall, who inherited about a quarter of a million acres of land in Ireland, becoming, as one account of his life describes him, 'the greatest landowner of his day', and who in 1791, before he inherited the family estate, reportedly had debts of more than £30,000.[50] There were, however, many more mundane examples. The payment of debts was an important part of estate financial management, and many marriage settlements made arrangements for this. The estate finances of the relatively modest Dufferin estate, for example, were so worrying that by 1825 the Blackwood family, who were not known for their flamboyance, had established a sinking fund to pay for debts and further expenditure, such as jointures of future wives. When Price Blackwood informed his father that he was to marry the portionless Helen Sheridan, his father protested that he could never approve such a match, as it was Price's duty to gain a portion with a wife, in order to help pay family debts.[51]

The arrangement of loans between members of the same class also occurred because, as has been noted by David Large, the principal business of the Irish banking system in the eighteenth century was exchange dealings, and the only exception to this was the La Touche bankers, who offered rent remittances to absentee landlords.[52] However, the trend was towards private loan arrangements. Furthermore, it was a normal part of family life for people in this class to use the services of solicitors. Marriages, last wills and testaments and estate conveyances were all managed by the family solicitor. Access to legal bonds and familiarity with the language of conveyance were part of aristocratic family life. Aristocratic women, as well as men, were involved in generating income, either from estate rental, if they were landowners, from rental of property or from investments in stocks. The more formal side of moneylending, which included lending money to friends and family via mortgage, charging interest and therefore making a profit, was an extension of these other activities. It was simply a good investment.

Single, married and widowed women all loaned money. There are, for example, several loan bonds among the papers of Lady Elizabeth Alexander, a wealthy single woman who was the daughter of James

Alexander, first Earl of Caledon, from County Tyrone. Married women who owned landed property in their own right, such as the Countesses of Antrim and Frances Anne Lady Londonderry, for example, borrowed money via bonds secured by mortgage on their estates. In fact, the widespread use of private settlements in this period rendered the lending of money by all women, whether single, married or widowed, unremarkable. Furthermore, married women borrowed money as a way to help other family members. For instance, in order to raise money to finance the entry of one of her younger sons into the navy, Arabella Ward, mother of the third Lord Bangor, sold some jewellery and borrowed some money or, as she expressed it, laid herself 'under obligation to two friends'.[53] However, the most extensive list of loans among the women surveyed were those due to a widow: Jane Creighton, Lady Erne, in 1800. These bonds are a lone example in the Erne papers of Lady Erne's income from moneylending. The existence of such a substantial loan network indicates that this form of financial business took place beyond the informal boundaries of family loan networks, as all of the recipients noted were from outside Lady Erne's immediate family. Born Jane King, she was the daughter of John and Rebecca King, of Charlestown, County Roscommon. She married firstly Arthur Acheson and secondly, in 1768, Abraham Creighton, Baron Erne of Crom Castle, in 1762, as his second wife. The Erne estate was in counties Fermanagh, Donegal, Mayo and Sligo and the family seat was Crom Castle, County Fermanagh. Between 1772 and 1799 Lady Erne conducted an extensive loan network, and her personal accounts indicate the extent of her charitable contributions to the poor on her estate and to public charitable institutions, as well as providing valuable information on her attitudes towards charity.

Charitable work was clearly another acceptable financial outlet for women. From the mid-eighteenth century to the mid-nineteenth century this was essentially conservative and paternalistic in nature, being confined to alleviating the circumstances of the poor rather than challenging the structure of society. In addition, the voluntaristic ethos that informed philanthropy by the end of the eighteenth century focused on the promotion of self-help and self improvement among the poor.[54] Such activities connected ideas of maternal benevolence with the perception that women had a natural propensity for the provision of moral and spiritual guidance.[55]

Poor-relief in Ireland was locally based until the 1840s, was commonly administered by local landowners on a voluntary basis and was characterised by ideals of self-help and self-improvement.[56] Government intervention was limited to support for local relief initiatives.[57] The problem of the indigent poor was dealt with by establishment of houses of industry, while the sick poor were dealt with by the establishment of dispensaries, county infirmaries and fever hospitals.[58] Private philanthropy offered a more socially acceptable outlet for women than institutional charity, and attracted women from all social backgrounds and from rural as well as urban areas.[59] Women were involved in a wide-ranging number of charitable causes, such as the establishment and maintenance of hospitals, schools or refuges for the care, education and moral guidance of the poor.[60] Upper-class women provided financial support through subscriptions and raised money through bazaars and fund-raising events. The role of women in the building and maintaining of schools was an important part of female charitable behaviour in this period. Elizabeth La Touche, wife of Peter La Touche, for example, was 'the great promoter of schools'.[61] In County Tyrone, in the early nineteenth century, Lady Mountjoy and Miss Gardner established a school for twenty-four girls. Sewing and spinning were taught, and 'moral duties' were 'strictly attended to'.[62] Such benevolence was not confined to women. Men also founded schools: Lord Mountjoy founded a night school 'for the purpose of instructing the labouring boys of the demesne, as planters' in 1783.[63] Although employment of such boys was an aim, 'the great object is, the preventing of idleness, which is always best accomplished by filling up the scraps of time.'[64] The foundation of the Magdalen Asylum by Lady Arabella Denny in 1765 was one of the earliest examples of women who had access to substantial financial resources reaching beyond fund-raising to establishing new institutions. However, in this period, despite the growth and development of institutional charities founded and run by women, the largest outlet for female charitable behaviour appears to have been private donations to the poor.[65] The six daughters of Henry Boyle, third Earl of Shannon, and Sarah Hyde, the 'ladies Boyle' from County Cork and Lady Elizabeth Alexander are examples of wealthy single women who directed some of their wealth towards charitable causes.

The primary concern of this book is to portray the diverse experience a group of women in the wealthy landed class had of property, and the complexity of familial power relations in this period. Within the small sample of families surveyed here there were significant differences in the wealth of women, their power within the family and the type of influence they exercised. Women's experience of property was therefore more complex than the arrangements laid out in family settlements suggest, and must be regarded within the multiple contexts of the law, family relationships and contemporary attitudes towards women and property. This survey therefore begins with an overview of women and the law in Ireland from the seventeenth century.

Notes

1 Marylynn Salmon, *Women and the law of property in Early America* (Chapel Hill and London: University of North Carolina Press, 1986), p. xii.

2 A. P. W. Malcomson, *The pursuit of the heiress: aristocratic marriage in Ireland 1740–1840* (Belfast: Ulster Historical Foundation, 2006); David Large, 'The wealth of the greater Irish landowners, 1750–1815', *Irish Historical Studies*, 15 (1966–67), pp. 21–47.

3 See, for example, Brian Fitzgerald, *Lady Louisa Conolly, 1743–1821: an Anglo-Irish biography* (London: Staples Press, 1950); Brian Fitzgerald, *Emily Duchess of Leinster 1731–1814: a study of her life and times* (London: Staples Press, 1949); Edith Stewart, Marchioness of Londonderry, *Frances Anne: the life and times of Frances Anne Marchioness of Londonderry and her husband Charles, third Marquess of Londonderry* (London: Macmillan, 1958); Frederick Blackwood, Marquess of Dufferin and Ava (ed.), *Songs, poems and verses by Helen, Lady Dufferin (Countess of Gifford)* (London: J. Murray, 1894); C. J. Hamilton, *Notable Irishwomen* (Dublin: Bryers and Company, 1904); Harold Nicholson, *Helen's tower* (London: Constable and Company, 1937).

4 Stella Tillyard, *Aristocrats: Caroline, Emily, Louisa and Sarah Lennox, 1740–1832* (London: Vintage, 1995); Sean Connolly, 'A woman's life in eighteenth-century Ireland: the case of Letitia Bushe', *Historical Journal*, 43:2 (2000), pp. 433–51.

5 Robert Twigger, 'Inflation: the value of the pound, 1750–1998', House of Commons Library Research Paper 99/20, 23 February 1999, p. 10; online at www.parliament.uk/commons/lib/research/rp99/rp99–020.pdf (accessed 12 November 2007).

6 John Bateman, *The great landowners of Great Britain and Ireland* (Leicester: Leicester University Press, 1971).

7 Large, 'The wealth of the greater Irish landowners', pp. 21, 25.

8 Malcomson, *The pursuit of the heiress*, p. 3.

9 Peter Roebuck, 'Rent movement, proprietorial incomes and agricultural development, 1730–1830' in Peter Roebuck (ed.), *Plantation to partition: essays in Ulster history in honour of J. L. McCracken* (Belfast: Blackstaff Press, 1981), pp. 82–101; W. H. Crawford, 'Landlord–tenant relations in Ulster, 1609–1820', *Irish Economic and Social History*, 2 (1975), pp. 5–21.

10 A. T. Harrison, 'The first Marquis of Dufferin and Ava: whig, Ulster landlord and imperial statesman' (D.Phil. thesis, University of Ulster, 1983), pp. 10, 656.

11 Vickery Gibb (ed.), The complete peerage of England, Scotland and Ireland, Great Britain and the United Kingdom (London: St Catherine's Press, 1916), iv, p. 575.

12 T. Jones Hughes, 'Historical geography of Ireland from c. 1700' in G. L. H. Davies (ed.), *Irish geography* (Dublin: Geographical Society of Ireland, 1984), p. 157.

13 See appendix A for biographical information about the families surveyed here.

14 W. E. Vaughan, *Landlords and tenants in Ireland, 1848–1904* (Dublin: Economic and Social History Society of Ireland, 1984), p. 6.

15 A. P. W. Malcomson, 'The gentle Leviathan: Arthur Hill, second Marquess of Downshire, 1753–1801' in Roebuck (ed.), *Plantation to partition*, p. 102.

16 Peter Jupp, 'County Down elections 1783–1831', *Irish Historical Studies*, 18 (1972–73), p. 181.

17 L. Proudfoot, 'Landownership and improvement c. 1700–1845' in L. Proudfoot (ed.), *Down: history and society: interdisciplinary essays on the history of an Irish county* (Dublin: Geography Publications, 1997), p. 208.

18 Public Record Office of Northern Ireland (hereafter PRONI), Downshire papers, D/671/D14/1/3a, marriage settlement of Arthur Hill, Viscount Fairford, and Mary Sandys, 20 June 1786.

19 PRONI, Londonderry Estate Office papers, D/654/G1/3, copies of affadavit in the Chancery case concerning the marriage of Frances Anne Vane to Charles Stewart, Lord Stewart, 1818; Malcomson, The *pursuit of the heiress*, p. 30.

20 Harrison, 'The first Marquis of Dufferin and Ava' p. 10; PRONI, Dufferin and Ava papers, D/1071/A/B6/3, rent schedules for the minority of Frederick Blackwood, 1841–47.

21 A. P. W. Malcomson, 'Absenteeism in eighteenth century Ireland', *Irish Economic and Social History*, 1 (1974), p. 17.

22 *Ibid.*, p. 16.

23 *Ibid.*

24 Large, 'The wealth of the greater Irish landowners', p. 41.

25 Henry Jephson, 'Irish statute reform', *Journal of the Statistical and Social Inquiry Society of Ireland*, 25 (July 1879), p. 377.

26 W. A. Maguire, *The Downshire estates in Ireland 1801–1845: the management of Irish landed estates in the nineteenth century* (Oxford: Clarendon Press, 1972), p. 28.

27 *Ibid.*, p. 110.

28 *Ibid.*, p. 72.

29 *Ibid.*, p. 73.

30 W. E. Vaughan, *Landlords and tenants in Ireland 1848–1904*, p. 5.

31 Susan Staves, *Married women's separate property in England, 1660–1833* (London and Cambridge, Massachusetts: Harvard University Press, 1990), pp. 1–26.

32 Amy Louise Erickson, *Women and property in early modern England*, (London: Routledge, 1993) pp. 3–45.

33 James Kelly, 'The abduction of women of fortune in eighteenth-century Ireland', *Eighteenth-century Ireland*, 9 (1994), pp. 7–43; Toby Barnard, *The abduction of a Limerick heiress: social and political relations in mid-eighteenth century Ireland* (Dublin: Irish Academic Press, 1998).

34 Barnard, *The abduction of a Limerick heiress*, p. 10.
35 Mary O'Dowd, 'Women and the law in early modern Ireland' in Christine Meek (ed.), *Women in renaissance and early modern Ireland* (Dublin: Four Courts Press, 2000), pp. 95–108.
36 Staves, *Married women's separate property*, p. 25. This view is also expressed in: Salmon, *Women and the law of property in Early America*; Eileen Spring, *Law, land and family: aristocratic inheritance in England, 1300–1800* (London: Chapel Hill, 1993); Erickson, *Women and property in early modern England*; Lori Chambers, *Married women and property law in Victorian Ontario* (London and Toronto: University of Toronto Press, 1996).
37 K. D. Reynolds, *Aristocratic women and political society in Victorian Britain* (Oxford: Clarendon Press, 1998).
38 A. P. W. Malcomson, 'A woman scorned? Theodosia, Countess of Clanwilliam (1743–1817)', *Familia*, 15 (1999), p. 3.
39 Amanda Vickery, *The gentleman's daughter: women's lives in Georgian England* (London and New Haven: Yale University Press, 1998), pp. 292–3.
40 Malcomson, *The pursuit of the heiress*; Large, 'The wealth of the greater Irish landowners'.
41 See appendix B for brief biographical information about the women surveyed here.
42 Staves, *Married women's separate property*; Spring, *Law, land and family*.
43 Jack Goody, 'Inheritance, property and women: some comparative considerations' in Jack Goody et al (eds), *Family and inheritance: rural society in Western Europe, 1200–1800* (Cambridge: Cambridge University Press 1973), p. 10.
44 A. R. Buck, 'Property, aristocracy and the reform of the land law in early nineteenth century England', *Journal of Legal History*, 16:1 (1995), p. 67.
45 Mary O'Dowd, *A history of women in Ireland 1500–1800* (Harlow: Longman, 2005), pp. 43–9.
46 PRONI, Clanwilliam/Meade papers, D/3044/D/1/20, fragment of a declaration by Theodosia Hawkins-Magill, Countess of Clanwilliam, undated; Malcomson, 'A woman scorned?', p. 3.
47 Stewart, *Frances Anne*; Jupp, 'County Down elections'.
48 Fitzgerald, *Lady Louisa Conolly*; Tillyard, *Aristocrats*.
49 Blackwood, *Songs, poems and verses*; Hamilton, *Notable Irishwomen*; Nicholson, *Helen's Tower*.
50 W. A. Maguire, *Living like a lord: the second Marquis of Donegall, 1769–1844* (Belfast: Appletree Press and the Ulster Society for Irish Historical Studies, 1984), p. 14.
51 PRONI, Dufferin and Ava papers, D/1071/D/12, Hans Blackwood to Price Blackwood, 27 June 1825.
52 Large, 'The wealth of the greater Irish landowners', p. 22.
53 PRONI, Ward papers, D/2092/1/10/54, Arabella Ward to William Ward, 3 December 1807.

54 Joanna Innes, 'State, Church and voluntarism in European welfare, 1690–1850' in Hugh Cunningham and Joanna Innes (eds), *Charity, philanthropy and reform from the 1690s to 1850* (Basingstoke: Macmillan, 1998), p. 21.
55 Rosemary Raughter, 'A natural tenderness: women and philanthropy in eighteenth-century Ireland' (MA thesis, University College Dublin, 1985), pp. 22–53.
56 *Ibid.*, p. 29.
57 Innes, 'State, Church and voluntarism', pp. 19–20.
58 Christine Kinealy, 'The poor law during the Great Famine: an administration in crisis' in Margaret E. Crawford (ed.), *Famine: the Irish experience 900–1900* (Edinburgh: J. Donald, 1989), p. 38.
59 Raughter, 'A natural tenderness'.
60 *Ibid.*; Maria Luddy, 'Women and charitable organisations in nineteenth century Ireland', *Women's Studies International Forum*, 11:4 (1988), pp. 301–5.
61 G. H. Bell (ed.), *The Hamwood papers of the Ladies of Llangollen and Caroline Hamilton* (London: Macmillan, 1930), p. 7.
62 John McEvoy, *Statistical survey of the county of Tyrone* (Dublin: Graisberry and Campbell, 1802), pp. 163–4.
63 *Ibid.*, pp. 164–5.
64 *Ibid.*, p. 166.
65 Raughter, 'A natural tenderness', pp. 3–20.

1

Women, marriage and statute law
in Ireland

In 1753 the 'act for the better preventing of clandestine marriages', otherwise known as 'Hardwicke's Marriage Act', passed into law in England. The Act reinforced paternal authority over children by introducing the necessity for parental consent for the marriage of minors, under twenty-one. It also undermined the previously private nature of marriage by making the publication of marriage banns compulsory. It was the first major state involvement in the regulation of the marriage contract, and was 'one of the most controversial and divisive measures' of eighteenth-century legislative history.[1] The regulation of the marriage contract in Ireland, however, predated 'Hardwicke's Marriage Act' by eighteen years, in a process of piecemeal regulation that had begun over a hundred years earlier in 1634, with no comparable debate. The reasons for the divergence in the otherwise similar English and Irish legal systems on the issue of marriage were the particular political situation in Ireland and the dominance of the Irish parliament by the interests of the protestant propertied elite. The regulation of marriage by statute law seems to contradict the basic assumption of liberal political theory that the family, as a 'natural' unit, was outside the scope of the law.[2] The reinforcement of paternal authority in the family also questions the assumption, by historians, of a trend towards 'affective individualism' and the 'egalitarian family' in landowning families.[3] If, as Lemmings argues, the passing of 'Hardwicke's Marriage Act' in England demonstrated that majority opinion in parliament favoured the patriarchal family, a similar patriarchal political elite was already in place in Ireland.[4]

English common law was established in Ireland by the sixteenth century in a process which culminated in Henry VIII declaring himself King of Ireland in 1541.[5] English marriage law reflected 'deeply held views on the role of women in society'.[6] Women's experience of property was determined to a large extent by the common law doctrine of coverture, by which the legal identity of a wife was 'literally covered' by that of her husband and her property passed into her husband's possession.[7] Married women were unable to acquire property or enter into contracts. The legal position of married women was described by one early eighteenth-century pamphleteer as 'lower than captivity itself'.[8] 'It was not the fact of being female', as Lee Holcombe notes, 'but the status of wife that entailed severe legal disabilities'.[9] Only upon the death of her husband did a widow regain her legal identity and become entitled to dower from her husband's estate until her death.

The legal disabilities of married women were mitigated by the existence of equity, which had developed to counteract perceived abuses of the common law system. The practice of arranging a separate estate for a woman during coverture for her own use, free from the control of her husband, developed through the use of equity in the Court of Chancery in the sixteenth century. The remit of equity was 'limited and peculiar'. It applied only to individual petitioners to the court and, although by granting property rights to women it effectively overruled coverture, it therefore did not challenge the general position of women in common law.[10] However, it offered relief from the legal disabilities inherent in coverture and was widely used by women in England and Ireland.[11]

The validity of marriage was initially within the jurisdiction of the Church. The Church assumed jurisdiction over marital matters from the fifth century, and a code of marriage developed as part of canon law in the twelfth and thirteenth centuries. Canon law regarded marriage as a sacrament and was concerned with the regulation of the person rather than property and therefore regarded marriage as essentially a private contract. Church thinking was based on the belief that verbal consent, freely given, should be the basis of the marriage contract. There was no need for ecclesiastical ceremony, parental consent or consummation of the union. The consent was to be given in the present tense, *per verba de presenti*, if the marriage was to be binding. If it was given in the future tense, *per verba de futuro*, it was considered to be only a promise to marry, or a pre-contract, which could be made indissoluble by a vow to marry made in the present tense, or by consummation. Marriage differed only from other contracts in that it was indissoluble. Both consent to marriage given in the present tense and pre-contract to marriage were considered binding by law.[12] A pre-contract to marry could therefore legally override a later agreement to marry given in the present tense.

The basis of a valid marriage was therefore consent, freely given. Minors under seven years old were excluded, as was marriage between close relations. The fourth Lateran Council in 1215 forbade marriage within the fourth degree of consanguinity and first degree of affinity. Bigamy was also disallowed, and the indissolubility of the marriage contract rendered a marriage void if one of the parties had contracted an earlier union.[13] In an attempt to regulate marriage by bringing known impediments to light, the Council also made the publication of banns a general requirement in a church marriage. However, the private nature of the marriage contract made regulation difficult, and marriages that did not adhere to church regulations, referred to as clandestine marriages, could be considered good in law, unless a case was taken to an ecclesiastical court to prove otherwise.[14]

In 1563 the Roman Catholic Church at the Council of Trent issued the *Tamesti* decree, which stated that, in addition to the publication of banns, the presence of the bishop of the diocese, or the parish priest, or another appointed priest was essential to validate a marriage. Two witnesses should also be present, and the marriage should be preceded by the publication of banns, except in cases where a licence had been acquired from the bishop.[15] From this date, marriages conducted without the presence of a priest and publication of banns were regarded as clandestine and subject to ecclesiastical censure. The Council of Trent had no bearing on English law, although the Catholic Church in Ireland accepted the *Tamesti* decree and the Convocation of the Province of Canterbury adopted the resolutions concerning the marriage ceremony in 1603.[16]

Post-Reformation ecclesiastical law was based on pre-Reformation canon law and jurisdiction over matrimonial matters remained with the ecclesiastical courts. Ecclesiastical law became the law of England in 1559, in a statute that was extended to Ireland in 1560.[17] The canon law on marriage was left in place in so far as it did not conflict with the law of the realm, and was subject to limitation and change by existing common law and statute. Verbal consent freely given therefore continued to form the basis of a legally binding marriage. Ecclesiastical solemnisation, although promoted by the Church, was not essential for a valid marriage.[18]

Early modifications of the marriage code in England focused on the jurisdiction of Rome in matrimonial matters and pre-contract as an impediment to a legal marriage.[19] Papal jurisdiction over matrimonial matters was overruled by statute in the 1537 'act of succession of the King and Queen Anne'[20] and in the 1542 'act for marriages', which noted that the 'usurped power of the bishop of Rome hath always entangled and troubled the mere jurisdiction and legal power of this realm of England . . . by making lawful which by God's word is lawful both in marriages and other things'. The Act overruled canon law on pre-contract as an impediment to marriage by stating that from 1 July 1540, marriages not within prohibited degrees, solemnised by the Church of Ireland and consummated were 'lawful, good and indissoluble, notwithstanding any precontract . . . not consummated with bodily knowledge

. . . [a]nd not withstanding any dispensation, prescription, law or other thing granted or confirmed by act or otherwise'.[21]

In Ireland, according to common law as modified by statute, only marriages that took place in the Church of Ireland were considered valid by law. The development of the Church of Ireland mirrored that of the Church of England, as Henry VIII declared himself head of both churches and ecclesiastical law came under the control of the monarch.[22] Uniformity of sacrament and worship with the Book of Common Prayer was established by statute in 1560 and again in 1665.[23] In 1665, after the English civil war, an 'act for the confirmation of marriages' declared that all marriages solemnised in Ireland since May 1642 were legitimate 'as if such marriages had been solemnised according to the rites and ceremonies established or used in the Church of Ireland'.[24] This was followed in the same year by the 'act for uniformity of public prayers and administration of sacraments', which established that the Church of Ireland should 'hold the same conformity of common prayers and administration of the sacraments, and other rites and ceremonies of the church, according to the use of the Church of England'.[25]

As well as ruling on the validity of marriages, ecclesiastical courts in Ireland, as in England, granted marriage licences and heard cases for the restitution of conjugal rights and separations or annulments. Jurisdiction on marriage was vested in the Archbishop of Armagh and the Prerogative Court, which also ruled on testamentary matters.[26] During the Commonwealth period, jurisdiction over all testamentary cases was taken over by appointed commissioners. On the Restoration, jurisdiction was returned to the court in Armagh, which continued to administer marriage licences until the disestablishment of the Church of Ireland and the creation of the Court for Matrimonial Causes and Matters in 1871.[27]

The difficulty for the Church of Ireland was that, statistically, it could not claim to represent the population of Ireland. It has been estimated that catholics made up between three-quarters and four-fifths of the population in the first half of the eighteenth century.[28] Catholic marriage was subject to regulation by the Catholic Church, indicating that Church of Ireland jurisdiction over marriage was at best partial, despite the 1666 Act of Uniformity. Non-conforming protestants also represented a problem for the Church. Of the 300,000 protestants in Restoration Ireland, 100,000 were Scots Presbyterian, and of the remainder only half belonged to the established Church.[29]

Ultimately, however, ecclesiastical jurisdiction over marriage was undermined and eventually eroded by the superiority of common law and statute. If we accept Martin Ingram's argument that that the decline of church courts after the Restoration in England was due to the 'growth of presbyterian and sectarian congregations during the civil war and interregnum, and the relatively narrow basis on which the Anglican Church was re-established in 1660–3', then the decline of spiritual jurisdiction in England can be attributed to its diminishing relevance to society.[30] Although ecclesiastical law had the full force of law, the principles of church law applied only to the individual and carried no sanction except excommunication, which could be effective only as a means of control only in an Anglican population.

Ecclesiastical law, in Ireland as in England, remained in place after the Reformation in so far as it did not conflict with common law, and it was subject to modification by statute. The indissolubility of the marriage contract was overridden in England from 1670, when divorce was made possible on the grounds of adultery and marriages could be dissolved by Act of Parliament.[31] The procedure was available to Irish petitioners, although, as in England, it was cumbersome and expensive, requiring a previous suit of 'criminal conversation' to be brought in a common law court.[32]

English policy in Ireland, and the interests of the Irish political elite which were represented in the Irish parliament, form the background to the development of Irish marriage law. Statute law in Ireland consisted of legislation enacted by the Irish parliament and legislation that originated in the English parliament either specifically for Ireland, or which was extended to Ireland as part of the United Kingdom. Marriage law in Ireland was a product of the constitutional inferiority of the Irish parliament to the English parliament and the political situation within Ireland following the 1652 commonwealth land settlement. Although English authority extended to the whole island from 1534, the Irish legal system was not identical to the English system. The constitutional superiority of the English parliament had been established by Poyning's Law in 1495, and was not to end until the Irish parliament achieved legislative independence in 1782.[33] In practice, appellate jurisdiction over matrimonial law lay with the English House of Lords, despite the fact that the Irish House of Lords had asserted its position in 1641.[34] This jurisdiction of the Irish House of Lords was legally removed by statute in 1720, restored in 1782 and removed again by the Act of Union in 1800.[35] Irish legislation originated in either Westminster or Dublin. Despite the restrictions of Poyning's Law the Irish parliament could draft legislation through the 'heads of bill' procedure, passing it to Westminster for ratification. Statutes originating in Westminster and extended to Ireland were of equal legal validity to statutes originating in the Irish parliament.[36]

By 1691, the Irish parliament was in effect a protestant parliament dominated by the landed elite. The commonwealth land settlement ensured that the majority of landowners in Ireland were protestant, therefore changing the political balance of power.[37] Protestants were 'now established as the landed class . . . and in the years ahead would come to define themselves as "the protestant interest".'[38] The source of protestant fears at this time lay in the Treaty of Limerick that followed the 1689–91 war. Although the Treaty left in place a 'protestant ascendancy', not all of the catholic gentry lost their estates. Catholic political power was therefore not totally destroyed, and from the perspective of the protestant interest, 'any settlement that left the estates and political power of a substantial section of the Catholic gentry intact could only mean that the conquest for supremacy would at some stage be renewed'.[39]

Initially, Irish statute law on marriage mirrored developments in England by establishing the necessity of consummation for a legitimate union during the sixteenth century. The monogamous character of marriage was also subject to statute in Ireland, as in England, with rulings on bigamy in 1634 and 1725.[40] However, in 1634, a specifically Irish statute made it unlawful for a woman under sixteen to marry without the consent of her father or guardian. The 1634 Act 'for the punishment of such as shall take away maidens that be inheritors' established punishment of two years' imprisonment for those found guilty of taking a minor out of the custody of her guardian, which was raised to five years if physical consummation or marriage took place.[41]

It is significant that the first Act in Ireland that impacted upon the marriage contract applied only to heiresses, and this suggests that the main concern in this case was the protection of protestant property interests. Two interrelated concerns are evident in the 1634 Act: the desire to strengthen paternal authority over children and concerns about the continuing problem of abduction in Ireland. The reinforcement of paternal authority over children was in accordance with other statutory reforms in this period. The concentration of paternal control over the disposal of family freehold property was reinforced by the 1634 Statute of Wills.[42] A particular family structure was therefore being promoted in which the father controlled family resources and exercised increasing authority over children.

The problem of the abduction of heiresses in Ireland was underlined by a combination of social and economic factors. According to James Kelly, abductors and victims of abduction were mostly protestant. Abductors tended to be the financially straitened sons of lesser gentry families, who regarded the abduction of an heiress, and the subsequent appropriation of her property, as a legitimate means to improve their meagre financial situation.[43] The underlying lawlessness in parts of

Ireland and the subordinate status of women helped create the conditions that facilitated the continuation of abduction throughout the eighteenth century.

The phenomenon of abduction in Ireland varied geographically. In the early eighteenth century, Dublin had the most recorded instances, followed by Limerick and Tipperary. This changed in the second half of the eighteenth century, when abduction was more prevalent in Tipperary, although Cork, Kilkenny and Dublin also had many recorded instances in this period.[44] The practice of abduction varied according to the level of violence experienced by the victim, with the worst cases resulting in the death of the victim. At the other extreme are instances when the victim was believed to have colluded in her own abduction, as a means of ensuring marriage to the 'abductor'.[45] Abduction was particularly problematic for women, as despite the violence endured by some women at the hands of their abductors, the victim was regarded as tarnished, with subsequent loss of value in the marriage market.[46]

The next statute dealing specifically with marriage law in Ireland was one of the first penal laws in 1697, the 'act to prevent protestants intermarrying with papists'. Under the terms of the Act a protestant woman in possession of an estate worth £500 forfeited her estate if she married a catholic. Her estate then passed to her next protestant heir. A man in possession of an estate who married a catholic woman also lost his estate, although the penalty was not automatic as he was given one year to convert his wife. The Act made it necessary for a protestant woman in possession of an estate when she married to have a certificate from the minister of the parish stating that her intended husband was a 'known protestant'. Any protestant or catholic minister who married such a woman without this certificate was liable to punishment of one year's imprisonment and a fine of twenty pounds.[47]

The 1697 Act demonstrates the political concerns of the protestant law-making elite. In the case of catholic–protestant intermarriage, the transfer of a woman's property to her husband on marriage was at odds with protestant property interests. The penal laws can be regarded as a series of piecemeal measures 'drawn up in response to a variety of immediate pressures and grievances', rather than an organised 'code' enacted by a unified protestant ascendancy.[48] The regulation of marriage was of particular political concern in Ireland, owing to the common law doctrine of coverture. As Sean Connolly has noted, the 1697 Act '[l]ike other bills of the 1690s . . . was essentially a defensive measure, closing off one of the avenues by which Catholics might supposedly subvert the Protestant interest'.[49] The Act is clearly focused on the protection of property interests, specifically noting that intermarriage would lead to 'the great ruin of such estates, to the great loss of many protestant persons to whom the same might descend'. By disinheriting a protestant woman who married a catholic and passing her estate to the next protestant heir, the political elite were keeping land in protestant ownership.

The Act also illustrates the potential conflict between patriarchal ideology and the interests of the protestant ascendancy. The law upheld contemporary ideology on the place of women in the family. By offering a protestant man who married a catholic woman one year to convert his wife before disinheritance, it made a distinction between men and women, which suggests that women occupied a subordinate position in the family and were subject to the rule of their husbands.[50] However, in contradiction of the patriarchal principle, the rights of a father to control his daughter's choice of marriage partner, along with a husband's right to take possession of his wife's property, were overruled if protestant property interests were threatened, as in the case of a protestant heiress marrying a catholic man.

In practice, this attack on the patriarchal nature of the family was met with reluctance by members of the Irish establishment. Mary O'Dowd notes several instances in which legislation which overturned the authority of fathers and husbands was criticised by the judiciary: '[a] man's control over his wife and family was clearly considered by members of the judiciary to be "right and proper" and they were uncomfortable enforcing laws which undermined that control'. Nevertheless, although these laws were sometimes mitigated in practice by a sympathetic judiciary, their existence on the statute books is significant, and 'when implemented they subverted the English legal code on family, property and women'.[51]

The complex relationship between the patriarchal ideology of women and the family and the interests of the protestant political elite can be seen in later legislation. The terms of the 1697 Act were extended in the 1703 'act to prevent the further growth of popery' to include marriage between protestants who had estates in Ireland with catholics outside Ireland.[52] However, in 1709, in an Act to explain the 1703 legislation it was ruled that a catholic woman married to a catholic man was entitled to up to one-third of his possessions after his death if she converted to protestantism 'notwithstanding any will or voluntary disposition made by such popish husband to the contrary'.[53] The patriarchal authority of a husband over his wife was therefore overturned when doing so would further protestant interests.

In an Act of 1707, the now entirely protestant parliament considered the 1634 legislation 'insufficient' to prevent the abduction of women. The principle of parental consent was upheld and more severe punishments were established for those who were involved in the abduction of women who possessed, or were due to inherit, real or personal property.[54] Offenders could be sentenced to three years in prison and barred from claiming profits from her estate. The abduction of an heiress followed by rape or forced marriage was made a capital offence 'without benefit of clergy'. Trustees in Chancery would then vest her estate for her. The Act also laid out penalties for clergy involved in such marriages. Church of Ireland clergy could be deprived of their benefices and be excluded from promotion. For catholic priests who conducted a marriage ceremony between two people 'knowing that either of them is of the protestant religion', the penalty was transportation, with a capital sentence if they returned to Ireland.

The severity of the 1707 Act indicates concern in the Irish parliament about the continuing problem of abduction in Ireland, and the associated threat to protestant property interests. As James Kelly has argued, the 1707 legislation broke new ground in Ireland by offering women protection from abduction.[55] The Act was unusual as a separate section relating to a specific abduction case was inserted by the English Privy Council. The case concerned the abduction in April 1707 of a thirteen-year-old heiress, Margaret MacNamara from County Clare, by John O'Bryan and 'diverse others'. O'Bryan, a catholic, is said to have forced MacNamara, a protestant, to marry him by threatening to rape her. The service was performed by a friar who had no legal entitlement to be in Ireland. In July 1707, MacNamara's mother applied to the House of Commons for relief, which resulted in the 1707 Act.[56] Practically and ideologically, however, the effect of the legislation is questionable. John O'Bryan and his accomplices were not brought to trial, owing to the reluctance of law officers in counties Galway, Clare, Limerick and Tipperary to pursue prosecutions.[57] Victims of abduction were also unwilling to initiate prosecution proceedings. Although the 1707 legislation enabled a victim of abduction to have her abductor brought to trial, in practice legal retribution did not mitigate the social and personal consequences of the loss of chastity outside marriage.[58]

The significance of the MacNamara abduction case is that legally the marriage was valid, and in this context the abduction of a protestant heiress by a catholic had implications for the protection of protestant property interests. As Kelly notes, the 'misfortunes of Margaret MacNamara created an enormous stir because they mirrored the insecurities of the protestant population at large'.[59] From the point of view of the political elite, the central problem of the abduction of an heiress was that the consequent marriage was considered legally valid. Despite the penalties established by statute, the problem of abduction continued, and adbuctors continued to get away with it. As Toby Barnard has noted, '[b]oldness did pay off'.[60]

The ineffectiveness of the law is indicated by the example of the abduction of the Limerick heiress Frances Ingoldsby in November 1743. After her abduction and forced marriage, Frances was rescued and her abductor, Hugh Fitzjohn Massey, was brought to trial. Massey, however, bought off jurors and eventually was released without charge to enjoy his wife's inheritance, estimated at an annual rental of £870.[61] The law could not stop abduction, and when the law was used, 'it tended to be invoked more to pursue and harass the malefactors than to recover the victim.'[62]

Furthermore, when abductors were successfully tried, as they were at the trial following the abduction of the Kennedy sisters in Kilkenny in 1785, this did not remove the double standard at work in Irish society. Catherine and Ann Kennedy, aged fourteen and fifteen respectively, were heiresses to a fortune of £2,000. In April 1779, they were abducted by James Strange and Garret Byrne, married by a couple-begging priest and raped. After being on the run for five weeks they were discovered near Wicklow. Strange and Byrne fled to Wales, where they were recaptured and returned to Ireland for trial. The two men, along with James Strange's brother, Patrick, were tried at the County Kilkenny Assizes in October 1780 and sentenced to death.[63] Although, as Kelly notes, critics of abduction outnumbered sympathisers of the three men, this was not the uniform response.[64] Alongside the viewpoint that the death penalty was perceived as the only way to curb this problem in Ireland, some commented upon the 'cruelty' of the Kennedy sisters. Dorothea Herbert recorded how the abductors were mourned as 'three very handsome young fellows of good families', while noting how 'everyone was disgusted at the ladies appearing so soon in public after so horrid a business'.[65]

The problem of abduction therefore became interrelated with the political agenda that aimed to prevent the intermarriage of catholics and protestants. The penalties against priests as established in 1707 were reinforced by legislation in 1709 that stated that if a catholic priest solemnised a marriage in which one party was protestant, it would be assumed the said priest was aware of this.[66] The next legislation dealing with marriage focused on the role of the officiating clergy at clandestine marriages. The number of reported abduction cases actually rose in the 1720s and this provided the political background for increasing statutory punishments for catholic priests.[67] In 1725 it was declared a felony, punishable by death 'without benefit of the clergy', for a catholic priest or a clergyman who had been degraded in rank and turned out of the clergy to marry two protestants, or a protestant and a catholic, as 'clandestine marriages are for the most part celebrated by popish priests and degraded clergymen, to the manifest ruin of several families within this kingdom'.[68]

The principle of paternal control re-emerged in 1735 in the 'act for the better preventing clandestine marriages'. The Act declared that all marriages undertaken by minors without the consent of 'the father (if living) . . . or, if dead, of the guardian' were 'absolutely null and void' if either of the parties was in possession of real estate valued at £100 or a personal estate valued at £500, or if their parents were in possession of real estate valued at £100 or a personal estate valued at £2,000. Sanctions were applied more widely in 1735 when it was noted that because 'the several laws made to prevent clandestine marriages have proved ineffectual', any minister 'in any church or chapel' who published banns of matrimony between a protestant and a catholic could be deprived of his spiritual livings.[69]

Until the 1735 legislation the common law in Ireland regarded marriage as a civil contract, accepting clandestine marriages as legally binding, although uncanonical. The 1735 Act, by making some marriages void by law, represented the first secular intervention into the issue of marriage validity. The Act also in some ways upheld the patriarchal structure of Irish society by placing the power of veto or consent with the father as head of the family. There is no mention of the place of mothers in this issue. The power of consent lay with the father, or if he was dead, the legal guardian. Unless a mother was appointed as legal guardian, she had no right of veto or consent over her child's marriage choices.

This patriarchal principle was partial in its application, as what was being promoted, especially from 1735, was the authority of fathers of protestant landed families. In this respect, the underlying principles of patriarchal society and the interests of the protestant political elite did not conflict. Paternal authority in the family was undermined when it conflicted with the requirements of the state, as in the case of a catholic husband's right to the property of his protestant wife. The protection of protestant property interests took precedence over existing common law provisions on marriage, which illustrates how the interests of the state were applied to what was ostensibly a private contract and challenged the status of the family as a natural, private unit, independent of government control.[70]

This is further indicated by an Act in 1745 in which the laws to prevent clandestine marriages were described as 'ineffectual'. The remedy was to declare marriage between a catholic and a protestant who had converted within twelve months or between two protestants celebrated by a catholic priest 'absolutely null and void'. The Act noted the difficulty of proving marriage or rape in cases of abduction and it was ruled that abduction 'with an intent to marry or defile' was punishable by death without benefit of clergy.[71]

Paternal control was further strengthened in 1749 when the right to annul marriages that had taken place between minors without parental consent was extended to cases where the married couple had absconded. The legislation made it possible for fathers or guardians to begin a suit for annulment in an ecclesiastical court of a clandestine marriage in the absence or death of the parties involved. The Act also asserted that although the validity of such marriages had now been overruled by statute law and the threat of property transmission from protestant women to catholic men was therefore blocked, a catholic priest who celebrated a marriage between a catholic and a protestant or between two protestants could still be found guilty of a felony.[72]

In practice, statute makers were concerned only with a marriage that involved at least one party who was a Church of Ireland protestant. Marriages between catholics, Quakers or Jews were considered valid by ecclesiastical law. With the exception of the legislation introduced by Henry VIII in 1540 prohibiting marriage within the fifteen degrees of kinship set out in the biblical Book of Leviticus, catholic marriages were not regulated by statute, being subject instead to conditions accepted by the Catholic Church at the Council of Trent. A marriage between two catholics, outside the Levitical degrees, celebrated by a catholic priest was valid in law.[73] Quaker and Jewish marriages were also not subject to statute intervention until the 1844 Marriage Act in Ireland, which established registration procedures for Quaker and Jewish marriages.[74]

Presbyterian ministers were subject to limiting statutes regarding marriage. The Irish Act of Uniformity in 1665 declared that marriages celebrated by Presbyterian ministers in possession of rectories and vicarages were considered valid until 29 September 1667. After this date, ministers celebrating marriages would be liable to penalties.[75] However in practice such marriages continued and were tolerated.[76] In 1719, the Irish Toleration Act established that protestant dissenting ministers who took an oath of allegiance and supremacy would be exempt from penalties for administering sacraments.[77] Presbyterian ministers were further relieved in 1737 by legislation exempting them from all prosecutions for marriages celebrated in their congregations by ministers who had qualified under the 1689 Toleration Act.[78] Although this Act did not legalise Presbyterian marriages, it did sanction their celebration and protect the officiating minister from prosecution. They were consequently assumed to be valid in practice, a situation which was confirmed by later legislation in 1782, which declared that marriages between Presbyterians by Presbyterian ministers were already valid in law.[79]

In practice therefore, until 1782, legal measures against Presbyterianism were unworkable, and Presbyterian marriages continued after 1667. However, the interference of the law in Presbyterian marriages was part of a wider attack on Presbyterianism. This included the blocking of access to employment in central and local government through the requirement to receive Holy Communion in the established church; preventing the children of Presbyterian families from being educated by those of their own religious persuasion; and the requirement that Presbyterian burials follow the service of the Church of Ireland.[80] Equality of Presbyterian and dissenter marriages to those of the established Church did not follow until 1842.[81]

The regulation of the validity of the marriage contract in Ireland therefore pre-dated the 1753 Hardwicke's Marriage Act, which declared all unions that did not fit the criteria of the Act to be legally void. The main terms of Hardwicke's Marriage Act concerned the marriage ceremony and the question as to what constituted a valid marriage by law. The Act established the necessity of parental consent for the marriage of minors under twenty-one. It also aimed to prevent clandestine marriages by making it a legal necessity for all individuals except Quakers or Jews to marry in a parish church according to the rubric in the Book of Common Prayer. The Act declared that after 1754 in England, pre-contract was no longer a legal impediment to a marriage that had been solemnised in a church ceremony. Hereafter, a legitimate ceremony took place in a parish of which at least one of the parties was a resident and was performed by legitimate clergy. The ceremony was to be preceded by the posting of banns in the parish church on three consecutive Sundays and the marriage was to be registered immediately after the solemnisation. Punishments, ranging from ecclesiastical censure to transportation, were established for clergy who solemnised unions not in accordance with the legislation.[82]

Hardwicke's Marriage Act was the first legislative intervention in the concept of what constituted a valid marriage in England, and overruled the ecclesiastical law on marriage, which regarded marriage as essentially a private contract up to 1753. The Act effectively removed the legal force of contracts both in present and future tense, and took away any remedy from the breaking of such contracts from the ecclesiastical courts. It was a controversial measure that prompted much debate both inside and outside parliament, because it established the necessity of a public marriage ceremony, by law, rendering all unions not celebrated in this way

legally void. The parliamentary debate on the issue has been summed up
as follows:

> Its passage through parliament was bitterly opposed, especially in the
> House of Commons, by men who claimed variously that it threatened the
> balance of the constitution; offended against the law of God; would weaken
> the English race in biology and numbers; promote fornication among the
> poor; and render innocent young women defenceless against treacherous
> seducers.[83]

Considering the level of debate in England, it is surprising that there
was not a similar debate on the marriage legislation already in existence
in Ireland. There are similarities between the passing of the Hardwicke's
Marriage Act and Irish marriage statutes. In both countries, statute regulation of marriage appears to have been motivated by a desire to protect
the interests of the propertied elite. David Lemmings has argued that
Hardwicke's Marriage Act 'was clearly drafted to maximize support
among the landowners predominantly represented in parliament' who
were concerned about the vulnerability of their estates under the ecclesiastical law on marriage. Lemmings also notes that the Act was motivated
primarily by a desire 'to prevent marriages among children of the social
elite which were not sanctioned by their parents and other relations'.[84]
However, despite the similar protection of propertied interests through
marriage regulation, there was no equivalent to Hardwicke's Marriage
Act in Ireland. As the Act did not apply to Ireland, the legal validity of
the private verbal marriage contract, *per verba de presenti*, and the pre-
contract to marriage, *per verba de futuro*, remained.

The key to this issue in Ireland is that only certain marriages were regulated. While the passing of Hardwicke's Marriage Act has been attributed to the interests of the propertied elite in parliament, in application
the Act affected all parts of society. In Ireland, however, the political
climate was such that the threat represented by clandestine marriage
applied only in the case of a propertied protestant woman marrying a
catholic man, and it was this scenario that Irish marriage legislation
aimed to avoid, initially by punishments to deter abductors, and clergy
performing such unions, and then by declaring these matches void. As
only certain marriages were thought to be a threat to the protestant
ascendancy, only certain marriages were regulated. The absence of a
public debate in Ireland further illustrates the different political circumstances that motivated marriage law in both countries. Irish marriage
statutes were essentially piecemeal measures dealing with specific perceived threats to protestant interests, and therefore marriage regulation

in Ireland had more in common with other penal legislation in Ireland than it did with Hardwicke's Marriage Act.

Changes in marriage law from the late eighteenth century were based on a change in government policy towards catholics to one of conciliation and 'gradual absorption into political society'.[85] By the end of the eighteenth century, catholics could testify allegiance under oath, inherit property, purchase land and vote for parliament. In 1781–82 it was reaffirmed that marriages between protestant dissenters were 'good and valid'.[86] In 1792 legislation on intermarriage was repealed to enable protestants and catholics to marry if the ceremony was performed by clergy from the established Church.[87] The relaxation in government policy that applied to Presbyterian ministers was not however extended to catholic clergy. The 1792 Act repealing legislation on intermarriage reaffirmed that a catholic priest was still forbidden by law to marry a catholic and a protestant and, although the death penalty for catholic clergy who celebrated such marriages was removed in 1833, such marriages remained void in law.[88] The protection of property interests therefore continued to form the basis of marriage legislation in Ireland until the 1830s.

Until the nineteenth century, there appears to have been little interest in Ireland in regulating marriage in general. The first Act which reduced the differences between English and Irish marriage law was in 1818, when section 13 of Hardwicke's Marriage Act, which dealt with contracts, was copied verbatim into Irish law, overriding the legality of private verbal contracts or marriage and pre-contract in Ireland.[89]

In the courts, the main consequences of a legal system that rendered some marriages void arose in prosecutions against bigamy. The most important case in this respect is *Regina v Milles*, heard in the Court of Queen's Bench in Ireland in 1842. The case centred on a charge of bigamy against George Milles, and the verdict was based on the validity of his first marriage, conducted by a Presbyterian minister. Milles was a member of the Church of Ireland, and his first 'wife', Hester Graham, was not a catholic, but it was not disclosed whether she was a member of the established Church or a protestant dissenter. Milles's second marriage took place in England, according to the rules of the established Church.

Cases of bigamy by necessity focused on the question of what constituted a valid marriage. In *Regina v Milles* it was held that a marriage contract *per verba de presenti*, though consummated, did not constitute a valid marriage in Ireland. A valid marriage by law required the presence of a clergyman in holy orders. A Presbyterian minister was not regarded as competent to celebrate the marriage between a member of the established Church and a Presbyterian. Milles's first marriage was therefore declared void and he was acquitted of the charge of bigamy.[90] The decision of the court in the Milles case was controversial and the authority of the ruling was questioned in later prosecutions.[91] The confusion surrounding the case led to the 1844 'act for marriages in Ireland; and for registering such marriages', which attempted to clarify the legal position of various marriages.

Following a similar Act in England in 1836, the 1844 Irish Marriage Act established a marriage registrar and provided for the registration of marriages outside the Church of Ireland. Regulations concerning Presbyterian, Quaker and Jewish marriages were also established.[92] It was ruled that a Church of Ireland protestant could marry a Presbyterian in a marriage ceremony conducted by a Presbyterian minister. The Act repealed the 1735 and 1749 legislation on clandestine marriage which had established parental authority to void the marriage of minors and replaced this with a general requirement for the marriage of minors.[93]

However the Irish Act differed significantly from the English Act in that it did not apply in any way to catholic marriages. Measures concerning degraded clergy and catholic priests were left in place and catholic marriages, subject to regulation by the Catholic Church, were to be 'celebrated in the same manner and subject to the same limitations' as before.[94] The English Act, in contrast, allowed for the registration of catholic marriages if they took place in a catholic church licensed as a separate building.[95]

The 1844 Act established the marriage registrar in Ireland and therefore provided the means for the legally recognised civil marriage ceremony. Church of Ireland marriages were to continue, as before, to be solemnised according to the Rubric of the Book of Common Prayer. The only difference was that instead of the publication of banns, notice was to be given to the newly established marriage registrar, except when a special Licence had been acquired by the Archbishop of Armagh.

Conclusion

The development of marriage law in this period illustrates a shift from the acceptance of marriage as a private contract, rendered legitimate by mutual consent freely given, to the idea of marriage as a matter of public interest, subject to statutory regulation.

English common law was informed by contemporary ideology that recognised the supremacy of paternal authority in the family.[96] By the common law doctrine of coverture, a married woman's property passed into the possession of her husband and therefore legally married women were placed in a position of dependence on husbands and fathers. The significance of statute law is that it was particular in application and far-reaching in consequence, as it changed the common law and overrode inferior laws such as ecclesiastical law.

The fact that Irish statute regulation of marriage predated English developments illustrates the different political contexts within which English common law operated. The development of Irish statute law reveals several concurrent concerns of the political elite. Clandestine marriage and abduction of heiresses were particularly problematic, considering the concern to protect protestant property interests that was at the heart of the political situation in Ireland at this time. By increasing paternal authority over the marriage choices of children, protestant landowners could veto intermarriage within their family. Furthermore, by creating exceptions to the common law on property, political concerns were dealt with, without upsetting the patriarchal balance of power within Irish families. Therefore, in particular situations, this patriarchal structure was overturned by Irish statute law: when a catholic man married a protestant woman, his common law entitlement to her property was removed, whereas a catholic woman who married a catholic man and then converted to Protestantism was legally entitled to claim one-third of his property.

The place of the family in Irish marriage law can be summed up as follows: where the requirements of the patriarchal family did not interfere with the needs of the political elite in Ireland, it was given the support of law. Marriage legislation in Ireland was focused on 'a particular class of people' who were regarded as a threat to protestant property interests.[97] The political situation in Ireland, coupled with the importance of marriage in a society which valued property as the basis of political power, motivated statute legislation that was concerned primarily with the protection of protestant property interests.

Notes

1 David Lemmings, 'Marriage and the law in the eighteenth century: Hardwicke's Marriage Act of 1753', *Historical Journal*, 39:2 (1996), p. 340.
2 Mary Lyndon Shanley, *Feminism, marriage and the law in Victorian England, 1850–1895* (London: Tauris, 1989), p. 11.
3 Lawrence Stone, *The family, sex and marriage in England, 1500–1800* (London: Weidenfeld and Nicolson, 1977), pp. 270–3.
4 Lemmings, 'Marriage and the law in the eighteenth century', p. 341.
5 33 Henry VIII, c. 1 (Ireland).

6   O'Dowd, 'Women and the law', p. 96.
7   Erickson, *Women and property* p. 24.
8   Sarah Chapone, *The hardships of the English laws in relation to wives with an explanation of the original curse of subjection passed upon the woman. In an humble address to the legislature* (Dublin, 1735), p. 32.
9   Lee Holcombe, *Wives and property: reform of the married women's property law in nineteenth-century England* (Toronto: University of Toronto Press, 1983), pp. 18–36.
10 *Ibid.*, p. 45.
11 Tim Stretton, *Women waging law in Elizabethan England* (Cambridge: Cambridge University Press, 1998), pp. 25–9, 130–1; Mary O'Dowd, 'Women and the Irish chancery court in the late sixteenth and early seventeenth centuries', *Irish Historical Studies*, 31 (November 1999).
12 J. H. Baker, *An introduction to English legal history* (London: Butterworths, 1990), p. 546.
13 S. L. Ollard, Gordon Cross and Maurice F. Bond (eds), *A dictionary of English church history* (London: Mowbray, 1948), pp. 364–9.
14 Art Cosgrove, 'Marriage in medieval Ireland' in Art Cosgrove (ed.), *Marriage in Ireland* (Dublin: College Press, 1985), p. 27.
15 Margaret MacCurtain, 'Marriage in Tudor Ireland' in Cosgrove (ed.), *Marriage in Ireland*, p. 63.
16 W. J. Byrne, *A dictionary of English law* (London: Sweet and Maxwell, 1923), p. 562.
17 2 Elizabeth I, c. 1 (Ireland).
18 Patrick J. Corish, 'Catholic marriage under the penal code' in Cosgrove (ed.), *Marriage in Ireland*, p. 68.
19 25 Henry VIII, c. 19 (England).
20 28 Henry VIII, c. 2 (Ireland).
21 33 Henry VIII, c. 6 (Ireland).
22 28 Henry VIII, c. 5 (Ireland).
23 2 Elizabeth I, c. 2 (Ireland); 17 & 18 Charles II, c. 7 (Ireland).
24 17 & 18 Charles II, c. 3 (Ireland).
25 17 & 18 Charles II, c. 6 (Ireland).
26 Henry Wood, *A guide to the records deposited in the Public Records Office of Ireland* (Dublin: His Majesty's Stationery Office, 1919), p. 222.
27 William R. Duncan and Paula E. Scully, *Marriage breakdown in Ireland: law and practice* (Dublin: Butterworths, 1990), p. 1.
28 Sean J. Connolly, *Religion, law and power: the making of protestant Ireland 1660–1760* (Oxford: Clarendon Press, 1992), p. 145.
29 J. G. Simms, 'The restoration, 1660–85' in T. W. Moody, F. X. Martin and F. J. Byrne (eds), *A new history of Ireland*, iii: *Early modern Ireland 1534–1691* (Oxford: Clarendon Press, 1991), p. 437.
30 Martin Ingram, *Church courts, sex and marriage in England, 1570–1640* (Cambridge: Cambridge University Press, 1987), p. 372.
31 Baker, *An introduction to English legal history*, p. 565.

32 W. G. Brooke, 'Rights of married women in England and Ireland', *Irish Law Times and Solicitors Journal*, 7 (1873), p. 280.
33 10 Henry VII, c. 10 (Ireland); 21 & 22 George III, c. 47 (Ireland).
34 F. H. Newark, *Notes in Irish legal history* (Belfast: M. Boyd, 1960), p. 16.
35 6 George I, c. 5 (Ireland); 21 & 22 George III, c. 47 (Ireland); 40 George III, c. 38 (Ireland).
36 W. N. Osbourough, 'The legislation of the pre-Union Irish parliament' in W. N. Osborough (ed.), *Studies in Irish legal history* (Dublin: Four Courts Press, 1999), pp. 85–6.
37 Patrick J. Corish, 'The Cromwellian regime, 1650–60' in Moody, Martin and Byrne (eds), *A new history of Ireland*, iii, pp. 357–61.
38 *Ibid.*, p. 386.
39 Connolly, *Religion, law and power*, pp. 264–5.
40 10 Charles I, c. 21 (Ireland); 12 George I, c. 1 (Ireland).
41 10 Charles I, c. 17 (Ireland).
42 10 Charles I, c. 1 (Ireland).
43 Kelly, 'The abduction of women of fortune', p. 10.
44 *Ibid.*, p. 41.
45 Barnard, *The abduction of a Limerick heiress*, p. 8.
46 *Ibid.*, p. 9.
47 9 William III, c. 3 (Ireland).
48 Connolly, *Religion, law and power*, p. 263.
49 *Ibid.*, p. 269.
50 O'Dowd, 'Women and the law', p. 105.
51 *Ibid.*, p. 107.
52 2 Anne, c. 6 (Ireland).
53 8 Anne, c. 3 (Ireland).
54 6 Anne, c. 16 (Ireland).
55 Kelly, 'The abduction of women of fortune', p. 11.
56 *Ibid.*, pp. 10–12.
57 *Ibid.*, p. 12.
58 *Ibid.*, pp.13–14.
59 *Ibid.*, p. 12.
60 Barnard, *The abduction of a Limerick heiress*, p. 8.
61 *Ibid.*, pp. 15–32.
62 *Ibid.*, p. 9.
63 Margaret Weiner, *Matters of felony: a reconstruction* (London: Heinemann, 1967).
64 Kelly, 'The abduction of women of fortune', p. 32.
65 Dorothea Herbert, *Retrospections of Dorothea Herbert 1770–1806* (Dublin: Town House, 1988), p. 112.
66 8 Anne, c. 3 (Ireland).
67 Kelly, 'The abduction of women of fortune', p. 16.
68 12 George I, c. 3 (Ireland).
69 9 George II, c. 11 (Ireland).
70 O'Dowd, 'Women and the law', p. 108.

71 19 George II, c. 13 (Ireland).

72 23 George II, c. 10 (Ireland).

73 The Queen v John Burke, 9 June 1843, *Irish law reports particularly of points of practice argued and determined in the courts of Queen's Bench, Common Pleas and Exchequer of Pleas during the years 1842 and 1843* (Dublin: R. Carrick, 1843), p. 549.

74 7 & 8 Victoria, c. 81 (Ireland).

75 17 & 18 Charles II, c. 6 (Ireland).

76 *Copy from Mr Gurney's short-hand notes of the argument in the case of the Queen v George Millis heard on the 13th, 14th, 16th and 17th February 1843* (Dublin, 1843), p. i.

77 6 George I, c. 5 (Ireland).

78 11 George II, c. 10 (Ireland).

79 21 & 22 George III, c. 25 (Ireland).

80 David W. Hayton, 'Exclusion, conformity, and parliamentary representation: the impact of the sacramental test on Irish dissenting politics' in Kevin Herlihy (ed.), *The politics of Irish dissent, 1650–1800* (Dublin: Four Courts Press, 1997), p. 53.

81 5 & 6 Victoria, c. 116 (Ireland).

82 26 George II, c. 33 (England).

83 Lemmings, 'Marriage and the law in the eighteenth century', p. 340.

84 *Ibid.*, p. 347.

85 Oliver MacDonagh, 'Ireland under the Union, 1801–70' in W. E. Vaughan (ed.), *A new history of Ireland* v. *Ireland under the Union, I: 1801–70* (Oxford: Clarendon Press, 1989), p. xlviii.

86 21 & 22 George II, c. 25 (Ireland).

87 32 George III, c. 21 (Ireland).

88 3 & 4 William IV, c. 103 (Ireland).

89 58 George III, c. 81 (Ireland).

90 *Report of the cases of Regina v Milles and Regina v Carroll in the Queens's Bench in Ireland in Easter and Trinity terms 1842* (Dublin, 1842).

91 W. Harris Faloon, *The marriage law of Ireland* (Dublin: Hodges and Figgis, 1881), p. 20.

92 7 & 8 Victoria, c. 51 (Ireland).

93 7 & 8 Victoria, c. 81 (Ireland).

94 *Ibid.*

95 6 & 7 William IV, c. 85 (England).

96 O'Dowd, 'Women and the law', p. 96.

97 *Report of the cases of Regina v Millis and Regina v Carroll*, p. 103.

2

Provisions made for women and children in family settlements

Women's ownership of property in the wealthy landed class in Ireland was determined by settlements that made provision from the family estate.[1] Such arrangements therefore provide a useful indication of property and power relations within families. Despite the evident desire to make adequate provision for family members, the primary concern in such arrangements was the protection of the family estate. Furthermore, methods used by landed families to make provision for women, as well as daughters and younger sons of a marriage, were characterised by the desire to consolidate the power of the husband or father over family landed property, while reinforcing his authority over family members.

Marriage settlements

In this period, provision for family members was primarily based on marriage settlements: private contracts drawn up by solicitors at the time of a marriage. These settlements could be added to by subsequent deeds, and were ultimately confirmed by the last will and testament of the husband or father. Marriage settlements were widely used among all classes by the early modern period in England, and there were several different types of settlement in use by different classes, but the type of settlement universally used by landed families in this period was the 'strict settlement', although this is a term used more by historians than contemporaries, who would have used the term 'marriage settlement' or 'family settlement'.[2] Strict settlement was developed by lawyers in England after 1650, and was in common use in wealthy landed families in Ireland at least from the early eighteenth century.[3]

By the eighteenth century, strict settlement had assumed a dual function: to transmit the family estate from one generation to another and to arrange provisions for the wife and children of the marriage.[4] The twin concerns of estate management and family provision have led to much debate among historians about the impact of strict settlement on family property relations. Lawrence Stone has argued that the guaranteed provision offered by strict settlement was an integral element in the affective family, and an indication of the importance of women's property rights in families.[5] In a similar vein, Lloyd Bonfield has argued that strict settlement proved to be advantageous to daughters and younger sons, as it ensured their provision from the family estate.[6] In contrast, Eileen Spring has argued that the share that daughters and younger sons could expect from family estates was reduced by the practice of strict settlement, as it enabled the previous generation to limit the amount of provision for younger children and therefore prevented the affection of the father from increasing the amount.[7] Spring has argued that strict settlement was predominantly concerned with the needs of the landed estate: '[w]hat landowners wanted was a means of preserving estates that allowed for some – but limited – provision for families'.[8] Spring's approach is the most useful here, as she regards women as individuals in their own right, whose interests were distinct from the family interest. Strict settlement can therefore be regarded as a tool that promoted the interests of certain family members while it excluded others. Furthermore, Spring's primary argument that the replacement of dower by jointure was symptomatic of a narrowing of women's property rights in this class reflects the experience of women in the twenty families examined here.

Marriage settlements appear to be cryptic documents, written in legal jargon and based on the use of trusts, and have been considered by one historian to be 'as uncommunicative as the lawyer who drew it up'.[9] The key to understanding these documents is to consider their specific function in the context of landed family financial arrangements. Marriage settlements were arranged by solicitors in accordance with the particular requirements of the family of the bride and bridegroom. They were essentially private contracts for the purpose of entailing landed estates on future heirs and arranging financial provision for women and younger children during the marriage and after the bridegroom's death. Such arrangements were created by the use of trusts that were recognised and upheld by equity in the Court of Chancery, a branch of law that generally protected the interests of those invisible in common law, such as married women. In accordance with English practice, jurisdiction over provisions made for women and children in marriage settlements was within the remit of the Court of Chancery in Ireland. Chancery regarded marriage settlements as 'heads or minutes of an agreement', the interpretation of which was influenced by 'the intention and design of the parties, rather than by what is the legal effect of the words'.[10] The status of marriage settlements in Chancery further influenced the content of such documents, as the provisions made represented the least amount a family were willing to be bound to, by law.

Although private, the settlements used by the sample families are all similar in structure and content. This similarity can be attributed to the widespread use by solicitors and family members of conveyancing manuals, the use of which, in English marriage settlements, has been noted from the seventeenth century to the early nineteenth century.[11] At least ten books on conveyancing were published in Ireland in the eighteenth century, including a third edition of Gilbert Horseman's *Precedents in conveyancing*. Irish landowners also had access to books published in England. Orlando Bridgeman's *Conveyances* was a seventeenth-century work that has been cited as a significant force behind the development of strict settlement.[12] It does not appear to have been published in Ireland, yet as it is listed in an inventory of the library at Castle Ward, County Down, in 1813, we can assume Irish landowners did have access to it.[13]

Marriage settlements can be regarded as a tool used by landowners to circumvent the effects of common law. By 1750, Irish property law was identical to practice in England. Before 1634 in Ireland, under common law, a landowner could not convey land to himself or his wife. It was therefore difficult to make settlements of land on his family. This problem was solved by conveying land to a third party, who then held the legal title of the land in question to the use, in other words to the benefit, of the actual owner. The actual owner to whose benefit the estates was being held, the *cestui qui use*, held the equitable right to the land as opposed to the legal title. The 1634 Irish Statute of Uses converted equitable estates into legal estates, therefore undoing the effectiveness of this method of conveyance.[14] The Irish Statute of Uses was identical in content to the English statute that had preceded it by a century, although the diminished significance of feudal dues had altered the context of the statute, and the Irish statute was motivated by a desire to bring Irish land law into line with English law.[15]

The main effect of the Statute of Uses was the introduction of trusts that enabled the actual owner to avoid legal title by the introduction of another party to the settlement, the trustees, while still ensuring the land remained for the benefit of the actual owner.[16] Trusts can therefore be regarded as an essential tool that landowners could use to protect their landed interests from the pitfalls of common law. Different types of trust were used for different situations. For example, one situation in which trusts could be used to circumvent the disabilities of Irish property law was in the case of the marriage of a Roman Catholic woman to a protestant man. According to Irish statute law, catholics had no legal right to own property. Documents belonging to the Nugent family of Portaferry, referring to one such possible marriage between Mr Savage, a protestant, and Mr McCartan's daughter, a catholic, some time around 1761, note that it was 'not advisable' for the father of the bride to make a settlement. According to statutory requirements, if Mr Savage married a catholic woman he would have been given one year to convert his wife to protestantism. After this time, he would have been contravening statutory requirements on the ownership of property in force in 1761, and a 'bill of discovery' could have been instigated against him, a process that could have led to the loss of his property. Mr Savage was advised to make alternative arrangements on the marriage using 'personal covenants', a promise of future payment made by private agreement.[17] The sanctions of the penal laws could therefore be avoided by the use of private agreements.

Strict settlement was also a useful instrument by which landowners could protect their estates from reckless heirs. By 1750, estates could be conveyed to a trustee as the legal owner, while a life interest was ensured for the heir and future generations. At the same time, measures were taken to protect the estate from being broken up due to the failure of male heirs, by the insertion of contingent remainders.[18] As one historian has noted, with reference to practice among the landed class in England, the importance of English land law 'was not so much what it said, as what it did not say; or in other words, the freedom of action it allowed.'[19]

Provision for the bride was also an essential part in the protection and consolidation of landed estates, as the status of women in common law had particular implications for a woman's property rights during marriage, as well as for the family property. According to common law, widows had a legal right to claim dower: a life interest in one-third of their husband's landed property on his death. Dower was regarded as 'inconvenient' by the landed class, as it bound estates with various dower provisions, and was therefore a 'great clog to alienations'.[20] Although dower was not formally challenged by statute until 1833, by the eighteenth century it was acceptable practice among the Irish landed class to bar dower and replace it with jointure. The Statute of Uses and the Statute of Wills allowed for the barring of dower in two ways: the provision of jointure by marriage settlement; or the provision of an annuity by last will and testament. In both cases the intention to bar dower had to be stated, along with the provision of an adequate jointure. If such arrangements took place before marriage, it was possible to bar dower. If arranged after the marriage had taken place, legally the wife had a choice of dower or jointure.

If the bride was a widow, it was socially acceptable for her to represent herself at the negotiation of a settlement. Otherwise, parties to a marriage settlement were the fathers of the prospective bride and bridegroom. If either father were deceased, the bride and bridegroom, if a minor, would be represented by whoever had legal control over their person and property. On the marriage of Robert Ward (1754–1831), a younger son of Bernard, Lord Bangor (1719–81), and Sophia Whaley (d. 1793) in 1782, both fathers were deceased. Robert Ward represented himself, and the two guardians of her person and property represented Sophia Whaley, as she was legally a minor at the time of her marriage.[21] Because she was a minor and a ward of the Court of Chancery, the marriage of Frances Anne Vane-Tempest (1800–65) and Charles Stewart (1778–1854) was considered by the Court of Chancery. Both guardians of Frances Anne gave evidence to the court, one opposing the match, and the Court made the final decision to support the marriage.[22]

The widespread use of marriage settlements in this period renders them essential documents in any survey of property relations in this class. The fact that all the families examined here used an almost identical format indicates that they shared the primary concerns of providing for the wife and children of a marriage while also preserving the interests of their landed estates.

Trustees

Trustees played a significant role in family financial business in this period and could be either family members, friends from another landed family or solicitors, and were uniformly male among the sample families. They were a crucial element in the settlement of property, as property could be devised to the trustee, who would then act as the legal owner, while the equitable ownership would be settled on the beneficiary. In landed transactions this was useful as it enabled landowners to avoid the limitations of the Statute of Uses and therefore to bequeath land. The use of trustees also enabled the person drawing up the settlement or last will and testament to restrict bequests of moveable goods by devising such items to trustees and devising limitations on the beneficiary. Therefore, when Robert Stewart, Marquess of Londonderry (1769–1822), bequeathed his house in St James's Square, London, to his widow, Amelia Stewart, Marchioness of Londonderry, for her life, he bequeathed all the jewellery, plate, ornaments and household goods to trustees for the use of Lady Londonderry while she lived in the house, and by doing so allowed her use of the items for the duration of her life interest while restricting her

Table 2.1 Guardians and executors in husbands' last wills and testaments, 1767–1855

Appointee	Guardian	Executor of will
Widow	6	5
Widow and heir	2	3
Widow and trustee	4	4
Heir	0	7
Heir and trustees	1	1
Younger son and trustees	0	1
Trustee	1	4
Widow and sister-in-law	1	0
Sister-in-law and heir	0	1
N/A or no details	13	2
Total[a]	28	28

Note: [a] This table was compiled from information in twenty-eight last wills and testaments from the twenty families surveyed here.
Sources: See appendix D.

ownership to use only. On her death, the house and contents passed to the use of the heir.[23]

As Table 2.1 demonstrates, trustees, although not numerically dominant, played a significant role in the testamentary affairs of these families. The one example of a trustee being nominated sole guardian and executor was from the same last will and testament, that of Richard Wingfield, Viscount Powerscourt (1730–88), in 1788. Similarly, the nomination of the heir as joint guardian and joint executor with trustees also appears in the same will and testament, that of John Creighton, Earl of Erne (1738–1828), in 1828. In at least two families, therefore, trustees undertook an integral role in landed family financial business, to the extent that they replaced the nomination of immediate family members, such as widows and sons, as guardians and executors. Although there is only one example here of a trustee being nominated sole guardian, trustees were as likely as widows to be appointed joint guardian. The guardianship of minors was divided into two areas of responsibility: guardianship of the person and guardianship of the estate. When trustees were appointed jointly with a widow it indicated that the widow was guardian of the person and that the trustees were guardian of the estate. Although the heir to the estate was most often appointed executor, it was equally possible that a trustee would be appointed as joint executor, either with elder sons or with widows, and it was probable that trustees who shared the duties of executor with widows would undertake financial business with the participation of the widow. The presence of trustees in testamentary documents as well as marriage settlements was therefore not merely a method of circumventing common law, and may indicate the diminishing authority exercised by widows in family financial business.

The role of mothers as guardians of the persons of their children, rather than their estates, indicates an assumption that mothers were the natural guardians of the welfare of their children, whereas a father exerted ultimate legal authority over his children's welfare and estates. The currency of this assumption is suggested by the fact that within the sample families, Harriet Douglas (d. 1833), widow of the son of the first Marquess of Abercorn and Countess of Aberdeen, used it as the basis for her petition to Chancery for the guardianship of her children in 1818.[24] In a more well-known case it also formed the basis of the appeal brought in 1839 by Caroline Norton (1808–77), the sister of Helen Blackwood, Lady Dufferin (1807–67), for increased rights of mothers to the guardianship of their children.[25]

However, there is no obvious pattern to suggest why widows were appointed executrix in certain families at particular times. The instances were not concentrated in a particular period, being seen throughout the period 1750–1850. Practice also varied between families and within families. Charles Brownlow (1757–1822) named his son as sole executor,[26] while his son, Charles Brownlow, Baron Lurgan (1795–1847), named his wife sole executrix.[27] Du Pre Alexander, Earl of Caledon (1777–1839), appointed his wife and eldest son joint executors.[28] Arthur Chichester, Marquess of Donegall (1739–99), appointed his younger son, along with trustees.[29] It is clear from such diversity that much depended upon the whim of the husband. Lord Donegall's appointment of his younger son as joint executor with trustees, for example, which went against the general trend in these families, was based solely on his personal dislike and distrust of his eldest son and heir.[30] The property brought to the marriage also does not appear to have been a relevant factor in the appointment of executrixes. Among the three Lady Dufferins, Dorcas (1726–1807), Anna (d. 1885) and Helen Blackwood, Dorcas brought the most property to her marriage with John Blackwood (d. 1799) in 1751, while Helen brought no portion. In his will, John Blackwood appointed his eldest son executor. Anna Blackwood's husband, James Stevenson Blackwood, the second Lord Dufferin (1755–1836) appointed trustees as executors in his 1836 will. After the death of Helen Blackwood's husband, Price Blackwood, Lord Dufferin (1794–1841), in 1841, she had the task of appointing an executor and agent to her husband's estates.

Jointure

By 1750, jointure had eclipsed the common law right to dower as the favoured method of providing for widows in landed families. All the women in the families surveyed here received jointure instead of dower. There is one example of jointure being settled after marriage, thereby legally enabling the bride to choose dower or jointure: the 1776 post-nuptial settlement of Letitia MacDonnell, Countess of Antrim (d. 1807). No settlement for jointure had been made prior to the marriage of Lady Antrim and Randall MacDonnell, Earl of Antrim. The aim of the settlement was to overrule Lady Antrim's right to claim dower by securing a jointure to which 'the said Countess hath agreed to accept . . . in lieu and bar of dower'.[31] Legally a post-nuptial settlement allowed the widow to choose between an annuity and dower. Practically, however, it was unlikely that a wife would disregard the wishes of her husband in such a matter. There is also one example here of a husband replacing a settled jointure with a life interest in land. Thomas Dawson, Baron Cremorne (1725–1813), replaced the jointure settled on his widow, Philadelphia, Lady Cremorne (d. 1826), with a life interest in freehold land, for the purpose of providing a larger income.[32] However, this is the only example of such a transaction. For the remaining women for whom information is available among the families studied here, provision on widowhood was provided by jointure.

Jointure was settled on a bride for her life only. It was intended as a maintenance payment, to which a widow was entitled by law, independent of the intentions of her family. The widow was empowered by the marriage settlement to claim this sum on her husband's death. It was typical for marriage settlements to note the right of a widow to receive the jointure settled 'peaceably and quietly' without 'suit trouble eviction or disturbance' of the heirs of her late husband. Reference to a widow's 'powers of distress and entry' to acquire the sum from the family estate if not paid to her after a set period of time, usually a standard twenty-one days, was also a common feature among the sample families.[33] In Ireland, jointure was either paid quarterly 'on several feast days of the annunciation of the blessed Virgin Mary, Saint John the Baptist, Saint Michael the Archangel and the birth of our Lord Christ', as in the case of Catherine Alexander, Countess of Caledon, in 1811,[34] or twice a year, as in the case of Anna, Lady Dufferin, who received payments on the feast days of the annunciation of the Virgin Mary and the nativity of Saint Michael the Archangel.[35]

Widows were entitled to retain their jointure if they remarried, and could also convey it to the use of another person if they wished. Anne

Dawson, Lady Cremorne (d. 1885), arranged for her £1,107 jointure to be divided between herself and her new husband, Colonel John Rawdon, on whom she settled £600, retaining the remainder for herself.[36] Widows could also bequeath arrears of jointure to another person. In her last will and testament, Letitia, Marchioness of Antrim, bequeathed the arrears of her jointure to her daughter.[37] Furthermore, a wife's claim on the jointure settled at the time of her marriage was not forfeited by adultery. When Lady Cecil Hamilton (1770–1819) married John James Hamilton, Marquess of Abercorn (1756–1818), as his second wife, in 1786, her jointure was settled at £2,000.[38] In April 1799, the Marquess divorced Lady Cecil by act of parliament on the grounds of her adultery. The jointure sum settled was not affected by the divorce, but required a separate deed of release. Subsequently, in May 1799, five days before she remarried, Lady Cecil Hamilton 'agreed to release and to give up the said annual sum or yearly rent charge of two thousand pounds'.[39] One year later the Marquess married again, taking as his wife Lady Ann Jane Hatton (1763–1827), and the sum of £2,000, in accordance with the original family settlement of 1786, was again settled as jointure.[40]

Portion

Jointure was arranged in most cases, though not all, on the basis of the portion brought by the bride to the marriage and can be regarded as the economic basis of financial provision made for the bride both during and after marriage. It appears to have been acceptable practice among the landed class for a match to be refused on the grounds that the provision for the bride was not worthy of her portion.[41] The portion can therefore be regarded as an essential bargaining tool to ensure the bride's economic security, and was more important in this instance than the nationality and the personal suitability of the prospective bridegroom.[42] This function is stated directly in some settlements, which noted that the arrangement of provisions for the wife and children of the marriage were made 'in consideration of the intended marriage and of the portion or fortune' of the bride.[43] Subsequent sections of the marriage settlement that arranged pin money, jointure and provisions for children of the marriage illustrate further the relationship of portion to financial arrangements made on marriage.

Historiographically, portion has been regarded as a static element of the marriage settlement in this class. Portions were used to purchase land, to provide portions for daughters in the husband's family, or to pay debts.[44] Evidence on portion from the sample families suggests that portion was also used, in some cases, as a source of income for brides. Portion can then be regarded as one method, in the context of a wider trend among the Irish aristocracy from the early nineteenth-century, of making marriages 'self-financing' from the point of view of the bride-groom's family.[45] However, in certain circumstances, families adopted a more flexible approach to portion and the arrangement of financial pro-vision in marriage settlements than either prevailing attitudes or the historiography of the subject suggests. Portion brought by the bride to her marriage could be in the form of either cash or land.[46] Details of portion in the arrangements made in thirty-one marriages are outlined in Table 2.2. On one occasion, portion was brought solely in the form of land.[47] In another case, it comprised land, investments and cash.[48] The majority of portions were in the form of cash. On two occasions, the respective marriages of Harriet Douglas to James Hamilton, Lord Abercorn (1786–1814), in 1809, and Jane MacNeill (d. 1878) to Charles Brownlow, Lord Lurgan (1795–1847), in 1828, a nominal, and possibly temporary, sum of £10 was used as a basis upon which provision was made. On one occasion, that of the marriage of Helen Sheridan to Price Blackwood, a future Lord Dufferin, in 1825, no portion appears to have been brought to the marriage.

Although portion in the form of land ultimately passed to the husband's family, it could also be a source of continuing income for brides. On both occasions when portion included land, the bride retained a life interest in the rental if she survived her husband. After the death of John Blackwood, Dorcas Blackwood received the rental of the 5,400 acres she had brought to her marriage, as a life interest, in addition to her jointure from the Dufferin estate. However, on this instance, on her death both her title, Baroness Dufferin and Clandeboye, and the estate passed to the next male heir, James Stevenson Blackwood, the second Lord Dufferin.[49] An even more favourable arrangement was made for Mary Sandys (1764–1836) on her marriage to Arthur Hill, Lord Fairford (1753–1801), the future Marquess of Downshire. Mary Sandys brought a cash portion of £41,486 in stock funds and an estate of land in England, inherited from her mother, Mary Trumbull, which had an annual rental of £2,930. Lord Fairford was to receive the rental for his life, and on his death it passed back to Mary Sandys, who had the power to bequeath it as she chose.[50]

The amount of portion brought to a marriage was partly a reflection of variations in wealth between the bride's and bridegroom's families, and, as Table 2.2 indicates, there was a significant variation in portion among these families. In 1765, Catherine Hall (d. 1843) brought £1,000 to her marriage to William Brownlow (1726–94), while Catherine Copely (d.

Table 2.2 Portion and jointure, 1747–1845[a]

Name	Date of marriage	Portion £	Settled jointure on estate £	Settled jointure portion %
Emily Lennox	1747	10,000	3,000	30
Dorcas Stevenson	1751	Land	500	N/A
Catherine Taylor	1755	5,000	1,000	20
Louisa Lennox	1758	10,000	2,500	25
Ann Hamilton	1761	5,000	2,000	40
Anne Lowry	1763	N/A	1,200	N/A
Catherine Hall	1765	1,000	500	50
Sarah Conway	1766	6,500	1,500	23
Philadelphia Hannah	1770	N/A	1,200	N/A
Frances Anne Pratt	1773	5,000	1,000	20
Letitia Trevor	1774	10,000	1,000	10
Charlotte Dillon	1777	5,000	1,000	20
Catherine Copely	1779	17,020	Investment	N/A
Mary Aylmer	1783	N/A	1,000	N/A
Mary Sandys	1786	Land, investments and cash	5,000	N/A
Barbara Godfrey	1790/91	N/A	2,000	N/A
Amelia Hobart	1794	20,000	2,500	12
Charity Forde	1795	6,000	700	12
Ann Jane Hatton	1800	5,000	2,000	40
Anna Foster	1801	10,000	1,000	10
Harriet Douglas	1809	10	2,000	N/A
Catherine Freeman	1811	10,000	1,500	15
Augusta Ann Wilmot	1816	N/A	3,000	N/A
Frances Anne Vane-Tempest	1819	£10,000	1,000	10
Augusta Charteris	1819	N/A	1,000	N/A
Mary Bligh	1822	10,000	1,200	12
Helen Sheridan	1825	N/A	1,000	N/A
Jane MacNeill	1828	10	1,200	N/A
Louisa Jane Russell	1832	12,000	5,000	42
Augusta Stanley	1841	5,000	2,500	50
Jane Alexander	1845	10,000	2,000	20

Note: [a] All percentages are rounded to the nearest unit.
Sources: See appendix C. 'N/A' denotes that the figure is not available from the sources used.

1791) brought £17,020 to her marriage to John James Hamilton, the future Marquess of Abercorn, in 1779.[51] The rental of the Brownlow estate at the time of this particular marriage was £6,808[52] while the rental of the Abercorn estate was £19,709.[53] However, variations in family wealth can only partly explain the amount of portion recorded in a marriage settlement. On the marriage of Frances Anne Vane-Tempest to

Charles Stewart, the future Marquess of Londonderry, Frances Anne brought a cash portion of £10,000. This represented a small proportion of the estate and associated income she brought to the Londonderrys. The jointure of £1,000 settled on this marriage was also a small proportion of the income received by Frances Anne on the death of her husband, as she had a significant separate estate. It therefore appears to be the case that the sum of £10,000 was used, as a token amount, for the purpose of arranging the marriage.[54] Furthermore, of the sixteen portions between the sums of £5,000 and £10,000 listed in Table 2.2, eight were exactly £10,000. It is possible that this was considered an appropriate sum on which to base provision for a future wife, or, alternatively, as the minimum amount to circumvent the bride's entitlement to common law dower.

It appears to have been standard practice that the amount of jointure to be settled was calculated in relation to the portion brought to the marriage. Anthony Malcomson has regarded jointure-to-portion ratio of 10 per cent as common among the Irish aristocracy in this period, and it is considered by Eileen Spring to be common by the late seventeenth century in England.[55] However, as Table 2.2 indicates, a 10 per cent ratio was not universally applied among the sample families, and, in fact, the ratio ranged from 10 per cent to 50 per cent. In three cases the ratio was 10 per cent, and in nine cases it ranged from 12 per cent to 15 per cent. Larger jointure-to-portion ratios can possibly be explained by non-monetary factors, such as the political and social advantages of the marriage to the bridegroom's family. Malcomson has noted how the 'condescension' of a bride from such a background could lead to the arrangement of a jointure proportionately much larger than the portion brought to the marriage.[56] The jointure settled on Frances Pratt (d. 1833) in 1773 was 20 per cent of the portion she brought to her marriage to Robert Stewart, Lord Castlereagh (1739–1821).[57] Frances Pratt was the daughter of Charles Pratt, Lord Camden (1714–94), who by this stage of his active political career in the British House of Commons had undertaken the offices of Attorney General and Lord Chancellor, and was also a close friend of the Whig politician and Prime Minister William Pitt 'the elder'. It can be assumed that the Stewart family recognised the potential for political advancement through the connections brought with the marriage. Such potential was realised in 1789 when Lord Camden obtained a peerage for Robert Stewart, and in 1798 when the son of Lord Camden, as Lord Lieutenant of Ireland, appointed Lord Castlereagh his acting Chief Secretary.[58]

The contractual nature of marriage settlements is highlighted by the use of nominal sums in two cases. On her marriage to Charles Brownlow in 1828, the portion brought by Jane MacNeill (d. 1878) was recorded as £10. Charles Brownlow settled a jointure of £1,200 sterling on the marriage, as he had been empowered to do by the will of his father. It is unclear from the settlement whether any future portion was to be paid, and it is most likely that alternative arrangements were made between Charles Brownlow and Jane MacNeill's father.[59] Similarly, on the marriage of Harriet Douglas to James, Viscount Hamilton, heir to the Abercorn title and estates, there is no record of portion, and, as a reflection of this, a nominal jointure of £10 was settled on the marriage.[60] What occurred here was that, because Viscount Hamilton's father, the first Marquess of Abercorn, was in England at the time of the marriage in 1809, complete arrangements could not be made. The Marquess of Abercorn was however concerned that dower should be barred at this stage, before his return. Before the marriage he wrote a codicil to his will indicating his intention that 'an adequate provision by way of jointure shall be settled on the said Harriet . . . in lieu and bar of her dower and thirds which she might become entitled to at common law or by any custom'. The codicil charged the estate with £2,000 jointure payment 'in order to guard against any accident that might happen' in the meantime.[61] The nominal jointure of £10 was increased by a later deed to £2,000.[62]

The use of nominal sums to permit the settlement of jointure indicates that the primary function of the marriage settlement, from the perspective of the bridegroom's family, was the barring of dower by the contracting of jointure for the bride. Post-nuptial agreements could be employed to make additional provision. Therefore, by the nineteenth century, although portion remained an important element for these families in the marriage settlement, the possibility of alternative arrangements on which to base provision for women did exist. This is further illustrated by the financial arrangements made on the marriage of Price Blackwood, the future fourth Lord Dufferin, and Helen Sheridan in 1825.

No settlement made prior to the marriage is extant among the Dufferin family papers at the Public Record Office of Northern Ireland. However, Blackwood family correspondence from this time indicates that negotiations preceding the marriage were acrimonious, and that Helen Sheridan's lack of portion was one reason for the Blackwood family's disapproval. Price Blackwood's father, Hans Blackwood (1758–1839), the future third Lord Dufferin, wrote to his son on the subject:

> In saying that the young lady's want of fortune is one cause you [and her family] also must take into their consideration that no settlement of jointure

or provision for younger children can be made upon such a marriage and I
am certain you ought to consider the deplorable situation should you have
a wife and family should any fatality occur to yourself.[63]

The Dufferin estate, which took a rental of £18,000 by the 1840s, was
increasingly in debt in the 1820s.[64] As a response to this, a family settlement of 1825 established a sinking fund to deal with the problem of
existing debt, and provision for future generations. An annual sum of
£2,000 from the estate rental was paid into the fund, which was conveyed to trustees for the purchase of government stocks.[65] Portions had
been used in the past to clear Blackwood debts, and it was expected that
on Price Blackwood's marriage his future wife would bring a suitable
portion for this purpose.[66] The use of portion to assist in clearing debts
of the bridegroom's family was a common arrangement for portions
received by other families: for instance, approximately half of the
£41,486 cash portion brought to her marriage in 1786 by Mary Sandys
was used to discharge the debts of the first Marquess of Downshire, and
the remainder was invested in government stocks for the use of Lord
Fairford.[67]

Crucially, Helen Sheridan's lack of portion did not prevent the marriage. At the time of the marriage in 1825, Price Blackwood was bound
to take out several life insurance policies during his time employed as a
captain in the Royal Navy, to ensure that his future wife received a jointure out of the family estate if she survived him, with his contributions
arranged according to income.[68] By 1837 he owned three insurance policies, with Guardian Assurance, the Law Life Assurance Society and the
Provident Assurance Society, the investment in which amounted to
£9,230 sterling, or £10,000 Irish.[69] This amount was equivalent to portions brought to other marriages within the Blackwood family, and
would ensure Helen Sheridan a jointure of £1,000 from the Dufferin
estate.[70]

The use of life insurance by Price Blackwood to compensate for his
wife's lack of portion in order to arrange jointure illustrates how a landed
family could arrange a marriage in the absence of a portion brought by
the bride. In two further cases among the families in this sample the jointure settled derived entirely from investments, and therefore did not represent a charge on the family landed estate. In the 1779 marriage
settlement of Catherine Copely (d. 1791) and John James Hamilton,
Marquess of Abercorn (1756–1818), £12,000 was invested in bank
annuities to provide jointure.[71] In 1782, Sophia Whaley's portion of
£12,000 was to be invested by Robert Ward, to purchase land or to be
invested in joint-stock companies, to provide jointure, provision for

younger children and additional income for Robert Ward.[72] On one occasion jointure settled on the family estate was supplemented with investments. The settled jointure of a £1,500 rent charge noted in Table 2.2, arranged for Catherine Freeman (1786–1863) on her marriage to Dupre Alexander, Earl of Caledon (1777–1839), in 1811 was only part of her settled jointure, which was supplemented with a further sum of £1,130 to be paid after the death of Lord Caledon by the Royal Exchange in London.[73]

The use of investments to supplement, or replace, jointure from landed estates reflects a desire among landowners to consider alternative forms of provision for family members. However, at the same time this type of provision may have had implications for women's control over their jointure, as it is possible that the less socially and economically prestigious a woman's husband was, the more control she exercised over her portion. The Downshires, for example, by the middle of the nineteenth century aimed to develop the family property and increase freedom in the management of the estates. This would require more land to be freed from the restrictions imposed by family settlements for the provision of widows and children.[74] In order to prevent an extra financial burden being placed on the estate, alternative arrangements were made on the marriage of one of the Marquess of Downshire's younger sons, Arthur Hill, to Mary Sutton in 1848. The £25,000 portion brought to the marriage was invested in government stocks by the bride's father to provide pin money, jointure and provisions for the younger children of the marriage. Mary Sutton was empowered by the marriage settlement to direct this sum, 'notwithstanding her coverture', and only in default of her direction could her husband control this sum.[75] In another example, on the marriage of Charlotte Boyle to Lord Henry Fitzgerald, a younger son of James Fitzgerald, Duke of Leinster (1722–73), and Emily Fitzgerald, Duchess of Leinster (1731–1814), in 1791, Charlotte's portion of £25,000 was to be held in trust for her during her marriage and she was to receive the dividends during her life and the gross sum on the death of her husband.[76]

The use of investments as a means of providing for women during and after marriage can be regarded both as a means of ensuring provision in the absence of landed property, and as a means of protecting the landed estate from being over-burdened by provisions for family members. Whichever perspective is taken, it appears to have been the case that when an income derived from investments rather than land, women enjoyed more control over payments and in some cases also controlled the principal sum.

The last will and testament

The contractual nature of marriage settlements indicates their usefulness and limitations as a historical source. Only property that the husband and wife were either in possession of, or due to inherit as heir at law, was of concern to conveyancers and future inheritance was not mentioned. A provision made in a marriage settlement was confirmed, and in many cases supplemented, by the last will and testament of the husband.

The power of the husband to dispose of property among the family was established by the Statute of Wills, passed in the Irish parliament in 1634.[77] This statute enabled landowners to dispose of all freehold property by will, and this provision included the freedom to bar dower. Although this could be achieved by landowners before 1634 by conveying land to trustees, the Statute of Wills was significant as it made such control easier for the landowner, thereby reinforcing the power and control that the head of the family wielded over family property.[78] This power also applied to personal property. As Eileen Spring argues, in England widows also lost their right to a share of their husband's personal property by 1725, by which time the male head of the family had the power to bequeath all personal property as he chose.[79] In Irish families it was acceptable practice for the head of the family to dispose of items such as household furniture and personal possessions, such as jewellery, as part of the estate. By increasing the range of items that were considered estate property, husbands could reduce a widow's common law inheritance.

A widow's common law right to inherit one-third of her deceased husband's landed property, and all of his personal property, was barred by the 1833 'act for the amendment of the law relating to dower', also known as the Dower Act. Although the use of marriage settlements and trustees had already effectively removed widows' common law rights, the Dower Act simplified the process for barring dower, as, from this time onwards, the intention of the husband to provide his widow with an annuity was sufficient legal evidence that dower should be barred.[80] Although the statute was not specifically extended to Ireland, neither was it withheld, and it can be assumed that English practice on this issue was followed in Ireland. The Irish Court of Chancery followed English practice, for example, in the 1841 case of *Hall v Hill*. In this case, although a widow's right to dower out of her deceased husband's estate was 'not expressly barred', Lord Chancellor Sugden ruled that it could be barred as her husband had made clear his intention in his will that she was to receive an annuity.[81] Therefore, although the Statute of Uses in Ireland and in England allowed for the barring of widows' common law right to dower only by pre-nuptial agreement, in practice landowners had more control over the barring of dower through the use of last will and testament.

Analysis of the relationship of jointure provision to the income of landed families from estate rental is hindered by the scarcity of reliable rental records for the period before 1850 among the sample families. It was not uniform practice in this period for landowners to record gross rental systematically. Furthermore, when it is possible to calculate gross rental, net rental presents an additional problem for the historian. Landlords may have had trouble actually receiving rents from tenants in times of hardship, such as the period following the Napoleonic wars, and changeable rental levels throughout this period make it difficult to reach an accurate figure regarding what income from rental may have been.[82] In most cases, when rental figures are available from the sample families, the dates do not correspond with what is required for the purpose of considering the relationship of jointure received to estate rental at the time of the husband's death. Because of the complexity of rental fluctuations, no attempt has been made here to estimate rentals accordingly. The figures used to calculate the percentages of settled and actual jointure received to rental, as listed in Table 2.3, are included primarily to enable tentative observations to be made on this issue.

As Table 2.3 indicates, the percentages of level of jointure, both settled and actually received by widows, and estate rental varied widely among the sample families. Of the seventeen women listed in Table 2.3, the actual jointure of five women was 25 per cent or more of estate rental and therefore almost equivalent to dower. If the rental of £12,000, derived from notes on accounts made by James, first Duke of Leinster, in 1766 and 1772, is accepted as a useful indication of the rental received by the Duke at his death in 1773, then the £3,000 settled on Emily, Duchess of Leinster, represented 25 per cent of rental, while her actual jointure of £4,000 was 33 per cent, and was therefore equivalent to the amount she would have received as dower.[83]

The percentages of jointure to estate rent for the remaining twelve women varied between 6 and 17 per cent. Most women in this sample therefore did not receive jointure that was equivalent to what they might have received as dower. The three women in the Blackwood family, Lords Dufferin, received jointure that was significantly less than what they would have been entitled to as dower. Among these three women, Dorcas Blackwood, Baroness Dufferin and Clandeboye, brought the most valuable portion, in the form of land, to her marriage to John Blackwood in 1751. Yet her jointure represented 6 per cent of the estimated Blackwood rental of £10,000 for the year 1800.[84] Anna Blackwood, Lady Dufferin,

Table 2.3 Percentages of settled and actual jointure to estate rental,
1747–1845[a]

Name	Date of marriage	Settled jointure: rental %	Actual jointure %
Emily Fitzgerald	1747	25	33
Dorcas Blackwood	1751	5	6
Louisa Conolly	1758	10	10
Catherine Brownlow	1765	6	28
Frances Anne Stewart	1773	13	43
Letitia MacDonnell	1774	10	15
Mary Creighton	1776	N/A	7
Mary Browne	1783	10	13
Barbara Chichester	1790	6	6
Mary Hill	1786	29	29
Anne Hamilton	1800	10	15
Anna Blackwood	1801	6	17
Catherine Alexander	1811	16	16
Augusta Westenra	1819	9	9
Helen Blackwood	1825	6	6
Jane Brownlow	1828	13	25
Jane Alexander	1845	13	13

Note: [a] N/A denotes that the figure is not available from the sources used.
Sources: See appendix C.

received a larger proportion, 17 per cent, of an enlarged rental, based on estimates for the minority of Frederick, fifth Lord Dufferin, in the period 1841–47.[85]

Although the evolving structure of family finances indicates a desire to consolidate landed property among the families surveyed here, the jointures noted also reveal an evident desire to provide an adequate income for women. Some women, such as the Duchess of Leinster, noted above, received generous jointure provision that was larger than what they might have received had they been entitled to dower. However, the level of jointures received by women in the sample families varied widely, and some women received jointure that was a fraction of the equivalent dower amount. As Table 2.3 suggests, this may have been as little as 6 per cent of the estate rental. This practice does not appear to have altered over this period. Women at both ends of the period 1750–1850 received both jointure that was equivalent to dower, and jointure that represented a small percentage of dower. Nor does family practice offer a satisfactory explanation. Catherine Brownlow (d. 1843), who married in 1765, and Jane Brownlow, Lady Lurgan (d. 1878), who married in 1828, both received jointures almost equivalent to dower. As noted above, Dorcas

Blackwood, Baroness Dufferin and Clandeboye, who married in 1751, and Helen Blackwood, Lady Dufferin, who married in 1825, both received small percentages of the Dufferin estate, while the jointure of Anna Blackwood, who married in 1801, was 30 per cent of the estate rental, and therefore almost equivalent to dower.

As noted in Table 2.2, the amount of jointure received by women in these families varied enormously, with annuities ranging from £600 to £5,000. In most cases, jointure was in the form of an annuity payable from estate rental. There are, however, two examples in this sample of jointure not being charged entirely on the family estate. John James Hamilton, Marquess of Abercorn, bequeathed to his widow Anne Hamilton, Marchioness of Abercorn, £1,000 from a trust fund as well as her jointure of £2,000 from the Abercorn estate.[86] The jointure of Anna Blackwood, Lady Dufferin, was increased from £1,000 to £3,000. The extra £2,000 was not charged on the Dufferin estate but was made up of a sum of £500 acquired from the interest on Anna, Lady Dufferin's portion, and a claim of money that her husband, James, Lord Dufferin, had from another landowner, from which he directed, when paid, that an annuity of £400 'may be procured for the life of my wife and for her sole use'. A further annuity of £1,100 was to be raised from his personal estate, 'to commence from the day of my death'.[87] While it was still common among these families to provide for widows from the rental of the family estate, these two examples indicate the possibilities available to supplement minimum jointure with other sources.

Despite the marginalisation of women's interests in the family estate that is evident in the structure of marriage settlements and testamentary power, the reality of the income received by women from their husbands estates is more complex. A powerful woman such as Theodosia Meade, Countess of Clanwilliam (1743–1817), was able to overturn the effects of a family settlement, for she believed her husband was not able to manage the property appropriately as a result of his growing indebtedness and drunkenness. The 1765 settlement made on the Countess's marriage to John Meade (1744–1800), according to Lady Moira, allowed her £1,000 pin money and a jointure of £3,500. In return, her husband took possession of her County Down estates at Gill Hall and Rathfriland, which were worth £4,000 a year in rental. However, during her marriage Lady Clanwilliam exerted her influence in the resettlement of these estates, after which they were to pass to her favourite second son rather than her eldest son as was customary, while she was to receive the rental for the rest of her life.[88]

Women received income from a variety of sources. As outlined in Table 2.4, additional interests, separate amounts from jointure, were also

Table 2.4 **Additional interests arranged for wives by husbands, 1747–1845**

Name	Date of marriage	Additional income settled on marriage	Additional income settled by husband's will
Dorcas Blackwood	1751	Life interest in land	
Louisa Conolly	1758		Life interest in freehold land
Anne Willougby Cole	1763		Interest in investment with power of appointment and capital interest in land
Catherine Boyle	1763		Share of investments and principal sum, with power of appointment
Theodosia Meade	1765	Life interest in land	
Philadelphia Hannah	1770		Life interest in land in place of jointure
Mary Creighton	1776	Life interest in land	
Catherine Copely	1779	Life interest in Investment	
Amelia Stewart	1794	Life interest in land	
Anna Blackwood	1801		Interest in investment with power of appointment
Frances Anne Vane-Tempest	1819		Capital interest in real and personal estate
Jane Brownlow	1828	£1,000 for house and gardens	Capital interest in land
Jane Alexander	1845	Life interest in investment	

Sources: See appendix C; PRONI, Clanwilliam/Meade papers, D/3044/D/1/20, fragment of a declaration by Theodosia Hawkins-Magill, Countess of Clanwilliam, undated.

settled on women, either on marriage or in their husband's wills. There are three instances in this study of capital interests in land being bequeathed to a widow by her late husband, and in all cases the land had been purchased by the husband during the marriage, or had been always held in *fee simple*. Charles, Lord Londonderry, bequeathed all his real and personal property to his widow, Frances Anne, Lady Londonderry, in 1854.[89] William Willoughby Cole, Earl of Enniskillen (1736–1803), bequeathed his 'estate and interest' in his house and lands in Bundoran, purchased during the marriage and held in fee simple.[90] Finally, Charles Brownlow, Lord Lurgan, bequeathed a personal estate of land in County

Armagh to his widow Jane Brownlow, Lady Lurgan.[91] Therefore, in addition to jointure, a widow might inherit an interest in an income from rental, or investments that had been enjoyed by her husband during his life. As with jointure, such interests were usually life interests. In five cases noted in Table 2.4, a widow received a life interest in the rental from a landed property. Louisa Conolly (1743–1817), for example, was bequeathed a life interest in her late husband's Castletown estate.[92]

A degree of caution is however required when considering such interests, as unforeseen events could affect a widow's receipt of such bequests. According to the terms of Lord Lurgan's will, Lady Lurgan was empowered to sell as she chose, to whomever she wanted, the land bequeathed to her in 1847 by her late husband's will, having first made an offer to her eldest son, who Lord Lurgan wished would purchase it 'for the benefit of the estate and advantage of my younger children'.[93] In practice, however, Lady Lurgan's power to sell the land was restricted, as her late husband had promised it as security for a loan. She was advised to receive the rental from the property for the period of the minority of the Brownlow heir, and take no further action until it could be reconsidered when her son inherited the Brownlow estates.[94] The interests of the succeeding heir may have also influenced the final outcome of testamentary bequests to a widow. In his last will and testament, John Creighton, Earl of Erne (1738–1828), confirmed the bequest of a life interest in a fee simple estate in Dublin to his widow Mary Creighton, Countess of Erne (d. 1842), as arranged in their marriage settlement.[95] Just after her husband's death, however, she gave up her claim to this life interest in return for an annuity of £486 from the Erne estate.[96]

Investments were an alternative source for providing for all family members, such as the heir and his bride if she survived him. On two occasions among the sample families, as noted in Table 2.4, interests in investments were settled on marriage. The marriage settlement of Catherine Copely to John James Hamilton, Marquess of Abercorn, arranged for the establishment of a trust fund, with a gross sum of £13,531 to be invested in consolidated bank annuities. The dividends were to be paid to Lord Abercorn during his life, and to his widow on his death.[97] On the death of her husband, Jane Alexander, Countess of Caledon (1825–88), received interest in a trust fund established with her portion.[98] On two occasions an interest in an investment was bequeathed to a widow by the last will and testament of her husband, along with the power of appointment. Anne Willoughby Cole, Viscountess Enniskillen (1742–1802), was entitled to the interest of a sum of £2,000 invested by William Willoughby Cole, Earl of Enniskillen, in 1778, for her life, and was also entitled to bequeath the interest in the sum.[99] In his last will and testament, James,

Lord Dufferin, established the right of his widow, Anna, Lady Dufferin, to receive dividends from a trust fund, the gross sum of which was £10,000 and which was hers to appoint in her last will and testament.[100]

Therefore, regarding provision made for women in Irish wealthy landed families, a complex picture emerges. Some women received interests in land or investments, although for most women jointure was settled in the form of an annuity from the main family estate. There was an evident desire to provide adequately for women in family settlements, and for some women jointure was equivalent to the income they could have expected to receive had they received dower. However, for some women jointure was much less, and in this period there was a perceptible marginalisation of provision for widows from family property. This was a continuation of a process that had begun in the seventeenth century, as dower was replaced by jointure and it became acceptable practice, as illustrated by these families, for bequests to widows of life interests in land to be relinquished in favour of annuities.

The role of executrix

As indicated in Table 2.1, heirs to the estate were most likely to be appointed executors of the last will and testament of the head of the family. There were five instances among the sample families of widows being appointed sole executrixes to their husbands' wills. However, numerically, when widows were appointed, this was more likely to be a joint appointment with either male heirs or trustees.

Amy Erickson argues that at this time the duties of the executrix were primarily moral and had lost all legal force by the eighteenth century.[101] It could be argued that, given the predominance of legal settlements in the financial affairs of landed families, the legal authority of the husband's will and the detailed instructions on bequests usually included in his will, the role of executrix did not carry much power anyway, beyond a symbolic gesture. However, in a wealthy landed family an executrix could be responsible for the management of substantial sums of money. The personal estate of the head of a landed family was potentially substantial: for example, that of William Brownlow was £38,739 on his death in 1794.[102]

The composition of property in landed families at this time combined rental from land with investments in shares, assurance funds and trust funds. Such funds were sometimes not immediately available, ensuring the involvement of the widow in her late husband's financial business for a number of years. When a widow was appointed executrix she enjoyed a degree of authority in relation to family property. Catherine Alexander,

Countess of Caledon, was co-executor and residuary legatee of the last will and testament of her husband, Dupre, Lord Caledon. As well as administering bequests, Lady Caledon was empowered to oversee, and change if necessary, the terms of a trust fund established by her husband amounting to the sum of £1,101, dividends of which were to be directed, via the parish church, to 'the poor' of the parish of Aghaloe in County Tyrone.[103] She corresponded with her late husband's bankers and organised the payment of legacies in her husband's will.[104] Lady Caledon was also entitled to the residue of her husband's personal estate by the terms of his will. She took responsibility for the legacies to the extent that when the codicil bequeathing them was discovered to be invalid, she personally paid the bequests which amounted to a sum of £1,685, from her own property.[105]

Jane Brownlow, Lady Lurgan, was sole executrix to the will of her late husband Charles Brownlow, Lord Lurgan, and sole legatee of his personal estate after his death in 1847. Her role as executrix included overseeing the payment of testamentary expenses and debts due to her late husband, managing his assets and 'full [and] ample powers to collect these assets [and] to compel payment of them'.[106] The assets over which Lady Lurgan had responsibility were divided according to the times at which they could be converted into money to facilitate the payment of debts and legacies. Assets such as unsold leases, livestock, the balance of Royal Exchange assurances, tithe and rent charge, arrears of rent, moss rent and ejectment costs to be paid by tenants could be converted into money within one year. The balance of this type of asset was £15,925. Assets such as shares in a gas company and household property such as plate, linen and farming implements could not be converted into money until five years had passed. The balance of this type of asset was £6,610. Out of the personal estate, debts had to be paid amounting to a total of £5,682, and were due to various people such as tailors, shoemakers and poultry suppliers, as well as for estate drainage and poor rate on arrears of rental.

The duties of executrix could therefore encompass several years and significant amounts of money. For example, a bond debt of £1,416 was due to be paid to Mr Greer, and it was noted that by the terms of the bond Lady Lurgan could not pay him until 1852. After the payment of all debts, the residue of Lord Lurgan's personal estate was calculated by her agent as £10,244 'at Lady Lurgan's disposal' within the first year, not including assets which would be converted within five years. It is likely that this sum was invested, as her agent calculated the annual sum which might arise out of an investment at 4 per cent, £419.[107]

Bequests made to widows

None of the women among the sample families married with the expectation of receiving dower, and although some women received jointure equivalent to what they would have received had they been able to claim dower, most received much less. Estate management policy in this period favoured the consolidation of estates because of the economic, political and social power that was associated with large landholdings. The replacement of dower with jointure is one example of how such practice worked to the disadvantage of many widows. It is significant that out of seventeen jointures listed in Table 2.3, five actual jointures and only two of the settled jointures were equivalent to dower. This suggests a practice of settling the minimum possible amount at the time of marriage, with the intention of increasing the amount by last will and testament. Crucially, such additions were added at the discretion of the husband. As outlined in Table 2.5, the type of property bequeathed to widows varied. Alongside jointure, widows were bequeathed additional annuities, legacies, paraphernalia and house interests. The type of interest in this property was either a capital interest, when a widow was bequeathed the complete ownership of the property with power to bequeath it, or a life interest, when she was bequeathed an interest in the property for life only, with no power to bequeath it. The bequests made to widows by their husbands indicate a desire on the part of husbands to make adequate provision for their wives, while at the same time protecting the family estates. The most effective way for a landowner to do this was to establish life interests in landed and moveable property, thereby securing an income for his widow during her life while ensuring the property passed securely to his heir on her death.

The financial reality for a widow was that the jointure payment might be delayed in the period following her husband's death. It was therefore usual practice among these families to bequeath a gross sum to the widow, such as the £500 bequeathed in 1790 to Letitia, Marchioness of Antrim, 'for her support' and the £500 bequeathed by John Creighton in 1828 to his widow Mary 'for her immediate accommodation'.[108] Such legacies differed from other gross sums, such as those bequeathed for the immediate accommodation of the widow, as by law a legacy was not due for payment until one year after the decease of the husband.[109] When Catherine Brownlow and the other Brownlow children took a case to Chancery for the payment of portions from the family property, her son William Brownlow (1755–1815), who had since inherited the Brownlow estates, argued that the personal property was insufficient to meet the cost of the portions and they would have to be raised on the real estate,

Table 2.5 **Types of bequest made to widows in their husbands' wills,
1767–1855**

Type of property	Number of bequests
Residue of personal estate	6
Gross sum	10
Capital interest in freehold land	3
Life interest in freehold land	5
Additional annuities charged on landed estate	12
Additional annuities charged on personal estate	1
Interest/dividends from investments	6
Legacies charged on landed estate	2
Legacies charged on personal estate	1
Capital interest in moveable property	13
Life interest in moveable property	13
Paraphernalia	10
Capital interest in house	1
Life interest in house	12
Temporary interest in house	1

Sources: See appendix D.

and as legacies they were not due for payment for a year. The amounts were paid, although this took place one year later.[110]

The bequest of a right of residence in one of the family houses is another feature of these wills. This practice has been referred to as a 'peculiarly Irish phenomenon', the exact legal status of which is vague. As Sheena Grattan notes, in accordance with jointure, such bequests were 'at best . . . passive "income" interests, conferring no capital entitlement on the beneficiary'.[111] The family home and other homes, often in London, Dublin or fashionable resting places such as Bath, were considered as part of the estate and were usually bequeathed as such to the heir. In thirteen wills that made reference to the right of residency, eleven specified that this was a life interest only. A further two examples of additional types of bequests were the right to live in the family house for one year bequeathed by Arthur Chichester, Marquess of Donegall, in 1795, and a capital interest bequeathed by Charles Brownlow to his widow Caroline Brownlow in 1822.[112]

The bequest of a right of residence indicates how control over all family property was concentrated in the hands of the male head of the family. In addition to the estate and lodge at Bundoran, near Ballyshannon, that was bequeathed to Anne Willoughby Cole, Lady Enniskillen, her husband William, Lord Enniskillen, bequeathed to her the use of household furniture, corn, hay and stock at the family seat, Florence Court, and 'the use and benefit of all the furniture, plate and house linen kitchen and other utensils' found in his house in Granby Row, Dublin, 'for and during her natural life'.[113] Family houses, and the contents that were indicative of status, as well as being objects used for living, were regarded as estate property. Household contents were considered as part of the family estate. Therefore, the bequest of residency rights was often, by necessity, accompanied by a life interest in household contents.

The temporary nature of a widow's residency rights is further illustrated by the issue of the widow's responsibility for 'wear and tear' of household furniture. William Brownlow, for example, specified in his bequest of the life interest in the Brownlow house in Merrion Square, Dublin, that his widow Catherine was to have the use of the house 'without being accountable for the same during her life'.[114] However, this is the only example of a husband's will ensuring his widow would not be liable for wear and tear of household property. Jane Alexander, Countess of Caledon, pursued this issue on the death of her husband in 1855. Lady Caledon was appointed guardian of the person of her son, the heir to the Caledon title and estates, James Alexander.[115] James lived with his mother at the Caledons' London house in Carlton House Terrace. It appears to have been the case that Lady Caledon was responsible for the wear and tear of household furniture and other items while she lived there. In 1857 she proposed an arrangement with the trustees of her late husband's estate that

> as long as her son lives with her in Carlton Terrace House, the furniture of that house which belong[s] to him, as part of the residue of the estate . . . ought not, as far as wear [and] tear goes, to be charged against her or be paid for by her though she is willing to make herself liable to the guardians [of the estate] for all damages beyond what is the natural consequence of the furniture being used.[116]

The trustees agreed this arrangement in 1857; consequently, for the period of her son's minority Lady Caledon was not liable for the replacement and repair of household items.

In seven cases the house was bequeathed as a life interest with no other conditions attached. The right to live in the family house for one year, bequeathed by Lord Donegall, was accompanied by a legacy of £8,000 to enable his widow, Barbara, Lady Donegall, to buy furniture.[117] However, in the other five wills, the right of residence was conditional. In his 1781 will, John Blackwood bequeathed the use of his house in Killyleagh, the family's second home, along with the furniture, plate, farm and garden produce to his wife Dorcas Blackwood for the duration of the time that 'she shall ch[oo]se . . . to reside with the said unmarried daughters'.[118] Randall, Marquess of Antrim, bequeathed the use of his house and furniture in Merrion Square, Dublin, to his wife Letitia, Lady Antrim, by his will dated 1790, for her use during the minority of their son and 'provided that she continues so long unmarried and uses the same for her own residence and does not let the same to any person or persons whatsoever'.[119]

The bequest of paraphernalia was not a feature of all wills. However, it is significant as it may indicate that there was an assumption that such personal property might be lost to the widow if it was not specifically bequeathed. A husband's personal property also, by law, included items that had been, in effect, a woman's property during her marriage, such as her clothes, jewellery and dressing table. William Brownlow bequeathed to his wife 'all her paraphernalia' in 1791, as did James, Lord Dufferin, in 1836. Alongside her paraphernalia Lord Dufferin also bequeathed to his wife Anna, Lady Dufferin, all her jewellery, with the added note that she could give it to her successor for a sum of £500.

Married women's separate property

Until the Married Women's Separate Property Acts in 1870 and 1882 it was not possible under common law for married women to own property, owing to the doctrine of coverture, which submerged the legal identity of a married woman into that of her husband. One of the problems for the married woman was that because of her loss of legal status during coverture, she was to a large extent dependent on the good will of her husband for financial support during marriage. It was, however, possible for private arrangements to be made for a married woman to receive a separate income for her own use during marriage, independent of her husband.

Separate estate originated in the sixteenth century and was arranged in equity by the use of trusts. This type of property differed from life interests in landed property or investments that were arranged for brides at the time of marriage. In the 1830s there were the beginnings of legal recognition that in some instances married women should be considered *femes soles*. The 1834 Irish 'act for the abolition of fines and recoveries', which is almost identical to the English Act of 1833, specified certain situations in which a wife could dispense with the requirement for her husband's consent in the disposal of her estate. A husband's insanity or absence, whether through imprisonment, transportation or estrangement, that is, when by law he was not able to give consent in a form that was legally valid, provided these conditions. Another exception to the requirement for the husband's consent was when the Court of Chancery was responsible for the wife's property.[120] The exceptional circumstances required for a wife to be considered legally *feme sole* meant that the spirit of the 1834 law was in accordance with the assumption that within the family, the husband was responsible for property matters. However, like its English counterpart of 1833, the act represented the first statute recognition in Ireland that in some instances a wife should be treated as a *feme sole* during property transactions.[121]

Separate estate was arranged by private contract and could therefore be 'drawn in an infinite variety of ways, with or without trustees, and with the payments dependent on more or less well-secured capital funds, or indeed not secured by any fund'.[122] However, particular wording was required if the settlement was to be considered valid by the Court of Chancery. As with all trusts, the key element of such arrangements was the clear expression of intention. Unless the boundaries of a married woman's ownership were clearly expressed, there was a danger that her rights over the separate estate could be curtailed.[123] When settling a separate estate on a married woman, the wording had to clearly express that it was for her 'sole and separate use'. To state solely that it was for 'her absolute use' was inadequate, as it was 'not the necessary unequivocal evidence of an intention to exclude the husband'.[124]

Irish marriage settlements are of limited use in considering the separate property of married women. Fewer than half of the marriage settlements from the sample families make any reference to any sum distinguishable as pin money or separate estate. A bride could only arrange her own separate property before her marriage took place, although such plans could be made on her behalf at any time during the marriage. For example, investments that provided a separate income could be bequeathed to married women by the last wills and testaments of family members.

Therefore, although there were two types of separate property owned by married women in this period, pin money and separate estate, it has not been possible to make a clear distinction between the two.[125] The term 'pin money' may have referred to more than one types of payment. In 1797, £1,000 was settled on Anne Katherine MacDonnell, Countess of Antrim, on her marriage to Henry Vane-Tempest 'for her sole and separate use and benefit by way of pin money'.[126] In 1811, £500 was settled on Lady Catherine Freeman on her marriage to Dupre Alexander, also 'for the separate use and by way of pin money'.[127] It is also possible that the meaning of 'pin money' changed over the course of the century. It may have represented a substantial income in the mid-eighteenth century, though by the mid-nineteenth century it had dwindled to represent a small sum of money.[128] As will be discussed below, pin money was a definable sum, while separate estate was more ambiguous. Therefore, for the purpose of this chapter, it may be useful to consider married women's separate estate as all other arrangements made in addition to pin money. This will make possible the identification of situations in which separate estate was settled as a distinct type of property.

Pin money

Pin money can be described as an annuity settled on a bride for the duration of her marriage that was paid in instalments, either biennially or quarterly, to the bride for the purpose of financing basic maintenance requirements such as clothes and other personal necessities. It was arranged using trusts, and came under the remit of equity in the Court of Chancery.[129] As Susan Staves has noted, conveyancers were concerned to establish a secure maintenance payment on married women that was viable in the courts while at the same time not undermining the authority of the husband during coverture.[130] Pin money was strictly intended for the maintenance of the wife and was therefore a specific type of payment, with particular rules attached to it. By the eighteenth century, it had evolved as a specific type of payment. Writing at the beginning of the nineteenth century, William Blackstone noted that the background to this provision was for the husband 'to provide his wife with necessaries' by law. This duty was so integral to the married state that a husband was also liable for his wife's debts if she purchased such 'necessaries'.[131]

The settlement of pin money did not feature in all marriage settlements examined here. One possible explanation for this absence is the fact that, unlike those governing jointure, the legal obligations surrounding pin money did not have immediate implications for the landed estate. However, it can be assumed that all women in the sample families did have arrangements made for pin money around the time of their marriage, and it is likely that a lower limit, based on requirements of rank, existed among these families.[132]

Where pin money does feature in these families, it is clear that its arrangement in Ireland followed English practice. It was standard practice for pin money to be subject to a rule of no arrears after a specified period, and this period varied among families. In the 1773 settlement on the marriage of Frances Pratt and Robert Stewart, arrears of pin money could not be claimed after one year.[133] In the 1841 settlement on the marriage of Augusta Stanley and Richard Dawson, Lord Dartrey, arrears could not be claimed after two years, and any arrears existing after that time were to sink into the family estate.[134] Also, unlike jointure, pin money could not be bequeathed by the bride. In the 1845 marriage settlement of Jane Grimston and James Du Pre, Earl of Caledon, it was specifically noted that the pin money of £400 was settled with the condition that Jane Grimston 'may not have power to anticipate or charge the said annual sum of £400 or any part thereof by appointment, assignment or otherwise'.[135] A bride's control over pin money was therefore limited to her use for maintenance during marriage.

The effectiveness of separate property arrangements in law appears to have been unclear to landowners at the time, as by law, any items purchased by a married woman belonged to her husband. The provision of pin money made for Anna Foster was noted specifically to be 'for her sole and separate use and benefit . . . to be disposed of by her for dress, clothes and such other uses as she shall think fit'.[136] In addition, Anna Foster was apparently empowered to spend the sum 'as she shall see fit'. However, despite this apparent independence, James Blackwood presumably did not trust the power of the marriage settlement, as he bequeathed to Anna 'all the paraphernalia and furniture of her dressing room she may desire'.[137]

Table 2.6 lists pin money arrangements made for thirteen women for whom details of portion are also available. In all these cases, pin money derived from the family estate. However, as in the case of jointure, there would have been exceptions to this. For example, as already noted, on the marriage of Mary Sutton to Arthur Hill, a younger son of the Marquess of Downshire, in 1848, £25,000 was invested in government stocks. From this sum Mary Sutton was to receive pin money of £400 or £500.[138] The percentage of pin money to portion ranged from 4 per cent to 10 per cent, a relatively small range compared with the differences of jointure among women noted in Table 2.3. The range in the amounts settled was also small, with the exception of three sums over £1,000. The remaining amounts ranged from £300 to £500 throughout this period, which suggests that, among this sample, most families considered this sum sufficient for a woman of this class.

The proportionately large pin money settled on Frances Anne Vane-Tempest Stewart, Lady Londonderry, is indicative of the confusion surrounding pin money and separate estate at this time. This sum clearly meant something different from the smaller sums settled on other women. In three cases noted above, in which women received pin money over £1,000, the women in question had brought portion in the form of land. It may sometimes have been the case that a large sums settled apparently as pin money was in fact a different type of annuity settled on a woman in compensation for her landed portion. The estates brought by Mary Sandys on her marriage to Arthur Hill, Lord Fairford, were entailed on her or her male heirs. If no male heirs were born during her

Tables 2.6 Pin money, 1747–1845

Name	Year of marriage	Portion £	Pin money £	Pin money portion %
Ann Chichester	1761	5,000	500	10
Sarah Stewart	1766	6,500	300	5
Frances Stewart	1773	5,000	300	6
Charlotte Browne	1777	5,000	300	6
Mary Hill	1786	41,486 + annual rental of £4,504	1,200	3
Amelia Stewart	1794	20,000	1, 600	8
Anna Blackwood	1801	10,000	500	5
Catherine Alexander	1811	10,000	500	5
Frances Anne Vane-Tempest	1819	10,000	2,000	20
Mary Brownlow	1822	10,000	400	4
Louisa Hamilton	1832	12,000	1,000	8
Augusta Dawson	1841	5,000	500	10
Jane Alexander	1845	10,000	400	4

Sources: See appendix C.

marriage to Arthur Hill, these estates were to pass into her ownership. In this event she would receive a reduced jointure from the Downshire estate of £1,900 instead of £5,000.[139] The large amount of pin money settled on Amelia Hobart's marriage to Robert Stewart in 1794 may reflect the fact that she was an heiress to her father's personal estates in Lincolnshire, the income from which was estimated as £18,000, as well as to the portion of £20,000 that she brought to the marriage.[140]

Separate estate

Separate estate could be arranged on behalf of a married woman at any time, either before, or during, her marriage. It was one method by which a father could ensure the financial independence of his daughter during her marriage. Because of the small size of the sample used in this study, it is impossible to generalise about the general practice regarding separate estate in this class in Ireland. It is clear that separate property arrangements were unconnected to the organisation of financial affairs concerning the main family estate, as separate property arrangements for brides are largely absent from the papers of the sample families. Acquiring information on the separate estate owned by women in this sample is further hindered by the fact that last wills and testaments written by women may be silent on the subject: separate estate enjoyed during marriage may have been alienated by the time the will was written, or devised in a separate document. Furthermore, the wording of separate estate arrangements was not uniform among the sample families. When Letitia MacDonnell, Marchioness of Antrim, bequeathed separate property to her married daughter Lady Charlotte Mark Kerr (1779–1835), this was stated to be for her 'sole and separate use on her receipt alone . . . notwithstanding her coverture'.[141] When Elizabeth Westenra, Lady Rossmore, settled a separate estate on her daughter, the deed so doing noted that it was to be established 'during the term of her natural life to and for her own sole and separate use and not in any wise [sic] subject to the controul [sic] of her husband'.[142]

However, it was possible to obtain information on the separate estate of eight women from these families, so some observations can be made. There were two types of separate estate in use among the sample families, land and investments, and women acquired their separate estate in several ways. The separate property of Anne Willoughby Cole, Viscountess of Enniskillen, Anna Blackwood, Lady Dufferin and Augusta Westenra, Lady Rossmore was, in all cases, based on a sum invested for their benefit by their husbands, either before or during marriage. On the deaths of their respective husbands, all three women would come into possession of the principal sum.[143] The separate property of Theodosia Meade, Countess of Clanwilliam, Mary Hill, Marchioness of Downshire, Anne Katherine MacDonnell, Charlotte Kerr and Frances Anne Vane-Tempest Stewart, Marchioness of Londonderry, all derived from their inheritance of family property.[144]

Provision of separate estate by investment took place throughout this period: Lady Enniskillen's separate estate was arranged in 1763 and Lady Rossmore's was arranged in 1841. This is in keeping with the separation of such arrangements from the landed property of the bride's father or her husband. Furthermore, in all cases where land was settled, the women concerned were heiresses to the family estate. In the absence of male heirs, therefore, a separate landed estate was conveyed to the use of a daughter; otherwise the preference among these families was to make such provision in non-landed form.

The settling of separate estate for a daughter's use was also a means of settling family property that the bride's father wished to be devised to her male heirs, such as her second son, but wished to keep separate from her husband's estate.[145] According to the terms of her father's last will and testament, Anne Willoughby Cole, Viscountess of Enniskillen, was a contingent remainder to her father's estates in County Fermanagh if her brother, Armar Corry, Earl of Belmore, died without issue. The Earl of Belmore had issue: his second but eldest surviving son from his first marriage inherited the estate. However, because of the possibility that she might inherit the estate, Lady Enniskillen wrote a will during her marriage which asserted her right to the estate as a separate property, in the event that the Earl of Belmore died without issue, 'for my own sole and separate use notwithstanding my coverture' and which could therefore be conveyed by her 'for such uses as I should think fit'.[146]

Younger children

The final section of the marriage settlement arranged provision for future daughters or younger sons of a marriage, the rights of whom to expect adequate provision from the family estate were within the remit of the Court of Chancery. By common law, daughters and younger sons would inherit by joint tenancy. However, equity favoured tenancy in common as a preferred mode of inheritance for younger children. There was no right of survivorship in tenancy in common, and each child had a distinct share in property settled. In contrast, the main feature of joint tenancy was that the shares of deceased children would automatically pass to their surviving siblings. This was believed to be 'an inconvenient mode of settlement'.[147] Following the 1751 case of *Rigden v Vallier* in the English Court of Chancery it was assumed that, in the absence of direction by last will and testament, a father would settle provision on his daughters and younger sons as tenancy in common.[148]

Practice in the Irish Court of Chancery followed the English courts. In 1803 the Irish Court referred to practice in the English courts, noting that 'of late, courts lean as much as possible to favour tenancies in common, as being found to answer the purpose of family dispositions, better than joint tenancies'.[149] Joint tenancy by common law could be overturned, and a tenancy in common established, primarily by the inclusion of words indicating that a tenancy in common was the intention of the settlement.[150] Words indicating the intention of tenancy in common were: 'equally, share and share alike, to and between and amongst'.[151] However, although Chancery supported the rights of daughters and younger sons to an adequate share of family property, it was at the same time clear that the testamentary wishes of their father could influence the court. Chancery was bound by the directions, and perceptible intentions, of the father as laid out in his last will and testament.

The legal obligation for parents to provide for their children explains the practice of bequeathing nominal sums in last wills and testaments. The justifications that accompany nominal bequests indicate further how prevalent the ideology of providing for one's children was among Irish landed families at this time. In his last will and testament John Creighton,

Earl of Erne, had power to dispose of £6,000 for the children of his marriage to Catherine Howard in 1799. In his last will and testament he bequeathed £1,999 to his son John and £4,000 to his daughter Catherine Creighton. His remaining daughter, Elizabeth, who was since deceased, was bequeathed £1, and this was because she had received £3,000 on her marriage.[152]

Testamentary practice among the sample families suggests that they desired to settle adequate provision for daughters and younger sons, while at the same time attempting to exert control over children through these provisions. Sums settled were subject to the direction of either the father or both parents, and only in default of direction by will would the money go to all younger children equally 'share and share alike'.[153] Furthermore, as with jointure, the amount settled on younger children was the minimum a family would commit to future children, and would be supplemented by last will and testament if provision were inadequate.

Practice, however, varied among the sample families. Provisions for children in nineteen marriages are listed in appendix E. In all cases, provisions were settled as tenancy in common only in default of parental direction by deed or last will and testament. Two of the wealthiest families in this sample, the Downshires and the Londonderrys, took different approaches to making provision for younger sons and daughters. On the marriage of Mary Sandys and Arthur Hill in 1786, provision was settled in accordance with the number of children born and £20,000 was settled for one younger child, £30,000 for two younger children and £40,000 for three or more younger children.[154] On the marriage of Frances Anne Vane-Tempest to Charles Stewart one sum of £10,000, equivalent to the portion brought to the marriage, was settled for younger children.[155] Of the seventeen examples of provisions listed in appendix E which detail the actual provision made for younger children, nine included supplementary provision made by the father's will. The division of the sum settled for younger children also varied between families. Charles Brownlow divided the sum he was empowered to settle on his one daughter and four sons equally. In his last will and testament, dated 1821, he distributed £14,000, requesting that his eldest son and heir make up the difference from the family estate. Each child received £3,000, except for one son who had already received £1,000 'paid for his advancement in the army'.[156]

Distinction was made in terms of gender and seniority in the division of the amount settled, and supplementary sums. In his will Bernard Ward divided his personal estate between his two younger sons, Robert and Edward Ward. The £8,000 settled for younger children on his marriage was to be divided among his daughters, who were to receive equal shares.

In addition to this they were to get another sum, the amount of which was higher for older daughters, with the eldest daughter receiving £4,000, the second daughter £3,000, and the two younger daughters £2,000 each. In addition to these amounts, Edward was to pay the eldest daughter, Anne Catherine, an annual sum of £50 until she married, and Robert was to pay the second eldest, Sophia, the annual sum of £50 until she married.[157]

In some families, distinction between children was made on the grounds of gender alone. In the 1781 will of John Blackwood, £3,000 was allocated to each of his three daughters, while payments to his five sons ranged from £500 to £2,000.[158] The reason for differentiation between children in the last wills and testaments is suggested by the will of Arthur Hill, Marquess of Downshire, which divided £40,000 settled for the younger children of his marriage in proportions of seven to ten, 'the boys to have the lesser, the girls the larger number'. His reasons for doing so were noted in the will: 'My wish is having by my settlements the power to divide £40,000 . . . as I may think fit and as my boys will serve their country and have many ways of providing for themselves and as the dear girls have not such opportunities but must patiently wait the caprice of love, or perhaps the avarice of some man to obtain a settlement.'[159]

The will of the Marquess of Downshire illustrates how differentiation between younger children on the grounds of gender could be based on a desire to increase the independence of daughters in relation to property. Such testamentary recognition was not, however, common. The treatment of daughters in wills varied among families, with some, as noted above, treating all children equally and some differentiating on the grounds of seniority. It was not a general rule therefore that daughters were treated more or less favourably than sons in the families examined. The ultimate authority of the father to decide on the allocation of provisions to younger children was, however, universally enforced. By his last will and testament a father was empowered to divide provision for daughters and younger sons in accordance to his perception of their needs.

The authority of the father over his children was further reinforced by the practice of attaching conditions to provisions. The most common condition attached to marriage settlements was the necessity of marriage with the consent of parents or guardian. Such conditions could be as general or specific as the father chose. In 1754, the will of John Dawson bequeathed two separate sums of £200 to his daughter and his son. The sum bequeathed to his 'beloved daughter', Elizabeth Dawson, was subject to the condition that 'she marry with the consent of my executors'. The sum bequeathed to his son, John Dawson, was subject to the condition that 'his behaviour until that time proves agreeable to my executor'.[160] John Cole, Lord Mountflorence, attached a more specific condition to the provision for one of his daughters, Elizabeth Cole. Elizabeth was to receive £2,490, her share of £8,000 settled for younger children, 'upon condition' that she 'shall not intermarry with Ponsonby Molesworth'.[161] The reason for Lord Mountflorence's objections to his daughter's possible marriage to Ponsonby Molesworth are not noted in his will. However, we can surmise that his motivation was at least partly financial: Ponsonby Molesworth was a captain in the army, but as he was the fifth son of his father, Sir Bysshe Molesworth, who was himself a younger son, his financial future may not have matched the expectations Lord Mountflorence had for his daughter. Elizabeth Cole obeyed her father's instructions and appears to have died unmarried, while Ponsonby Molesworth married another woman from a less prominent family, Susannah, sister of Sir Roger-Hale Sheaffe, an American-born general in the British Army.[162]

The image of parental harshness presented by conditions imposed in wills is mitigated by examples that suggest that such conditions were not always fully adhered to. A codicil to the will of John Dawson stated that if his daughter married without consent, she would lose only half of the money bequeathed to her.[163] Both younger daughters of James Stevenson, the father of Dorcas, Lady Dufferin, were married when James Stevenson made his final will, one with consent and one without consent. The will attached a condition that additional sums would only be paid 'provided always that if the said Ann or Margaretta or either of them shall happen to marry in my lifetime without my consent first had in writing that she so marrying without such consent shall not be entitled to the said sum of fifteen hundred pounds'.[164] Ann Stevenson, who married with consent, received the £1,000 settled on her by her parents' marriage settlement along with the additional £1,500, making a total of £2,500 to be paid to her on the death of her father. Margaretta Stevenson married without consent and received only the £1,000 she was entitled to by the marriage settlement of her parents. The additional sum of £1,500, which she would have received, was to be settled on the children of her unconsented marriage 'for their maintenance and support'. This payment was conditional upon the consent of Margaretta's mother, Anna, who was appointed as guardian to the children.[165]

The type of property bequeathed to daughters and younger children also varied among families. When daughters did inherit land, it was in default of sons. As noted in Chapter 4, in a sample of six wills in which bequests were made to both daughters and younger sons, younger sons were more likely to receive land, while daughters received legacies. However, the information in Table 2.7 indicates that within the sample

Table 2.7 Bequests to younger children, 1767–1855

Name	Date of will	Type of bequests to daughters	Type of bequests to sons
Lord Mountflorence	1767	Legacies	
Earl of Kildare	1768	Legacies	Land
Lord Bangor	1779	Legacies	Land
Sir John Blackwood	1781	Legacies	Legacies
Earl of Antrim	N/A	Land	
Earl of Antrim	1791	Land	
Earl of Donegall	1795		Land
William Brownlow	1799	Legacies	Legacies
Marquess of Downshire	1801	Legacy	Legacy
Earl of Caledon	1802	Legacy	
Earl of Enniskillen	1805	Legacies	Land, legacies
Earl of Shannon	1807	Land, legacies	Land, legacies
Earl of Kenmare	1812	Legacies	Legacies
Marquess of Abercorn	1818	Legacies	Legacies
Charles Brownlow	1821	Legacy	Legacy
Earl of Erne	1828	Legacy, investment	Land
Lord Rossmore	1843	Legacies	Land
Lord Lurgan	1847	Legacies	Legacies
Earl of Caledon	1855	Legacies	Legacies

Sources: See appendix E.

families, both younger sons and daughters received only legacies in most cases from the family estate. This suggests that, as in the experience of widows, it was acceptable practice to restrict the involvement of younger children in the landed estate.

Provisions made for daughters and younger sons varied among families. Distinction between children on the grounds of gender, age or perceived need was possible. It was also possible that daughters and younger sons would be treated equally. However, the main feature of the experience that younger children had of family property was of the power of the father to direct provision. Parental authority was established in marriage settlements and confirmed by the primacy of a father's wishes as expressed in his last will and testament.

Conclusion

The methods by which Irish landowners provided for family members had much in common with those used in English families. Irish families used strict settlement to secure their estates for future generations, and

by 1750 jointure had replaced dower as the preferred method of provision for widows. Future children were also provided for at the time of
their parents' marriage.

Regarding the power structure of these families, the examples presented in this chapter concur with Spring's conclusion about the nature
of English landed families. In Irish families, despite an evident desire to
provide for wives and children, husbands and fathers, as heirs to estates
and heads of families, exercised most power in the distribution of family
property, and the interests of women and younger sons, while not
uniform, were in most cases increasingly removed from the landed estate.

By replacing dower with jointure and bequeathing cash legacies to
daughters and younger sons, landowners consolidated their control over
landed family property. The practice of settling a minimum provision on
brides and younger children, which could be supplemented by last will
and testament, enabled the husband and father to exert a degree of
control over provisions and consequently over family members. This
control was supported by the use of trustees in family settlements to
convey land, moveable family property and other heirlooms considered
integral to the family title and estate, thereby enabling a landowner to
limit the interests of family members in such items to life only. Trustees
also acted as guardians and executors, roles otherwise taken by widows
and elder sons. The developing structure of family settlements therefore
also reflects the displacement of widows, and in some cases elder sons,
from integral roles in family financial management.

The actual provisions made for wives, daughters and younger sons
within this structure suggest a less uniform picture. In some cases,
women did receive jointure equivalent in amount to what they would
have received as dower. Some women had access to substantial separate
estates, and therefore presumably exercised significant financial independence from family control during and after marriage. However, most
women in this study received jointure that was a fraction of what the
equivalent dower would have been, which indicates a reduction in financial independence. Additional bequests to supplement jointure were a
common feature, but were usually life interests, intended for maintenance and, in effect, dependent on the whim and means of the husband.
Other property bequeathed to the widow could be subject to conditions
that required her to remain unmarried or would be extended to her as
long as she lived with her unmarried children.

Provisions for daughters and younger sons suggest a similar picture.
Parental authority was established by marriage settlement and confirmed
by the father's last will and testament. There are three cases among these
families of daughters inheriting the family estate in default of male heirs,

although for most children provision was limited to what was settled on their parents' marriage, with additional bequests made by the last will and testament of their father. There are some cases of land and investments being bequeathed to younger children, but it was more common for fathers to bequeath fee simple land to younger sons and interests in investments to daughters. However, in most cases both daughters and sons received only legacies from the family estate. As in the case of widows, provision for younger children was similarly dependent on the whim and means of the father. Conditions were attached, such as requirements for good behaviour and marriage with consent, which, if disobeyed, could lead to a substantial reduction in the provision received.

Notes

1 The information upon which this chapter is based has been extracted from extant marriage settlements and last wills and testaments from the twenty families used in this thesis, the details of which are outlined in appendices D, E and F.

2 Amy Erickson, 'Common law versus common practice: the use of marriage settlements in early modern England', *Economic History Review*, second series, 53:1 (1990), p. 21; Gilbert Horseman, *Precedents in conveyancing, settled and approved by Gilbert Horseman . . . and other eminent counsel, in three volumes* (Dublin: Knapton, 1764).

3 Lawrence Stone, *An open elite? England 1540–1880* (Oxford: Clarendon Press, 1984), p. 73; Malcomson, *The pursuit of the heiress*, p. 2.

4 Lloyd Bonfield, 'Marriage, property and the "affective" family', *Law and History Review*, 1:1 (spring 1983), p. 298.

5 Stone, *The family, sex and marriage*.

6 Lloyd Bonfield, 'Affective families, open elites and strict family settlements in early modern England', *Economic History Review*, 38:3 (1986); Lloyd Bonfield, 'Strict settlement and the family: a differing view', *Economic History Review*, 41:3 (1988), pp. 461–6.

7 Eileen Spring, 'The family, strict settlement and historians', *Canadian Journal of History*, 18 (December 1983); Eileen Spring, 'The strict settlement: its role in family history', *Economic History Review*, 41:3 (1988).

8 Eileen Spring, 'Law and the theory of the effective family', *Albion*, 16 (1984), p. 11.

9 Malcomson, *The pursuit of the heiress*, p. 2.

10 The judgment of Lord Chancellor Manners in *Dillon v Dillon*, 26 January 1809, cited in Thomas Ball and Francis Beatty, *Reports of cases argued and determined in the High Court of Chancery in Ireland in the time of Lord Manners* (London: W. Clarke, 1813), p. 89.

11 Erickson, *Women and property*, pp. 104–6; Staves, *Married women's separate property*, pp. 56–94.

12 H. J. Habakkuk, 'Marriage settlements in the eighteenth century', *Transactions of the Royal Historical Society*, fourth series, 32 (1950).

13 Queen's University Belfast, Special Collections, Catalogue of books in Castle Ward library, July 1813.

14 10 Charles I, 2, c. 2 (Ireland); J. C. W. Wylie, *Irish land law* (Abingdon: Professional, 1986), pp. 79–82.

15 27 Henry VIII, c. 10 (England); Wylie, *Irish land law*, p. 81.

16 *Ibid.*, pp. 79–82.

17 PRONI, Nugent of Portaferry papers, D/552/B/2/1/223, fragment of a letter referring to an intended marriage between Mr Savage and Mr McCartan's daughter [1761].

18 Habakkuk, 'Marriage settlements in the eighteenth century', p. 15; Christopher Clay, 'Marriage, inheritance and the rise of large estates in England, 1660–1815', *Economic History Review*, second series, 21 (1968), p. 509.

19 Buck, 'Property, aristocracy and the reform of the land law', p. 70.

20 William Blackstone, *Commentaries on the laws of England*, I (London: Clarendon Press, 1809), p. 136.

21 PRONI, Clanmorris papers, D/421/E/2, marriage settlement of Sophia Whaley and Robert Ward, 30 April 1782.

22 PRONI, Londonderry Estate Office papers, D/654/G1/3, copies of affadavit in a Chancery case concerning the marriage of Frances Anne Vane to Charles Lord Stewart, April 1818.

23 PRONI, Londonderry Estate Office papers, D/654/40, last will and testament and probate of Robert Stewart, Marquess of Londonderry, 7 June 1794, probate granted 10 May 1823.

24 PRONI, Abercorn papers, D/623/B/2/32, copy of the petition made to the Barons of the Exchequer from the Earl of Aberdeen and Countess of Aberdeen regarding the guardianship of her children, 23 May 1818.

25 Pearce Stevenson [Caroline Norton], *A plain letter to the Lord Chancellor on the Infant Custody Bill* (London, 1839).

26 PRONI, Brownlow papers, D/1928/T/3/6), last will and testament and one codicil and probate of Charles Brownlow, will dated 20 December 1821, probate granted 22 October 1822.

27 PRONI, Brownlow papers, D/1928/T/3/8, last will and testament and probate of Charles Brownlow, Lord Baron Lurgan, will dated 8 June 1832, probate granted 1 July 1847.

28 PRONI, Caledon papers, D/2433/B/11/2, solicitor's copy of the last will and testament of Dupre Alexander, Earl of Caledon, probate granted 1840.

29 PRONI, Rose Cleland papers, T/761/18, copy of the last will and testament of Arthur Chichester, Marquess of Donegall, and two codicils, will dated 7 August 1795; Maguire, *Living like a lord*, pp. 7–8.

30 *Ibid.*, pp. 7–8.

31 PRONI, Earl of Antrim papers, D/2977/1/1/27, deed to secure jointure for Letitia MacDonnell, Marchioness of Antrim, 25 June 1776.

32 Public Record Office, London (hereafter PRO), PROB/11/1542, last will and testament of Thomas Dawson, Viscount Cremorne, extracted from the will registers of the Prerogative Court of Canterbury, will dated 29 May 1812, probate granted 31 March 1813.

33 See for example the copy of the marriage settlement of Jane MacNeill and Charles Brownlow, 27 June 1828, PRONI, Brownlow papers, D/1928/T/17.

34 PRONI, Caledon papers, D/2433/A/1/371/1, marriage settlement of Dupre Alexander, Earl of Caledon, and Lady Catherine Freeman, 15 October 1811.

35 PRONI, Dufferin and Ava papers, D/1071/A/N2/1, copy marriage settlement of James Stevenson Blackwood, Lord Dufferin and Anna Foster, dated November 1801.

36 PRONI, Dartrey papers, D/3053/1/8/7, instructions for counsel to settle the draft deed of settlement on the marriage of Lord Baron Cremorne with Augusta Stanley, undated [1841].

37 PRONI, Earl of Antrim estate papers, D/2977/1/2/4, copy of the last will and testament and probate of Letitia MacDonnell, Marchioness of Antrim, dated 31 July 1799, extracted from the Prerogative Court of Canterbury.

38 PRONI, Abercorn papers, D/623/B/2/22, indenture of release of the jointure of Lady Cecil Hamilton, 18 May 1799.

39 *Ibid.*

40 PRONI, Abercorn papers, D/623/B/2/23, marriage settlement of John James, Marquess of Abercorn, and Lady Ann Jane Hatton, April 1800.

41 Malcomson, *The pursuit of the heiress*, p. 4.

42 Erickson, *Women and property*, p. 150.

43 PRONI, Caledon papers, D/2433/A/1/371/1, marriage settlement of Dupre Alexander, Earl of Caledon, and Lady Catherine Freeman, 15 October 1811.

44 Habakkuk, 'Marriage settlements in the eighteenth century', p. 27; Clay, 'Marriage, inheritance and the rise of the large estates in England', p. 509.

45 Malcomson, *The pursuit of the heiress*, p. 4.

46 Although the Irish and British currencies merged in 1826, Irish families continued to use Irish pounds in family settlements. The pounds noted here are therefore Irish, unless stated otherwise.

47 PRONI, Dufferin and Ava papers, D/1071/A/N1/17a, copy of the marriage settlement of John Blackwood and Dorcas Stevenson, dated 1751.

48 PRONI, Downshire papers, D/671/D14/1/3a, marriage settlement of Arthur Hill, Viscount Fairford, and Mary Sandys, 20 June 1786.

49 PRONI, Dufferin and Ava papers, D/1071/A/N1/17a, copy of the marriage settlement of John Blackwood and Dorcas Stevenson, dated 1751; PRONI, Blackwood papers, D/1071/A/N3/3b, copy of the last will and testament of John Blackwood, 31 December 1781.

50 PRONI, Downshire papers, D/671/D14/1/3a, marriage settlement of Arthur Hill, Viscount Fairford, and Mary Sandys 20 June 1786.

51 PRONI, Brownlow papers, D/1928/T/2/10, marriage settlement of William Brownlow and Catherine Hall, 4 November 1765; PRONI, Abercorn papers, D/623/B/3/25, last will and testament and probate of John James Hamilton, Marquess of Abercorn, 18 March 1809, probate granted 9 May 1818.

52 See appendix C for details of the Brownlow rental.

53 PRONI, Abercorn papers, D/623/C/4/1, rental account book for the manor of Strabane, County Tyrone, 1794–1810; PRONI, Abercorn papers, D/623/C/4/3, rental account book for the manor of Donelong, County Tyrone, 1794–1810; PRONI, Abercorn papers, D/623/C/4/5, rental account book for the manor of Cloghogel, County Tyrone, 1794–1810; PRONI, Abercorn papers, D/623/C/4/8, rental account book for the Donegal estate, 1794–1810.

54 PRONI, Londonderry Estate Office papers, D/654/F1/25a–c, marriage settlement of Charles Stewart, Baron Stewart of Stewart's Court and Ballylawn, and Frances Anne Vane, 27 March 1819; Malcomson, *The pursuit of the heiress*, p. 30.

55 *Ibid.*, p. 4; Spring, *Law, land and family*, p. 50.

56 A. P. W. Malcomson, *John Foster: the politics of the Anglo-Irish ascendancy* (Oxford: Oxford University Press, 1978), p. 23.

57 PRONI, Londonderry Estate Office papers, D/654/F1/11, marriage settlement of Frances Pratt and Robert Stewart, Lord Castlereagh, 6 June 1773.

58 Malcomson, *The pursuit of the heiress*, p. 13.

59 PRONI, Brownlow papers, D/1928/T/17, copy of the marriage settlement of Jane MacNeill and Charles Brownlow, 27 June 1828.

60 PRONI, Abercorn papers, D/623/B/2/29, settlement of annuity of Harriet Douglas on her marriage to John James Hamilton, Earl of Abercorn, 1809.

61 PRONI, Abercorn papers, D/623/B/3/25, last will and testament and probate of John James Hamilton, Marquess of Abercorn, 18 March 1809, probate granted 9 May 1818.

62 PRONI, Abercorn papers, D/623/B/2/30, appointment by the Marquess of Abercorn to Viscountess Hamilton of a further rent charge of £1,200, 14 May 1811; PRONI, Abercorn papers, D/623/B/2/31, appointment by the Marquess of Abercorn to Viscountess Hamilton of a further rent charge of £800, 14 May 1811.

63 PRONI, Dufferin and Ava papers, D/1071/D/12, Hans Blackwood to Price Blackwood, 27 June 1825.

64 PRONI, Dufferin and Ava papers, D/1071/A/B6/3, rent schedules for the minority of Frederick Blackwood, 1841–47.

65 PRONI, Dufferin and Ava papers, D/1071/A/H2/40/1, copy of schedule of Blackwood family settlement, 3 May 1825.

66 PRONI, Dufferin and Ava papers, D/1071/A/N2/1, copy of the marriage settlement of James Stevenson Blackwood, Lord Dufferin, and Anna Foster, dated November 1801; PRONI, Dufferin and Ava papers, D/1071/D/12, Hans Blackwood to Price Blackwood, 16 June 1825.

67 PRONI, Downshire papers, D/671/D14/1/3a, marriage settlement of Arthur Hill, Viscount Fairford, and Mary Sandys 20 June 1786.

68 PRONI, Dufferin and Ava papers, D/1071/F/B2/1/1, copy of letter from Price Blackwood to Helen Blackwood, dated 11 July [1833]; PRONI, Dufferin and Ava papers, D/1071/D/1-11, Price Blackwood's insurance documents for 1834 in assorted correspondence of Price Blackwood.

69 PRONI, Dufferin and Ava papers, D/1071/A/N2/11a&b, appointment of new trustees to the marriage settlement of Price Blackwood and Helen Blackwood, 9 March 1837.

70 PRONI, Dufferin and Ava papers, D/1071/A/H2/40/1, copy of schedule of Blackwood family settlement, 3 May 1825.

71 This settlement is noted in the last will and testament and probate of John James Hamilton, Marquess of Abercorn, 18 March 1809, probate granted 9 May 1818, PRONI, Abercorn papers, D/623/B/3/25.

72 PRONI, Ward papers, D/4216/E/2, marriage settlement of Robert Ward and Sophia Whaley, 30 April 1782.

73 PRONI, Caledon papers, D/2433/A/1/371/1, marriage settlement of Dupre Alexander, Earl of Caledon, and Lady Catherine Freeman, 15 October 1811.

74 Maguire, *The Downshire estates in Ireland*, pp. 23–4.

75 PRONI, Downshire papers, D/671/D14/1/20, marriage settlement of Arthur Hill and Mary Sutton, 26 June 1848.

76 PRONI, De Ros papers, MIC/573/31/3/1, extract of settlement made previous to the marriage of Lord Henry Fitzgerald and Charlotte Boyle, 1791.

77 10 Charles I, c. 17 (Ireland).

78 Wylie, *Irish land law*, pp. 79–80.

79 Spring, *Law, land and family*, pp. 62–3.

80 3 & 4 William IV, c. 105.

81 Cited in William Drury and Robert Warren, *Reports of cases argued and determined in the High Court of Chancery in Ireland during the time of Lord Chancellor Sugden* (Dublin: Hodges and Smith, 1843), pp. 94–133.

82 Large, 'The wealth of the greater Irish landowners', pp. 21, 25; Roebuck, 'Rent movement, proprietorial incomes and agricultural development', p. 82; Crawford, 'Landlord–tenant relations in Ulster', pp. 12–21.

83 National Library of Ireland (hereafter NLI), Leinster papers, MS 631, notes on debts and expenditure of the Leinster estate by James Fitzgerald, Duke of Leinster, dated 1766 and 1772; Malcomson, *The pursuit of the heiress*, p. 10.

84 Harrison, 'The first Marquess of Dufferin and Ava', p. 10.

85 PRONI, Dufferin and Ava papers, D/1071/A/B6/3, rent schedules for the minority of Frederick Blackwood, 1841–47.

86 PRONI, Abercorn papers, D/623/B/3/25, last will and testament and probate of John James Hamilton, Marquess of Abercorn, 18 March 1809, probate granted 9 May 1818.

87 PRONI, Dufferin and Ava papers, D/1071/A/N/3/1, copy of the last will and testament and probate of James Stevenson Blackwood, Lord Dufferin, dated 5 March 1836.

88 PRONI, Clanwilliam/Meade papers, D/3044/D/1/20, fragment of a declaration by Theodosia Hawkins-Magill, Countess of Clanwilliam, undated; Malcomson, 'A woman scorned?', p. 3.

89 PRO, PROB/11/2189, last will and testament of Charles William Vane, Marquess of Londonderry, extracted from the will registers of the Prerogative Court of Canterbury, will dated 20 May 1852, probate granted 11 April 1854.

90 PRONI, Enniskillen papers, D/1702/1/27/7a, last will and testament and probate of William Willoughby, Earl of Enniskillen, 21 June 1793, probate granted 25 July 1805.

91 PRONI, Brownlow papers, D/1928/T/3/8, last will and testament and probate of Charles Brownlow, Lord Baron Lurgan, will dated 8 June 1832, probate granted 1 July 1847.

92 PRO, PROB/11/1482, last will and testament of Thomas Conolly, extracted from the will registers of the Prerogative Court of Canterbury, probate granted 15 July 1808.

93 PRONI, Brownlow papers, D/1928/T/3/8, last will and testament and probate of Charles Brownlow, Lord Baron Lurgan, will dated 8 June 1832, probate granted 1 July 1847.

94 PRONI, Brownlow papers, D/1928/T/17, report of the present state of Lady Lurgan's finances, by her agent, undated [1847].

95 PRONI, Erne papers, D/1939/25/1/12, last will and testament and probate of John Creighton, Earl of Erne, will dated 11 November 1828, probate granted 1829.

96 PRONI, Erne papers, D/1939/24/2/8, conveyance of Lady Erne's life estate in certain hereditaments in the City of Dublin held in fee farm, 13 October 1829.

97 PRONI, Abercorn papers, D/623/B/3/25, last will and testament and probate of John James Hamilton, Marquess of Abercorn, 18 March 1809, probate granted 9 May 1818.

98 PRONI, Caledon papers, D/2433/A/1/566/1, marriage settlement of James Dupre, Earl of Caledon, and Jane Grimston, 4 September 1845.

99 PRONI, Enniskillen papers, D/1702/1/27/3a, last will and testament of Anne Lowry, Countess of Enniskillen, 15 September 1793.

100 PRONI, Dufferin and Ava papers, D/1071/A/N/3/1, copy of the last will and testament and probate of James Stevenson Blackwood, Lord Dufferin, dated 5 March 1836.

101 Amy Louise Erickson, 'Property and widowhood in England 1660–1840' in Sandra Cavallo and Lyndan Warner (eds), *Widowhood in medieval and early modern Europe* (Harlow: Longman, 1999), p. 160.

102 PRONI, Brownlow papers, D/1928/T/3/5, statement of the personal fortune, debts and legacies of William Brownlow, deceased [1794].

103 PRONI, Caledon papers, D/2433/B/11/2, solicitor's copy of the last will and testament of Dupre Alexander, Earl of Caledon, probate granted 1840.

104 PRONI, Caledon papers, D/2433/B/11/29, account of Messers Coutts with the executors of the late Earl of Caledon [1840].

105 PRONI, Caledon papers, D/2433/B/11/34, John Gibson to Catherine Alexander, Countess of Caledon, 26 June 1839, with annotations dated 1 January 1843 and 20 February 1849.

106 PRONI, Brownlow papers, D/1928/T/2/17, report as to the present state of Lady Lurgan's finances and her powers and duties as executrix and guardian of her children [1847].

107 *Ibid.*

108 PRONI, Earl of Antrim papers, D/2977/1/2/2, last will and testament and probate of Randall MacDonnell, Marquess of Antrim, 14 August 1790, probate granted 15 August 1791; PRONI, Erne papers, D/1939/25/1/12, last will and testament and probate of John Creighton, Earl of Erne, will dated 11 November 1828, probate granted 1829.

109 PRONI, Brownlow papers, D/1928/T/3/5, documents relating to a case in the Court of Chancery over the terms of the last will and testament of William Brownlow, 1799–1800.

110 *Ibid.*

111 Sheena Grattan, 'Of pin money and paraphernalia, the widow's shilling and a free ride to mass: one hundred and fifty years of property for the Irish wife' in Norma Dawson et al (eds) *One hundred and fifty years of Irish law* (Belfast: SLS Legal Publications, 1996), p. 224.

112 PRONI, Rose Cleland papers, T/761/18, copy of the last will and testament of Arthur Chichester, Marquess of Donegall, and two codicils, will dated 7 August 1795; PRONI, Brownlow papers, D/1928/T/3/6, last will and testament and one codicil and probate of Charles Brownlow, will dated 20 December 1821, probate granted 22 October 1822.

113 PRONI, Enniskillen papers, D/1702/1/27/7a, last will and testament and probate of William Willoughby, Earl of Enniskillen, 21 June 1793, probate granted 25 July 1805.

114 PRONI, Brownlow papers, D/1928/T/3/5, solicitor's copy of the last will and testament of William Brownlow, and two codicils, will dated 1791, probate granted 1794.

115 PRO, PROB/11/2217, last will and testament of James Dupre, Earl of Caledon, and two codicils, extracted from the will registers of the Prerogative Court of Canterbury, will dated 21 June 1855, probate granted 23 August 1855.

116 PRONI, Caledon papers, D/2433/B/22/1, document concerning furniture in house at Carlton Terrace House, dated 24 June 1857.

117 PRONI, Rose Cleland papers, T/761/18, copy of the last will and testament of Arthur Chichester, Marquess of Donegall, and two codicils, will dated 7 August 1795; Maguire, *Living like a lord*, pp. 33–4.

118 PRONI, Dufferin and Ava papers, D/1071/A/N3/3b, copy of the last will and teatament of John Blackwood, 31 December 1781.

119 PRONI, Earl of Antrim papers, D/2977/1/2/2, last will and testament and probate of Randall MacDonnell, Marquess of Antrim, 14 August 1790, probate granted 15 August 1791.

120 4 & 5 William IV (Ireland).

121 John Fraser MacQueen, *The rights and liabilities of husband and wife* (Dublin: Hodges and Smith, 1848), pp. 113–22.

122 Staves, *Married women's separate property*, p. 139.

123 Frederick Albert Lewins, *A practical treatise on the law of trusts* (London: Sweets and Maxwell, 1879), p. 662.

124 *Ibid.*, p. 645.

125 Staves, *Married women's separate property*, p. 133.

126 PRONI, Earl of Antrim papers, D/2977/1/2/3, copy of the marriage settlement of Anne Katherine MacDonnell, Countess of Antrim, and Henry Vane-Tempest, 24 April 1797.

127 PRONI, Caledon papers, D/2433/A/1/371/1, marriage settlement of Dupre Alexander, Earl of Caledon, and Lady Catherine Freeman, 15 October 1811.

128 Erickson, *Women and property*, p. 103.

129 Staves, *Married women's separate property*, p. 133.

130 *Ibid.*, pp. 131–61.

131 Blackstone, *Commentaries*, p. 442.

132 Staves, *Married women's property*, p. 131.

133 PRONI, Londonderry Estate Office papers, D/654/F1/11, marriage settlement of Frances Pratt and Robert Stewart, 6 June 1773.

134 PRONI, Dartrey papers, D/3053/1/8/14, marriage settlement of Augusta Stanley and Richard Dawson, Lord Dartrey, 10 July 1841.

135 PRONI, Caledon papers, D/2433/A/1/566/1, marriage settlement of James Dupre, Earl of Caledon, and Jane Grimston, 4 September 1845.

136 PRONI, Dufferin and Ava papers, D/1071/A/N2/1, copy of the marriage settlement of James Stevenson Blackwood, Lord Dufferin, and Anna Foster, dated November 1801.

137 PRONI, Dufferin and Ava papers, D/1071/A/N/3/1, copy of the last will and testament, and probate, of James Stevenson Blackwood, 5 March 1836.

138 PRONI, Downshire papers, D/671/D14/1/20, marriage settlement of Arthur Hill and Mary Sutton, 26 June 1848.

139 PRONI, Downshire papers, D/671/D14/1/3a, marriage settlement of Arthur Hill, Viscount Fairford, and Mary Sandys, 20 June 1786; PRONI, Downshire papers, D/671/D14/2/18b, draft will of Mary Hill, Viscountess Fairford, undated [1787]; PRONI, Downshire papers, D/671/D14/2/22a&b, probate of the last will and testament of Mary Hill, Marchioness of Downshire, 1837.

140 PRONI, Londonderry Estate Office papers, D/654/F1/14a, marriage settlement of Robert Stewart and Amelia Hobart, 7 June 1794; Malcomson, *Pursuit of the heiress*, p. 33.

141 PRONI, Earl of Antrim papers, D/2977/1/2/4, last will and testament of Letitia MacDonnell, Marchioness of Antrim, 31 July 1799, probate dated 10 February 1802.

142 PRONI, Verner–Wingfield papers, D/2538/C/12, copy of the marriage settlement of William Verner and Harriet Wingfield, dated 18 October 1819.

143 PRONI, Enniskillen papers, D/1702/1/27/3a, last will and testament of Anne Lowry, Countess Enniskillen, 15 September 1793; PRONI, Dufferin and Ava papers, D/1071/A/N/3/1, copy of the will and probate of James Stevenson Blackwood, Lord Dufferin, dated 5 March 1836; PRO, PROB/11/1947, last will and testament of Augusta Westenra, Lady Rossmore, extracted from the will registers of the Prerogative Court of Canterbury, will dated 1 July 1840, probate granted 8 June 1841.

144 PRONI, Clanwilliam/Meade papers, D/3044/D/1/20, fragment of a declaration by Theodosia Hawkins-Magill, Countess of Clanwilliam, undated; PRONI, Clanwilliam/ Meade papers, D/3044/D/1/51, photocopy of a letter from Theodosia, Countess of Clanwilliam to Robert Meade, 21 October 1808; PRONI, Downshire papers, D/671/D14/2/221&b, last will and testament of Mary Hill, Marchioness of Downshire, 3 May 1832, probate granted September 1836; PRONI, Earl of Antrim papers, D/2977/2/1/24/1&2, state of the title to the Antrim lands sold under the decree of the Court of Chancery of Ireland, 23 December 1803; PRONI, Earl of Antrim papers, D/2977/2/1/23/14, rental of the estate of Anne Katherine MacDonnell, Countess of Antrim, 1815; PRONI, Earl of Antrim papers, D/2977/2/1/23/9, legal opinion of the estate of Anne Katherine MacDonnell, Countess of Antrim, 1815; PRONI, Earl of Antrim papers, D/2977/2/4/3/13, the opinions of counsel on the right of [Frances Anne Vane, Marchioness of] Londonderry to the estates of her mother the late [Anne Katherine MacDonnell] Countess of Antrim, on the harbour of Carnlough, 1834.

145 Malcomson, *The pursuit of the heiress*, p. 30.

146 PRONI, Enniskillen papers, D/1702/1/27/3a, last will and testament of Anne Lowry, Viscountess Enniskillen, dated 1793.

147 Taggart v Taggart, 1803, in *Reports of the cases argued and determined in the High Court of Chancery in Ireland during the time of Lord Redesdale* (London: J. Butterworth, 1806), pp. 84–90.

148 *Rigden v Vallier*, 25 March 1751, in John Tracey Atkyns, *Reports of cases argued and determined in the High Court of Chancery in the time of Lord Hardwicke* (London: J. Wenman, 1782), pp. 693–8.

149 Taggart v Taggart, 1803, in *Reports of the cases argued and determined in the High Court of Chancery in Ireland during the time of Lord Redesdale*, pp. 84–90.

150 Wylie, *Irish land law*, p. 387.

151 Cited in *Campbell v Campbell*, 4 July 1792, in William Brown, *Reports of cases argued and determined in the High Court of Chancery* (Dublin: E. Lynch, 1795), pp. 15–19.

152 PRONI, Erne papers, D/1939/25/1/12, last will and testament and probate of John Creighton, Earl of Erne, will dated 11 November 1828, probate granted 1829.

153 PRONI, Downshire papers, D/671/D14/1/3a, marriage settlement of Arthur Hill, Viscount Fairford, and Mary Sandys, 20 June 1786.

154 *Ibid.*

155 PRONI, Londonderry Estate Office papers, D/654/F1/25a–c, marriage settlement of Charles Stewart, Baron Stewart of Stewart's Court and Ballylawn, and Frances Anne Vane-Tempest, 27 March 1819.

156 PRONI, Brownlow papers, D/1928/T/3/6, last will and testament and probate of Charles Brownlow, will dated 20 December 1821, probate granted 22 October 1822.

157 PRONI, Clanmorris papers, D/4216/F/1, last will and testament and two codicils and probate of Bernard Ward, will dated 30 August 1779, probate granted 1781.

158 PRONI, Dufferin and Ava papers, D/1071/A/N3/3b, copy of the last will and testament of John Blackwood, dated 31 December 1781.

159 PRO, PROB/11/1363, last will and testament of Arthur Hill, Marquess of Downshire, extracted from the will registers of the Prerogative Court of Canterbury, will dated 30 September 1801, probate granted 7 October 1801.

160 PRONI, Dartrey papers, D/3053/1/2/7, copy of last will and testament of John Dawson, dated 19 December 1754.

161 PRONI, Enniskillen papers, D/1701/1/27/4a, last will and testament of John Cole, Lord Baron Mountflorence, 7 April 1767.

162 John Debrett, *Debrett's complete peerage of the United Kingdom of Great Britain and Ireland* (London: J. G. and F. Rivington, 1836), p. 502.

163 PRONI, Dartrey papers, D/3053/1/2/7, copy of the last will and testament of John Dawson, dated 19 December 1754.

164 PRONI, Dufferin and Ava papers, D/1071/A/N3/1, copy of the last will and testament, and probate, of James Stevenson, dated 25 December 1768.

165 *Ibid.*

3

Women and legal guardianship

When the heir to a landed estate was a minor, or was declared insane, the management of her or his welfare and landed estate came within the remit of the Court of Chancery. The prevailing structure of the family, in which control over family property was exercised by the husband and father, was therefore suspended and there were increased opportunities for women to undertake an expanded role in the management of family property as guardians of minors, or as committees responsible for the affairs of the insane.

Legal guardianship of minors

The legal guardianship of children has been recognised as an important issue among landed families from the fourteenth century onwards, and women have acted as guardians at least from that time.[1] The involvement of Chancery in the legal guardianship of minors represented, as Caroline Norton noted in 1839, the one instance when the state did intervene in 'the "divine prescriptive right of the father"'.[2] The degree to which Chancery was involved was determined by the amount of property owned. In 1809, a case in the Court of Chancery in London noted that petitions for appointing a guardian were not dependent on a reference to the Master only if 'the property of the infants did not exceed £1500'.[3] The involvement of Chancery was an option that landed families appeared eager to avoid, as it was an expensive and time-consuming process. The Court could also prove inflexible. For example, if the minor wished to visit abroad, it was possible that the Court would refuse permission for the ward to go outside its jurisdiction. The direct involvement of the Court in family affairs could be avoided by the appointment of a guardian by the father in his last will and testament. In practice, a minor who was heir to a landed estate could have one guardian or several. In the latter case, the functions of the several guardians were usually divided between guardianship of the person, which included the maintenance and education of the minor, and guardianship of the estate.

The position of women as legal guardians of propertied minors was paradoxical. There was no assumption in law that on the death of her husband a woman would be guardian to her children. This decision rested with the father as stated in his last will and testament. If a father had died without appointing a guardian to his children, guardianship passed by law to the nearest male relatives and a mother could contest this only if these guardians by default refused to act as such.[4] Furthermore, the division of responsibility in the affairs of minors, between guardianship of the person and guardianship of the estate, suggests that the role of widows as guardians in the wealthy landed class declined during the period under discussion. However, alongside the legal assumption of a father's natural authority as guardian, the natural role of the mother to act in the child's best interests and to provide the best care was recognised. Therefore, when Harriet Douglas, Countess of Aberdeen, petitioned the Scottish Court of Chancery for guardianship of her three children, the eldest of whom was the heir to her first husband's father, the Marquess of Abercorn, she did so on the grounds that, as mother of the children, she was 'the most natural and proper person to be appointed one of the guardians of her own children, as no individual can be supposed to be more warmly interested in the care of their persons and preservation of their fortune'.[5]

Harriet Douglas was the wife of James, Viscount Hamilton, heir to the Abercorn estates in counties Tyrone and Donegal as well as Scottish estates. Viscount Hamilton was survived by his father, John Hamilton, the first Marquess of Abercorn. One year after his death, in July 1815, Harriet married, as her second husband, George Gordon, fourth Earl of Aberdeen. Through the early death of his father, Harriet's eldest son, James Hamilton (1811–85), the grandchild of the first Marquess, became the next heir to the family estates. He succeeded as the second Marquess in 1818 when he was seven years old. James, Viscount Hamilton, had died without appointing guardians to his children, and the nearest male relatives on both the father's side and the mother's side had, in accordance with the law, been appointed legal guardians by default. They had consequently renounced this role, thereby clearing the way for Harriet and her husband to petition the Court of Chancery in Scotland in May 1818 for the right to act as joint guardians to the children.

As a married woman Lady Aberdeen was in a problematic position. A legally accepted assumption, according to the laws of Scotland, was that, as 'she herself is subjected to the powers of a husband she is incapable of having any person under her power'. [6] The outcome of the Aberdeen case was, however, determined by the fact that Harriet's second husband, the Earl of Aberdeen, was appointed sole guardian while the case was being decided. In this situation the power of the husband would not be increased but 'on the contrary is to be shared with the person in the world who ought most naturally to be entrusted with the charge of their persons, and is most interested in their welfare'. [7]

The Court's assumption of the 'natural' predisposition of the mother to act in her children's interests was at odds with the legal position of mothers. Yet this was also the argument used by Caroline Norton in 1839 to promote her Child Custody Bill. Caroline Norton was the younger sister of Helen Blackwood, Lady Dufferin. A writer by profession, Caroline Norton was also involved in the instigation of the Married Women's Property and Divorce Act passed in 1857. The campaign to get the law on infant custody changed was motivated by her own domestic situation: she had separated from a violent husband who had refused to allow her access to their three children.

Caroline Norton had married George Norton in 1827, and three children were born during the marriage: Fletcher, Brinsley and William. The Norton marriage was stormy and Caroline attempted to leave her husband several times before finally leaving in 1836. George Norton then instigated a 'criminal conversation' case against the then Prime Minister, Lord Melbourne, with whom he alleged his wife had committed adultery. 'Criminal conversation' cases were the first step in divorce proceedings, although in this case Norton was unsuccessful. After he lost the case, he denied Caroline access to their three children. Thomas Talfourd, MP for Reading, agreed to introduce the Infant Custody Bill into the House of Commons. After being rejected once by the House of Lords, the bill passed into law in 1839.

When the House of Lords initially rejected the bill, Caroline wrote *A plain letter to the Lord Chancellor on the Infant Custody Bill*, published under the pseudonym Pearce Stevenson. In it, she argued that a mother was the best person to be entrusted with the care of her children, and that this was especially the case when the father in question was violent and immoral: 'She is under God, responsible for the souls and bodies of the new generation confided to her care; and the woman who is mother to the children of a profligate and tyrannical husband, is bound by her duty, even if she were not married by the strong instinct of her own heart, to struggle against the seizure of her infants. It is not her happiness alone that is involved, *theirs* is also at stake [emphasis in original].' [8]

Until the passing of the Infant Custody Act in 1839, mothers had no rights of custody or access to their children by law. The Infant Custody

Act was the first legislation that questioned the total authority of a father over his children, although, as has already been noted, propertied minors were exempt from such unchallenged paternal authority. However, the Act granted only limited rights to women. A mother had the right to custody of a child up to seven years old, and the right of access to a child up to the age of sixteen, in the event of a separation from her husband. This applied only in cases where she had not been found guilty of adultery. Paternal supremacy in the matter of children's guardianship remained in place in Ireland until the 1886 Guardianship of Infants Act, which declared that a mother could be guardian to her children on the death of her husband, either solely or jointly with any other guardian appointed by her husband.[9]

The duties and powers of the guardian

In practice, the role of women as guardians varied among wealthy landed families. Women acted as sole guardians of both the estates and the personal welfare of their children, or as joint guardians. In the case of joint guardianship, women's responsibility was limited to the welfare of their children, while estate affairs were entrusted to the heir or trustees.

Jane Brownlow, Lady Lurgan, was appointed sole guardian of the persons and property of all three of her children in her husband's last will and testament. There were three children of the marriage: Charles, the eldest son and heir; Edward; and Clara Brownlow. Charles Brownlow was sixteen years old when his father died in 1847, and came of age in 1852. Lady Lurgan received the income of all three children from the Lurgan estate, and was solely responsible for their maintenance and education. In addition, she was responsible, along with two trustees, for the management of the Lurgan estates for the remaining period of Charles Brownlow's minority. By the terms of her husband's will, Jane had the power of appointment of one of the trustees, so that they 'may aid her with counsel and advice'.[10]

The Lurgan estates in County Armagh at this time took an annual rental of £15,484. One of Lady Lurgan's duties as guardian was to ensure the payment of the various charges on the Brownlow estate during the minority period, such as interest on amounts settled on the estate, tithe rental, crown rent, poor rates and expenses connected with rent collection. To fulfil the requirements of the Court of Chancery in her son's affairs, several criteria had to be met. The key issue was 'the management of the estate and the maintenance and education of the minor out of his net income', and it was essential to ensure this could be achieved, and that Lady Lurgan would be accountable for it: '[t]he great and fundamental role of [g]uardianship is that the property should in every respect be managed in the way most beneficial for the minor, [and] that no expense should be incurred, the advantage of which *to him* cannot be proved if questioned [emphasis in original]'.[11]

Lady Lurgan's role in the management of her son's future estate was primarily that of a caretaker. She did not have the authority to develop or invest in the estate, and she did not exercise direct control over leasing, as this was vested in trustees.[12] However, for some women guardianship of a son's estates was an extension of an already powerful role in the management of family property. Only women with substantial separate properties wielded such influence. Anne Skeffington, Countess of Massereene, was guardian of the Massereene estate during the minority of her eldest son, Clotworthy Skeffington, the future second Earl of Massereene. Lady Massereene was a landowner in her own right; the estate she possessed in Derbyshire was valued at £50,000 in 1772 and she used her separate property to aid it.[13] Lady Massereene's control over these estates continued after the second Earl reached majority, owing first to his absence while travelling in Europe and then to his imprisonment in Paris for debt. Clotworthy Skeffington signed over the management of his affairs to Lady Massereene, although he attempted to revoke this in 1769, before eventually signing over control of the estate to a lawyer sympathetic to her interests.[14] The extent of Lady Massereene's control over the estate was such that, when the borough of Antrim was disenfranchised by the Act of Union in 1801, she and her three younger sons successfully claimed the £15,000 compensation, in opposition to Clotworthy, Earl of Massereene, on the grounds that she had taken a prominent role in the estate's management while he had been absent.[15]

Similar control over the family estate was exercised by Mary Hill, Marchioness of Downshire. When the second Marquess of Downshire died in 1801, his son and heir, Arthur Hill, was a minor. In accordance with the late Marquess's last will and testament, the Downshire estates were vested in Chancery, and Lady Downshire was appointed guardian of the persons and estates of Arthur Hill in 1803.[16] Just as Lady Massereene had been the owner of a substantial estate in her own right, Lady Downshire was also the owner of a separate estate in Worcestershire, and after her husband's death she also took a prominent role in Downshire estate matters until her son reached majority in 1809. This included the authorisation of estate expenditure, receiving estate rental lodged in banks to her credit and correspondence with agents over the management of leases. This involvement extended beyond estate administration as Lady Downshire vigorously promoted her family's interests in local politics, when members of other families remained largely absent from their property and relied on rank and patronage to exert their influence.[17] The predominance of Lady Downshire in Hill family affairs has been regarded as driven by her belief of the wrongs inflicted upon her family by the Act of Union, of which the late Marquess had been a staunch opponent. As Peter Jupp notes, '[t]he Downshires . . . could not have attained greater popular martyrdom when the Marquess, having been stripped of his county dignities and seeing his friends dismissed their posts, died on 7 September 1801'.[18]

The interests of the Downshires and the Londonderrys governed County Down politics at this time. The Downshires were the wealthier of the two families, and an important aspect of Lady Downshire's electoral strategy was the management of 'permanent and temporary allies amongst the gentry'.[19] In 1805 Lady Downshire backed the independent candidate Colonel John Meade, a younger son of Theodosia, Countess of Clanwilliam, in an alliance that led to the defeat of Lord Castlereagh.[20] A year later she requested her agent to undertake a survey of political interests of tenants on the Downshire estates in King's County, Westmeath and Kildare, 'stating the names of the leading proprietors in each, the probable amounts of their rentals and the number of votes each can bring forward'.[21] In the 1807 and 1808 elections, candidates backed by Lady Downshire, Mr Savage and Colonel Meade won both seats in County Down.[22] In 1806, Lady Downshire wrote to Arabella Ward (d. 1813), wife of Edward Ward (d. 1812), who was at that time managing the interest of Lord Bangor in the county, to thank her for her family's support, and to hope 'that our families may preserve a most friendly intercourse'.[23]

Three points can be made here about the estate management of Lady Massereene and Lady Downshire during the minorities of their sons. First, both women were experienced in estate matters, as they were owners of substantial landed property in their own right. The assumption of responsibility for their sons' estates was not therefore an unusual step within the context of their place in family property relations. Secondly, both women promoted the family interest. In fact, it could be argued that the interests of Lady Massereene and Lady Downshire were inextricable from their family interests. This is especially the case for Lady Downshire, who continued to oppose the Londonderrys after her son, the second Marquess of Downshire, had formed an alliance with them, stating that Lord Castlereagh was 'a name which every member of my family ought to shun and condemn'.[24] This is related to the third point: it was crucial for a guardian to be seen to be acting in the minor's interests. The estate management of Lady Downshire during her eldest son's minority took place within the context of her son's best interests.

In April 1804, she wrote to the agent of her estates, John Reilly, of her desire to 'do everything in my power, and that depends on me, to improve and regulate my dear son's estates'. Referring to building projects on the estate, she noted: 'I can only say that I am ready to authorize such sums to be expended on them as may be necessary for the improvement of the estates and the benefit of my son'.[25]

When a widow's appointment of the guardianship of her children was limited to their persons, her responsibility may have included the right to choose the guardian of the estate, and she may have been able to appoint a guardian sympathetic to her own interests. In 1812, Arabella Ward was advised in the appointment of guardians to the estate of her eldest son, Edward Ward, who was heir to the Castle Ward estate in County Down, that 'it appears probable that you may have a friend nominated to the care of Castle Ward who will admit you to a considerable share in the benefit of that wardship, looking on himself as your trustee'.[26]

However, in situations where a widow did not wield significant influence over estate matters, she may have been pressured by family members in making this appointment. Helen Blackwood, Lady Dufferin, was also nominated joint guardian of the 'persons and estates' of her only child, Frederick Blackwood, the future fifth Lord Dufferin. When Frederick came of age in 1847, Helen wrote a humorous letter referring to the deeds that transferred the Dufferin estate into his possession. Before sending them to him she had 'peeped into one of them, and found that I have apparently, in the most liberal manner presented you with a fine landed property somewhere'.[27] Practically, however, she had no involvement in estate matters during Frederick's minority. The guardianship was shared with Frederick's uncle, James Blackwood, then Lord Dufferin, who predeceased Price, Lord Dufferin. Lady Dufferin then had the duty of appointing another guardian. She appointed her late husband's uncle William Blackwood, on the basis of what she claimed was 'the just and natural view of the case': William Blackwood's good reputation within the family, his experience in estate matters and the fact that he was the next heir, and therefore had an interest in acting for the benefit of the estate.[28] William Blackwood was, however, as later noted by Frederick, Lord Dufferin, 'not at all a sympathetic person to my mother'.[29]

The remit of the guardian of the person was limited to the maintenance and education of the minor.[30] In the case of Lady Dufferin this was in some ways an extension of the financial authority she exercised over her son during her husband's absences. Between 1831 and 1835, Helen assumed his role in Frederick's upbringing, taking on such tasks as buying Frederick's clothes and paying his tutor.[31] The primary difference was in the legal basis of the relationship, rather than the detail. As Helen noted, her authority was now legal, as much as it was maternal: '[w]hen you are a man (if it please God to spare your life) you will be well off and able to indulge yourself in *moderately* expensive whims, as well as reasonable desires, but until that time, you are dependent on *me* for the education you receive, and the indulgences you enjoy [emphasis in original]'.[32]

The appointment of a mother as guardian of her children by her husband's last will and testament may have been made conditional upon her remaining a widow. The legal reasons for this were that, in the event of a widow remarrying, her legal status was once more subsumed into that of her husband. Considering the financial control a guardian, even if limited to the person, had over her children, this was undesirable from the perspective of the late father. When the first Duke of Leinster died in 1773 there were eleven children in the Fitzgerald family, nine of whom were minors. The eldest son, William, had come of age, and had succeeded his father as second Duke of Leinster. The eldest daughter, Emily, was twenty-one and due to marry. By the terms of the Duke of Leinster's last will and testament, the guardianship of the 'estates and fortunes' of the nine children was to be held by the seven trustees nominated by the late Duke, one of whom was Charles, Duke of Richmond, the brother of Emily Fitzgerald, Duchess of Leinster, the late Duke's widow.

The Duchess of Leinster was nominated guardian of the persons of the children, and was to receive the interest of their portions for the children's maintenance and education as long as she remained a widow. In his will, the Duke of Leinster arranged for Emily to have interest in Carton House, the use of the property at Blackrock for her younger children and her jewellery, with the condition that she did not remarry.[33] The practice of making a widow's interest in family property conditional upon her not remarrying was acceptable practice among these families, and it is also likely that the Duke of Leinster suspected that his wife would remarry. From around 1771, Emily had been having an affair with William Ogilvie, who had been a tutor to the Fitzgerald children from 1767.[34] She married him in secret in August 1774.[35] The marriage was scandalous within the Fitzgerald family as well as in Dublin society, owing to the difference in class between Emily and William Ogilvie, and his previous position in the family as tutor. In order to avoid the scandal, and possibly also to save money, Emily and Ogilvie moved immediately after the marriage to France, where they lived on an estate belonging to Emily's brother, the Duke of Richmond, for a number of years. Following her remarriage, however, Emily continued to act as the guardian of her children. She received an annual sum of £400 for each of the children for their education and maintenance, to be spent at her own discretion. Her continuation as guardian was arranged without the 'necessity of any application to the Chancellor'.[36] There may have been concern in the Fitzgerald family over the proximity of Emily's second husband, William Ogilvie, to the Fitzgerald family's financial affairs. As a widow with her own money in the form of a substantial jointure from the Leinster estates, Emily was more economically independent than a young woman marrying for the first time. However, as a married woman once more, she was by law subject to the rule of her husband. And it appears to have been the case that William Ogilvie did take care of all financial matters, including Emily's jointure, giving her £200 a year pin money from it.[37]

Emily's continuation as guardian to her children was possible only because the estates of the children were managed separately by the trustees nominated by the Duke of Leinster in his last will and testament. Also, her eldest son, William Fitzgerald, Duke of Leinster, was the new head of the family and, as such, was empowered, although to a limited degree, to make decisions about the guardianship of the Fitzgerald children. Emily's role as guardian of the persons of her children, responsible for their maintenance and education, was in any case regarded as acceptable as she was their mother. For example, in 1774 one of Emily's sons, Charles Fitzgerald, wrote to her requesting an increase in his allowance. His appeal to Emily was to his mother rather than to his legal guardian: 'I don't address you as a guardian, but as an affectionate mother who has my interest at heart, and who would do anything she thought would make me happy.'[38]

Emily's eldest son, William Fitzgerald, Duke of Leinster, was also able to reduce other losses that she suffered after her second marriage, in particular the loss of her right to live at Carton House, which Emily managed to exchange with her son, before her marriage was made public, for a sum of money rumoured to be £40,000 and possession of the buildings, as yet unfinished, at Blackrock.[39]

Three of the younger sons of the late Duke of Leinster, Charles, Henry and Robert Fitzgerald, were devised interests in landed property by his last will and testament. In 1776 Charles Fitzgerald reached the age of fourteen and, using his legal right to choose his own guardian, he chose his brother William, the second Duke of Leinster, as his guardian rather than Emily. The result of this decision was that the matter of the guardianship of the Fitzgerald children was brought to the Court of Chancery.[40] The outcome of the case was that William Fitzgerald, Duke of Leinster, was appointed guardian of the person and estate of Charles Fitzgerald. The renegotiation of the family power structure that followed an eldest son superseding his mother's control over her children is illustrated by William Fitzgerald's attempt to ameliorate the impact of Emily's loss of guardianship over Charles Fitzgerald.

In February 1776 William wrote to Emily on the subject of Charles's upbringing, stating that he would 'take no step in regard to his education without your advice; but as I advance him the money I thought it was better for him to look upon himself as controlled by me'.[41] In March 1776, he explained that the necessity of control over the children's estates resting with him was due to the fact that according to the last will and testament of the first Duke of Leinster, William was responsible for the debts and the jointure of Lady Kildare, which had been settled on the estate, and 'it would be rather hard on me not to know what becomes of the money these estates produce'.[42] In May 1776 William assured Emily that it was better for the Leinster estate that he was Charles's guardian as he was responsible for the payment of various jointures and annuities, and the 'authority of enquiry' into the children's estate that would be granted if he were guardian would make the organisation of the estate easier. He believed that the Chancellor would agree to Emily being guardian of her remaining children, and he also wished this 'excepting in regard to Henry and Robert's estate'.[43] Despite William Fitzgerald's attempts to console his mother, it is clear that Emily's authority over the children of her marriage to the first Duke of Leinster would be accepted insofar as she had no access to the landed estate of her three sons.

As the examples of Helen, Lady Dufferin, and Emily, Duchess of Leinster, illustrate, when a widow was joint guardian, she was responsible for the maintenance and education of the minor, an area of responsibility that was in accordance with prevailing ideas about the role of women in the family. Also, although sympathetic relatives could improve a woman's position in the family, ultimately the role of a woman in the management of the affairs of a minor who was heir to landed property operated within the boundaries of the Court of Chancery, and was determined by the last will and testament of the husband. However, some widows, such as Lady Massereene and Lady Downshire, exercised considerable authority over their sons' estate affairs. For these women, the family interests were interconnected to their own personal interests. They wielded considerable power in their families, and it was in their interests to promote their families' interests. Despite these examples of powerful female guardians, however, widows were less likely than men in this period to be appointed sole guardians of their children, and estate interests tended to be entrusted to elder sons or trustees.

Guardianship of the insane

Jurisdiction over the affairs of the insane in this period also rested with the Court of Chancery. When someone had been declared insane that person lost her or his legal identity and his or her landed property was vested in Chancery for the duration of her or his insanity, or for the rest of her or his life. As there was a chance that the heir might regain sanity, the landed estate was frozen for the duration of the insanity, or the life-time of the heir. The Court then appointed a committee, usually made up of family members, to be responsible for the welfare of the insane person and the management of their personal estate. The division of responsi-bilities between two committees was an attempt to prevent the concen-tration of power in one individual. As a further check on the committees, petitions would be considered by Chancery only if there were no oppo-sition from family members. The relationship between the committee and the estate of the insane was amended twice in this period by English statute law, suggesting recognition of the needs of landed prop-erties outside Chancery. In 1771, Chancery was empowered to enable guardians or committees of the insane to renew leases, accept surrenders of old leases and grant new leases. In 1803, guardians and committees were enabled to sell or mortgage estates, again subject to the consent of Chancery. While both statutes increased the power of committees, however, the primacy of Chancery and the sole objective of Chancery to protect the interests of the insane remained firmly in place.[44]

The insanity of Nicholas Ward, second Viscount Bangor (1750–1827), and the consequent changes to the management of his financial affairs illustrate the impact that intervention by Chancery had on landed family property matters. The history of the Ward family at this time is illustra-tive of what occurred when the traditional family structure was sus-pended. During the time of Nicolas Ward's insanity various competing interests interacted within the Ward family, and all sides had to negoti-ate with the Court of Chancery.

The Ward family had been created Barons Bangor in 1770 and Viscounts Bangor in 1781. By 1802, the Castle Ward estate, which had been in the family's possession from the sixteenth century, took a rental of £6,629. Bernard Ward, first Viscount Bangor (1719–81), extended the estates in the 1770s by his purchase of further land in Lecale and Ards, both also in County Down. In 1747 Lord Bangor married Ann Magill (1728–89), widow of Robert Hawkins-Magill and mother of Theodosia Meade, Countess of Clanwilliam. There were seven children of the mar-riage, three sons, Nicholas, Edward and Colonel Robert Ward (1754–1831), and four daughters: Anne Catherine, Sophia, Sarah and Emily. In 1766, Lord and Lady Bangor separated and Lady Bangor left Ireland to live in Bath, where she died in 1789.

The commission that established Nicholas Ward's insanity noted that he had been insane since 1774, and the Ward family appears to have been aware of his deteriorating mental health from the early 1770s. Legally, nothing but a private Act of Parliament could have prevented Nicholas Ward from inheriting the Castle Ward estate after his father's death, as the land was entailed on male heirs. However, in response to the insanity of his heir, Bernard, Lord Bangor, devised the estate which he had purchased in Lecale and Ards, and which was therefore not entailed, to his younger sons Edward and Robert Ward. The Castle Ward estate was charged with the jointure of £700 for Nicholas's mother, Ann, Lady Bangor, and £8,000 for his five sisters.[45]

Following the death of Bernard, Lord Bangor, in 1781, a commission of lunacy was issued against Nicholas, Lord Bangor, and the Castle Ward estate was vested in Chancery. Two committees were established: one to be responsible for the welfare of Lord Bangor, and the other to manage his personal estate, which in this case was the demesne at Castle Ward. The primary concern of the Court was the welfare of Nicholas, Lord Bangor, and his estate, which was effectively frozen for the duration of his insanity. This extended to Lord Bangor's personal wealth. For example, although Nicholas's mother and sisters who were living in 1781 were entitled to a share of his personal estate, they had no settled interest as Nicholas might survive them. Savings from his personal estate, which amounted to an annual sum of £1,200, were to be invested for his own benefit, and only on his death would they pass to his next of kin.[46]

Initially, the second son, Edward Ward, was appointed committee of the person, with responsibility for the welfare of Lord Bangor and of the portion of Castle Ward required for his maintenance. However, as Edward lived mainly in England at this time with his wife Arabella and their eight children, the arrangements were changed, and by 1791 he was acting committee of the demesne, while the youngest son, Robert, acted as committee of the person. As committee of the demesne, Edward received an allowance of £300 from the demesne for the repair and maintenance of the house and grounds at Castle Ward, which was estimated to be 461 acres.[47] Robert Ward lived on his estate in County Down while acting as committee of the person and received £700 for the health, safety and general welfare of Nicholas.

Despite the limitations placed on committees by Chancery, both men attempted to serve their own financial interests by applying to the Court to have their allowances from the Bangor estate increased on several occasions between 1781 and 1812. The interests of Edward and Robert Ward divided the Ward family into two competing camps. In 1802, Edward Ward presented a petition to the Court of Chancery in Dublin, requesting an increase in his allowance from the estate, on the grounds that the income for the upkeep of the demesne at Castle Ward was not sufficient to enable him to support his family. His petition was refused by the Court on the grounds that the requirements of Edward Ward's family were not the concern of the Court, '[t]he interest of the lunatic alone, and the case and judgment of his estate being the only object which the Chancellor ought to have in view'.[48] In 1808, Edward petitioned the Court once more on similar grounds, and he was again warned by his solicitor that 'the Chancellor has no power to grant an allowance for the support or the education' of his family. However, he was advised this time to ask for the amount ostensibly 'for the support of the demesne', while at the same time making private explanations to the Ward family of 'the true object of the petition'.[49] Crucially, while the petition of Edward Ward was unacceptable in Chancery, it was acceptable within the Ward family. When Edward's petition failed in 1802, Arabella blamed Robert's 'evasive manner' for Edward's defeat, and justified her husband's application with 'the necessities of a large family'.[50]

At the same time as Edward Ward's unsuccessful petition in 1802, Robert Ward petitioned, also unsuccessfully, to increase his allowance for the care of Lord Bangor from £700 to £1,400 and to extend the area at Castle Ward allotted for the use of the committee of the person.[51] Robert Ward's petition alarmed family members who were concerned about his influence at Castle Ward. This alarm led to the appointment of Hugh Montgomery, the husband of Lord Bangor's youngest sister Emily, to act alongside him as committee of the person, in an attempt to check Robert's attempts to increase his sphere of influence at Castle Ward.[52] As another committee of the person of Lord Bangor, Hugh Montgomery diluted Robert's authority, and Robert regarded him as a usurper 'who took on himself acts of commander not adviser' and enjoyed an unacceptable degree of authority.[53] Thus a particular view of legitimate financial need in relation to the Castle Ward estate existed within the Ward family. This viewpoint supported the specific interests of some family members – on one side the heir, Edward, and on the other his younger brother, Robert, whose interest would not have been given such prominence had Lord Bangor not been declared insane.

Initially, women in the Ward family took an informal role, as checks on the power of committees. Financial negotiations and observations were a prominent feature of family life. Requests for increased allowances, loans and other financial matters were discussed among family members, and the expenditure of certain family members was an acceptable subject of correspondence. Hugh Montgomery, the husband of Emily Ward, was also a trustee of the marriage settlement of Edward and Arabella Ward and therefore played a prominent part in Ward family financial arrangements. As trustee of Edward and Arabella Ward's marriage settlement, Hugh Montgomery invested money for Arabella and advised her on financial matters such as the purchase of debentures and her income from the estate.[54] This was sometimes relayed through his wife Emily, for example when she wrote on behalf of her husband in March 1802 because he was ill and 'unable to do it himself'.[55]

The informal role assumed by women in financial business was expanded because of the bearing that knowledge of the activities of the committees had on the management of Lord Bangor's affairs. During Robert Ward's 1802 petition, Emily Montgomery, who clearly opposed the expansion of his authority, kept Arabella informed of Robert's intentions at Castle Ward, advising her to raise a 'prudent clamour' against Robert and to write to the Countess of Clanwilliam and Anne Catherine Ward to 'gain them over to your side'.[56] When Robert successfully petitioned in 1807 for an increase in his allowance from £700 to £1,400, it was without Hugh's knowledge and therefore without the possibility of his opposition.[57] As at least one successful petition appears to have been concluded without the knowledge of some family members, it may have been the case that the onus was on family members to object.[58] In this case, what may appear as 'gossip' could become important information passed between family members and invaluable in the management and control of financial business.

There were degrees of influence within this informal role. In 1812, Theodosia, Countess of Clanwilliam, who as step-sister to Nicholas maintained a voice in family affairs, refused to agree to Robert Ward's proposed change to the management of the estate's sinking fund, even when it had been agreed by all other family members.[59] Importantly, this is the only example of opposition being exercised at such an advanced stage of a petition, a factor that may be explained by the fact that the Countess of Clanwilliam, as a step-sister, was outside the main family structure and therefore was free from the restrictions that power structures within families imposed. More importantly, however, the Countess was also the only family member, apart from Edward and Robert, who was the owner of a large estate in her own right and was therefore possibly more confident in asserting her authority in estate matters. The necessity of the consent of family members therefore elevated the importance of family debate for financial arrangements. As a result, women in the Ward family exercised a degree of control in relation to family financial matters that they might not have otherwise experienced.

Between 1781 and 1813 there were no female members of the committee of the person, or of the estate. However, in 1812, a more direct role in the management of Lord Bangor's affairs by women was taken when, after the death of Edward Ward in November 1812, new committees were appointed. There were important differences between the boundaries within which the appointment of new committees were established in 1812 and those of the original appointments of Edward and Robert Ward in 1781. From 1810 until his death in November, Edward, with the consent of Robert, lived at Castle Ward with Lord Bangor while his family remained in England. Although he was never formally appointed, he acted as committee of the person, presumably along with his role as committee of the demesne.[60] The reasons behind this act were undoubtedly financial, as the allowance for the care of Lord Bangor was significantly higher than that for the demesne.

On the death of Edward, his widow, Arabella Ward, asserted her interest, on behalf of her children, in Lord Bangor's estate on the grounds that it was Edward's 'last wish' that she should act in his place as committee of the Castle Ward estate.[61] One of the immediate concerns facing Arabella as a new widow was provision for her own income and that of her children, and she discussed with Robert Ward her fear of 'beggary' after her husband's death.[62] In his last will and testament, Edward appointed his wife sole guardian of their children and executor of his will. Little provision had been left for his children and it was calculated in 1812 that on Arabella's death they 'would be reduced to the pitiful sum of £700 a piece'.[63] The careers of her four younger sons needed to be financed and allowances needed to be settled on her two daughters on their marriage.[64] This financial situation was exacerbated by the fact that the death of Edward resulted in Arabella's eldest son Edward Southwell Ward (1790–1837) becoming heir at law to the Ward title and estate, with the resulting social requirement that her other children needed to be provided for in accordance with their proximity to the peerage. From 1802 there had apparently been an income of £5,000 from the estate, and Arabella secured that the remainder should be settled on her and her children.[65] After the death of Lord Bangor and the division of his property, Arabella's eldest son, who was heir to the Ward title and estate, could eventually have an income of £10,000.[66]

Arabella petitioned Chancery by the end of December 1812 with the intention that her late husband's interest in Castle Ward be granted to her.[67] By claiming her right to act in her husband's place, rather than campaigning for a new grant, Arabella may have been acting in accordance with what was perceived to be acceptable behaviour for a widow. Nevertheless, she was immediately involved in a power struggle within the Ward family.

Robert Ward opposed Arabella's memorial, on the grounds that he wished her to join with him in the committee of the person of Lord Bangor 'as a natural and proper mode'. He argued that it was 'the only way you can have any present advantage out of L[or]d B[angor]'s property', as the demesne needed extensive repairs and would be expensive to manage.[68] Although he argued that it was not his intention that Arabella should 'have confin[e]d yourself to residence at C[astle] W[ard], but to have considered it as a place to visit occasionally with your family', it is likely that his position was influenced by his desire to weaken the influence of Hugh Montgomery at Castle Ward by establishing Arabella there.[69]

Other women in the Ward family acted as advisers and confidants to Arabella. Immediately after Edward's death, the Countess of Clanwilliam offered the use of her Dublin house to Arabella, advising her to 'come to Ireland without loss of time and in *Dublin* confidentially confer with some man of business [emphasis in original]'.[70] Emily Montgomery advised her to act quickly to establish her right as she 'would have a better chance of . . . getting the benefit of the *domain* [sic] for the advantage of yourself and family, by being on the spot [emphasis in original]'.[71]

This dispute was settled in December 1812: Arabella was appointed committee of the demesne and granted £750 per annum for the upkeep of the house and demesne.[72] At this time, Arabella made clear her interest in protecting the interests of her family, as well as fulfilling her role as committee of the demesne: 'I mean to pay as much attention to that portion of C[astle] W[ard] which is granted to me as I would to the inheritance of one of my sons. It is not expected I should build hot houses or green houses. I shall never allow a tree to fall by the one but continue to plant moderately. Of course I shall lay by for my unprovided children as much as I can spare out of my income but not to the injury of C[astle] W[ard].'[73]

A more direct position of influence was assumed by Nicholas Ward's sister, Anne Catherine Ward, when she was appointed as another member of the committee of the person in January 1813. Anne Catherine was a supporter of Robert Ward's interests. While the Countess of Clanwilliam and Emily Montgomery were 'suspicious' of Robert and advised Arabella not to trust him or cooperate with him, Anne Catherine argued that Robert meant no harm and was 'certain Robert wishes to serve you'.[74] In February, Anne Catherine announced her intention to extend the proportion of the mansion house at Castle Ward and demesne allocated for the sole use of committee of the person, and in the following months both she and Robert prepared a petition, which reached Chancery in April 1813, for 'exclusive possession of the house', an increased allowance from the estate from £1,400 to £2,000 and, crucially, 200 acres from the Castle Ward demesne to be allocated for the sole use of Nicholas Ward.[75]

The problem with this petition from Arabella's perspective was that it was such a large proportion of the Castle Ward estate that, if successful, it would make Arabella's position as committee of the demesne financially untenable. Also, though Anne Catherine's petition was most feasibly motivated by the desire to make room for Robert Ward to become sole manager of Castle Ward, both she and Robert presented their case as based solely on their interest in the welfare of Lord Bangor.[76] Robert Ward argued that 'the female committee' would not take more than necessary, and that 'nearly an entire new establishment must be made' for the use of Nicholas.[77] Anne Catherine Ward argued that the previous allowance of £1,400 was 'insufficient for a nobleman in any situation'.[78] The status of her brother also had implications for patronage on the estate: 'If I am thought worthy to have the care of my brother', she argued, 'I should not like to undertake it without a liberal allowance that would enable me to benefit in some degree the people on his estate'.[79]

The petition of Anne Catherine and Robert Ward was therefore, ostensibly at least, in accordance with the remit of the committee as its stated concern was the welfare of Lord Bangor. Although acceptable outside Chancery, Arabella's assertion of her family's interest in Castle Ward and her intention to provide for her children from the income she received from the demesne were at odds with the conditions imposed by Chancery on the committees, and could not therefore form the basis of a defence against the encroachment of her interest at Castle Ward by Anne Catherine and Robert. Arabella was advised to move into Castle Ward or else submit to the demands of Anne Catherine if they were reasonable.[80] She consequently moved to Ireland to live at Castle Ward.

The petition by Anne Catherine and Robert Ward was rejected in May 1813, on the grounds that it would make the arrangement already made for Arabella in December 1812 untenable, and would harm the interest of her children in the estate. It was also argued that the division among the committee of the person was not serving the interests of Lord Bangor. Arabella's opinion on her new role as committee of the person, which she had previously avoided, was that it was a necessary compromise based on financial need 'though driven by necessity to accept of a residence here . . . and seclude my unprovided family from the advantages of society . . . as I was not allowed by Robert's objections to live in England without giving up so much of my income, I resolved to finish my course at this beautiful place . . . The rights of my family as elder branches I must ever support.'[81]

Alongside the division in the family between the respective claims of Edward and Robert Ward, other interests existed. Crucially, these outside interests were not accepted by the two main camps in the Ward family. Emily Montgomery and Anne Catherine Ward disapproved of the expenditure of their step-sister Theodosia Meade, Countess of Clanwilliam. Consequently, when she requested a loan from the sinking fund in November 1802, Emily noted wryly her annoyance at 'the rate the Earl and Countess go on'.[82] The financial behaviour of Sophia Ward was also frowned upon. Sophia's assertion of her financial rights by asking for 'the repayment of a loan of £2,000', and demanding the allowance she was owed from the estate, was met with the derisive comment: 'Sophy [sic] is always scheming about money.'[83] Sophia justified her financial negotiations as the wish only 'to get my money to promote peace and avoid future wrangling'.[84] Therefore, there was a distinction within the Ward family between the unnecessary financial needs of a single woman such as Sophia Ward and the legitimate financial interests of Edward Ward and his family. Arabella Ward's successful petition to act as committee of the estate at Castle Ward indicates the primacy granted to family title and inheritance by the Court of Chancery. The needs of a large family had not previously been considered valid by the Court in Edward Ward's petitions in 1802 and 1808, yet in 1813 Arabella presented herself as 'but an agent for my unprovided family'[85] and on her success thanked the Chancellor for this decision 'in favour of my family . . . the advantage of my children . . . is so closely connected with my care of the family inheritance, that I do not think I shall ever lose sight of it . . . I trust that as far as I am concerned family union may be preserved'.[86]

Conclusion

The organisation of the legal guardianship of minors and of insane people within the wealthy landed class therefore illustrates the formal and informal boundaries within which family financial affairs operated. Families negotiated the imposition of standards from outside, while maintaining their own definitions of what was acceptable.

Formal boundaries were established by the Court of Chancery, which was concerned primarily with estate matters. The role of a woman in the guardianship of minors was determined by the degree of authority accorded them by her husband's last will and testament. Within the families surveyed here, the appointment of widows as guardians of the estates of their children diminished in favour of the appointment of elder sons or trustees. Yet there was a variety of experience among women. Jane Brownlow, Lady Lurgan, exercised significant control over her late husband's estate as guardian of her eldest son. Powerful and independently wealthy women such as Anne Skeffington, Countess of

Massereene, and Mary Hill, Marchioness of Downshire also exercised considerable authority over family estates during their sons' minorities. Emily Fitzgerald, Duchess of Leinster, and Helen Blackwood, however, were restricted to the guardianship of the welfare and personal care of their children.

The reorganisation of the financial structure of the Ward family that followed the vesting of the Castle Ward estate in Chancery had the effect of elevating the role of women in the family. The necessity of consent for petitions highlights the importance of informal networks of communication and financial advice in families, in which women played a significant part. Women such as Arabella Ward and Anne Catherine Ward also exercised formal authority by acting as part of the committees of the estate and person of the insane, thereby exerting influence over family financial matters that they might not have had otherwise. At the same time, family interests regarding property were particular and definite. The interests of single women, such as Sophia Ward, were regarded as unimportant, while the family interests of Edward and Arabella Ward were regarded as legitimate.

Notes

1 Scott L. Waugh, *The lordship of England: royal wardships and marriages in English society and politics 1217–1327* (Princeton, New Jersey: Princeton University Press, 1988), pp. 194–231.
2 Norton, *A plain letter to the Lord Chancellor*, p. 2.
3 Wheeler ex parte, 1809, cited in Francis Vesey, *Reports of cases argued and determined in the high Court of Chancery from the year 1789 to 1817, v 16, 1809–10* (London: Brooke and Clarke, 1827), p. 266.
4 O'Keefe v Casey, 1803, cited in *Reports and cases argued and determined in the high Court of Chancery in Ireland during the time of Lord Redesdale* (Dublin: J. Butterworth, 1810), p. 106.
5 *Ibid.*
6 PRONI, Abercorn papers, D/623/B/2/32, copy of petition to the Barons of the Exchequer from Earl of Aberdeen and Countess of Aberdeen regarding the guardianship of her children, 23 May 1818.
7 *Ibid.*
8 Norton, *A plain letter to the Lord Chancellor*, p. 108.
9 49 & 50 Victoria, ch. 27, *The law reports; the public general statutes passed in the forty-ninth and fiftieth years of Her Majesty Queen Victoria, 1886* (London, 1886), pp. 55–8.
10 PRONI, Brownlow papers, D/1928/T/2/17, report as to the present state of Lady Lurgan's finances and her powers and duties as executrix and guardian of her children, by her agent [1847].
11 *Ibid.*

12 *Ibid.*
13 Anthony Malcomson, *The extraordinary career of the second Earl of Massereene, 1743–1805* (Belfast: Her Majesty's Stationery Office, 1972), p. 29.
14 *Ibid.*, pp. 26–30.
15 PRONI, Foster/Massereene papers, D/562/2871, memorandum of legal case papers concerning the Massereene family, c.1801.
16 PRONI, Downshire papers, D/671/D14/2/20a, last will and testament of Arthur Hill, Marquess of Downshire, extracted from the will registers of the Prerogative Court of Canterbury, 24 November 1797, probate granted 7 October 1801; PRONI, Downshire papers, D/607/I/21, Thomas Handley to James Brownbrigg, 10 June 1803.
17 Jupp, 'County Down elections', p. 191.
18 *Ibid.*, p. 184.
19 *Ibid.*, p. 191.
20 Malcomson, 'A woman scorned?', p. 12.
21 PRONI, Downshire papers, D/607/I/42, Thomas Handley to James Brownbrigg, 25 March 1806.
22 Jupp, 'County Down elections', p. 185.
23 PRONI, Ward papers, 2092/1/10/46, Mary Hill, Marchioness of Downshire to Arabella Ward, 22 November 1806.
24 PRONI, Downshire papers, D/607/J/59, Mary Hill to Thomas Handley, 14 November 1812.
25 PRONI, Downshire papers, D/607/I/25, Mary Hill to John Reilly, 9 April 1804.
26 PRONI, Ward papers, D/2092/1/11/16, Richard Tighe to Arabella Ward, 15 November 1812.
27 PRONI, Dufferin and Ava papers, D/1071/F/A1/8/1, Helen Blackwood to Frederick Blackwood, undated [1847].
28 PRONI, Dufferin and Ava papers, D/1071/F/A3/2, Helen Blackwood to Henrietta Sheridan, 25 August 1841.
29 PRONI, Dufferin and Ava papers, D/1071/F/A3/1, note by Frederick Blackwood in a typescript copy of a letter from Helen Blackwood to Henrietta Sheridan, 25 August 1841.
30 PRONI, Dufferin and Ava papers, D/1071/F/A3/2, Helen Blackwood to Henrietta Sheridan, 11 September 1841.
31 PRONI, Dufferin and Ava papers, D/1071/F/A2/1, copy of a letter from Helen Blackwood to Price Blackwood, 24 December 1831; PRONI, Dufferin and Ava papers, D/1071/F/B2/1/1, copy of a letter from Price Blackwood to Helen Blackwood, 31 July 1834.
32 PRONI, Dufferin and Ava papers, D/1071/F/A1/7/1, Helen Blackwood to Frederick Blackwood, undated [1842].
33 PRONI, Downshire papers, D/671/D14/2/17, copy of the last will and testament of James Fitzgerald, Duke of Leinster, 9 February 1768.
34 Tillyard, *Aristocrats*, p. 50.

35 *Ibid.*, p. 309.
36 NLI, Brian Fitzgerald papers, MS 13,022, typescript of letter from William Fitzgerald to Emily Fitzgerald, Duchess of Leinster, 8 February 1775; Fitzgerald, *Emily Duchess of Leinster*, p. 143.
37 Louisa Conolly to Emily Fitzgerald, Duchess of Leinster, 1 April 1776, printed in Brian Fitzgerald (ed.), *Correspondence of Emily, Duchess of Leinster (1731–1814), iii Letters of Lady Louisa Conolly and William Marquis of Kildare* (Dublin: Stationery Office, 1957), p. 193.
38 NLI, Brian Fitzgerald papers, MS 13,022, typescript of letter from Charles Fitzgerald to Emily Fitzgerald, Duchess of Leinster, 22 November 1774.
39 Tillyard, *Aristocrats*, p. 308.
40 NLI, Brian Fitzgerald papers, MS 13,022, typescript of a letter from William Fitzgerald to Emily Fitzgerald, Duchess of Leinster, 25 February 1776.
41 *Ibid.*
42 NLI, Brian Fitzgerald papers, MS 13,022, typescript of a letter from William Fitzgerald to Emily Fitzgerald, Duchess of Leinster, 7 May 1776.
43 *Ibid.*
44 11 George III, c. 20 (Ireland, 43 George III, c. 75 (Ireland).
45 PRONI, Clanmorris papers, D/421/6/F/1, last will and testament and two codicils and probate of Bernard Ward, will dated 30 August 1779, probate granted 1781.
46 PRONI, Ward papers, D/2092/1/9/93, legal opinion by Stephen Radcliffe on finances of Ward family [c.1802].
47 PRONI, Ward papers, D/2092/1/9/88, summary of evidence relating to Lord Bangor's lunacy and Edward Ward's income [1802]; PRONI, Ward papers, D/2092/1/11/78, Matthew Franks to Arabella Ward, 12 May 1813.
48 PRONI, Ward papers, D/2092/1/9/88, summary of evidence relating to Lord Bangor's lunacy and Edward Ward's income [1802].
49 PRONI, Ward papers, D/2092/1/10/67, Matthew Franks to Arabella Ward, 24 June 1808.
50 PRONI, Ward papers, D/2092/1/10/93, copy of a letter from Arabella Ward to Robert Ward [May 1808].
51 PRONI, Ward papers, D/2092/1/10/21, Emily Montgomery to Arabella Ward, 6 June 1802.
52 *Ibid.*
53 PRONI, Ward papers, D/2092/1/11/19, Robert Ward to Arabella Ward, 29 November 1812.
54 PRONI, Ward papers, D/2092/1/10/27, Emily Montgomery to Arabella Ward [March 1802].
55 PRONI, Ward papers, D/2092/1/10/24, Emily Montgomery to Arabella Ward [March 1802].
56 PRONI, Ward papers, D/2092/1/10/20, Emily Montgomery to Arabella Ward, 23 May 1802.

57 PRONI, Ward papers, D/2092/1/11/81, Hugh Montgomery to Richard Keown, 13 May 1813.

58 PRONI, Ward papers, D/2092/1/11/81, Hugh Montgomery to Richard Keown, 13 May 1813.

59 PRONI, Ward papers, D/2092/1/10/103, Theodosia, Countess of Clanwilliam to Arabella Ward, 24 November 1812.

60 PRONI, Ward papers, D/2092/1/11/31, Robert Ward to Arabella Ward, 31 December 1812.

61 PRONI, Ward papers, D/2092/1/10/119, Robert Ward to Arabella Ward, undated [November 1812].

62 PRONI, Ward papers, D/2092/1/10/111, Robert Ward to Arabella Ward, 28 February 1812; PRONI, Ward papers, D/2092/1/10/124, Robert Ward to Arabella Ward, 29 May 1812; PRONI, Ward papers, D/2092/1/10/108, Robert Ward to Arabella Ward, 21 January 1812.

63 PRONI, Ward papers, D/2092/1/11/30, Matthew Franks to Robert Ward, 29 December 1812.

64 PRONI, Ward papers, D/2092/1/10/125, copy of a letter from Arabella Ward to Robert Ward, 26 December 1812.

65 PRONI, Ward papers, D/2092/1/10/108, copy of a letter from Arabella Ward to Robert Ward, 21 January 1812.

66 PRONI, Ward papers, D/2092/1/10/107, copy of a letter from Arabella Ward to Robert Ward, 20 January 1812.

67 PRONI, Ward papers, D/2092/1/11/28, Richard Tighe to Arabella Ward, 28 December 1812; PRONI, Ward papers, D/2092/1/10/125, copy of a letter from Arabella Ward to Robert Ward [26 December 1812].

68 PRONI, Ward papers, D/2092/1/11/23, Robert Ward to Arabella Ward, 4 December 1812.

69 PRONI, Ward papers D/2092/1/11/26, Robert Ward to Arabella Ward, 4 December 1812; PRONI, Ward papers, D/2092/1/11/28, Richard Tighe to Arabella Ward, 28 December 1812.

70 PRONI, Ward papers, D/2092/1/11/10, Theodosia, Countess of Clanwilliam, to Arabella Ward, 7 November 1812.

71 PRONI, Ward papers, D/2092/1/10/87, Emily Montgomery to Arabella Ward, 12 November 1812.

72 PRONI, Ward papers, D/2092/1/11/6, copy of the draft of Mr King's report upon Robert Ward's petition [May 1813].

73 PRONI, Ward papers, D/2092/1/11/35, copy of a letter from Arabella Ward to Robert Ward, dated January 1812.

74 PRONI, Ward papers, D/2092/1/10/87, Emily Montgomery to Arabella Ward, 12 November 1812; PRONI, Ward papers, D/2092/1/10/117, Anne Catherine Ward to Arabella Ward, 14 April 1813.

75 PRONI, Ward papers, D/2092/1/11/67, copy of order to the Master in Chancery to report an increase in Lord Bangor's establishment, 7 April 1813.

76 PRONI, Ward papers, D/2092/1/11/51, Matthew Franks to Arabella Ward, 26 February 1813.

77 PRONI, Ward papers, D/2092/1/11/62, Robert Ward to Arabella Ward, 30 March 1813.

78 PRONI, Ward papers, D/2092/1/11/67, copy of order to the Master in Chancery to report an increase in Lord Bangor's establishment, 7 April 1813.

79 PRONI, Ward papers, D/2092/1/10/117, copy of a letter from Anne Catherine Ward to Arabella Ward, 14 April [1813].

80 PRONI, Ward papers, D/2092/1/11/51, Matthew Franks to Arabella Ward, 26 February 1813.

81 PRONI, Ward papers, D/2092/1/11/108, copy of a letter from Arabella Ward to Anne Catherine Ward, 1 July [1813].

82 PRONI, Ward papers, D/2092/1/10/19, Emily Montgomery to Arabella Ward, 8 November [1802].

83 PRONI, Ward papers, D/2092/1/10/82, Emily Montgomery to Arabella Ward, 12 June 1808; PRONI, Ward papers, D/2092/1/10/28, Anne Catherine Ward to Arabella Ward [undated].

84 PRONI, Ward papers, D/2092/1/10/41, Sophia Ward to Arabella Ward [1802].

85 PRONI, Ward papers, D/2092/1/11/72, draft letter from Arabella Ward to Stewart King, 12 April 1813.

86 PRONI, Ward papers, D/2092/1/11/8, copy of Lady Arabella Ward's letter to the Chancellor 'on leaving Dublin' [1813].

4

Single women and property

Legally, both widows and single women were *femes soles* and had the right to own and control their own property, make contracts, sue and be sued. However, as a history of single women in early modern England has noted, modern historians of women have neglected the fact that 'although a single woman and a widow were both unmarried women, people in early modern England did not think of these two groups of women in the same way'.[1] The term 'spinster' carried negative connotations in this period. The age at which a single woman became an 'old maid' averaged at thirty-five and, as another history of single women has noted, the 'shame and scorn with which spinsters were regarded in the past often makes them virtually invisible'.[2] It has also been speculated that the labelling of single women as 'old maids' was the result of an ideology that encouraged women to 'yield possession and control of their earthly goods . . . to men'.[3]

In Ireland it is clear that the dismal image associated with spinsters in this period was related to their financial situation. The *Retrospections of Dorothea Herbert*, for example, is the memoir of a spinster from a middle-class rectory family, written when the author was about thirty years old, in the period after the death of her father and indicating her increasing isolation as a spinster who was economically dependent upon her family.[4] It is unclear whether wealthy single women in Ireland experienced the shame associated with spinsterhood to the same degree as their poorer contemporaries, although it has been observed that many rich women married to avoid the stigma of spinsterhood.[5] It may have been the case that wealthy spinsters were protected from such influences by their economic independence. Single women are absent from family genealogies that focus on marriage and the transmission of land from one generation to the next. However, as daughters, single women can be found in family settlements. The single woman's experience of property can also be traced through various deeds and property-related documents such as tax receipts, as well as personal correspondence and last wills and testaments. Such documents reveal a more complex life than images of lonely spinsterhood suggest, as single women are revealed as active, independent women who controlled their own property, generated extra income through loans and lived independent lives outside the family estate with connections to wide networks of friends and extended family.

Single women and family property

In the wealthy landed class the main source of income for an unmarried daughter was the amount settled for younger children in her parents' marriage settlement, and the final distribution of this fund by her father's last will and testament. This amount formed the basis of a portion for daughters if they married, or for their income if they remained single. It was also usual practice in these families to make further provision for actual daughters and sons during the marriage by separate deeds and in last wills and testaments. The main effect of this trend, as in the case of widow's jointure, was that family members were to a degree dependent on the head of the family to provide regular payments. The level of provision was to a large extent determined by the financial circumstances of the family and, more particularly, by the preferences of the father. Some families treated all siblings equally while some differentiated on the grounds of gender or seniority. Therefore, until they reached the age of twenty-one, unmarried women were legally and economically subject to the control of their parents, and especially their father, who could exact obedience from children, for example by making provisions dependent on marriage with consent, or good behaviour.

Paternal control over provision for younger children was to a certain extent diluted by the fact that parents were obliged by law to provide maintenance, protection and education for their children in accordance with their rank.[6] As with married women, such rights could be asserted in the Court of Chancery. Chancery tended to favour the rights of children to adequate financial provision, even if this provision was not expressed in their father's last will and testament. When James Alexander, first Earl of Caledon, bequeathed £30,000 to his only daughter, Elizabeth (d. 1852), to be paid by his son, Du Pre Alexander, the second Earl, one year after his death, he neglected to provide her with maintenance for the year preceding the payment of the legacy.[7] When the extent of the legacy was questioned in Chancery by Du Pre Alexander, the Court ruled that despite the silence of Lord Caledon's last will and testament on the subject, Elizabeth had the power to devise the legacy, even if she died before it was payable, and she was also entitled to claim the interest on the legacy for the period following her father's death to enable her to 'defray her maintenance for that year'.[8] This decision reflected Chancery practice on contingent or vested legacies, which for her, 'being a child [and] without provision would be decreed by the Court of Equity interest at 5 per cent, on the legacy from testators', and was, significantly, applicable even if it had not been the late Lord Caledon's intention to allow interest.[9]

In the last wills and testaments of fathers in these families, land tended to be settled on the eldest son, while younger sons and daughters were provided for by annuities and legacies. This trend was mostly followed in the wills of mothers, although mothers were more likely than fathers to bequeath land to daughters. An analysis of twenty wills from men and women in these families indicates that when there was a male heir to the family estate, it was increasingly unusual for land to be bequeathed to daughters or younger sons. Daughters were more likely to be bequeathed chattel property and legacies, while younger sons, although also receiving annuities and legacies, were additionally bequeathed capital and life interests in land.[10] Furthermore, if we consider last wills and testaments in cases where both male and female siblings from the same family received bequests, the difference between the type of property bequeathed to sons and daughters is more starkly shown. In a survey of six wills dated between 1768 and 1837, three written by women and three written by men, daughters were bequeathed only legacies, while younger sons were bequeathed land and chattel property, as well as annuities and legacies.[11]

The preference for bequeathing land to younger sons reflects the concern to keep land 'in the family', and to consolidate smaller 'cadet' estates, rather than breaking them up in order to provide for numerous children. Anne Skeffington, Countess of Massereene, wished to settle fortunes for her younger children on an estate the Countess inherited from her father. On consulting with her Irish lawyers, she was advised: '[w]hen your ladyship comes to aid your younger children's fortunes by means of that estate it may be done without either selling or dividing of it by leaving to any one of them entire, charging it with fortunes for the rest as you think fit'.[12]

The preference in these families for the consolidation of landed property, and the provision for daughters, and on occasion younger sons, by legacy was such an acceptable part of estate management that even if land had been settled on daughters and younger sons, a father who was determined to enlarge and unify his landed estate could override this. Therefore, when Louisa Ward, the second wife of Robert Ward, settled an estate of land on her husband, with remainders specifically limited to the children of that marriage, her wishes were not guaranteed to be met.[13] Louisa pre-deceased her husband, and in his last will and testament, Robert Ward arranged a sum of money, equal in amount to £9,230, to be paid out of his personal assets to each of his children 'in full lieu and satisfaction of my promise they or any of them may be entitled to or any claim they may have under my marriage settlement'. By accepting this payment the six children from his marriage to Louisa Symes would give up their legal claim to the estate, and it could be settled, as Robert intended, on his eldest son from his first marriage, Michael Edward Ward.[14]

The exception to the practice of extensive estates being bequeathed to elder sons occurred when daughters inherited in default of male heirs. Mary Hill, Marchioness of Downshire, and Frances Anne Vane-Tempest Stewart, Marchioness of Londonderry, were two of the most obvious examples of women among the sample families who inherited substantial landed estates. There is however no example here of an heiress to an estate with a rental over £10,000 who did not marry, and it is probable that such heiresses had no choice but to marry. In such large estates an heiress was a substitute for an elder son, and the estate would be settled on her male heirs. Even for smaller landed estates, however, the unmarried heiress may have represented an anomaly at this time. Jill Liddington notes, in relation to the heiress Anne Lister, that in addition to her ability to live openly as a lesbian and her 'unorthodox marriage to Ann Walker', her journals and letters suggest the 'freedoms that an independently propertied woman . . . was able to enjoy in pre-Victorian England'.[15]

Single women who did inherit landed property were active in its management. When Montague Blundell, Viscount Blundell, died without issue in 1756, his estate in County Down and King's County passed to his three daughters, two of whom were married and one of whom, Anna, remained unmarried. After a dispute arose in 1766 over the payment of arrears on the estate, Anna and her sisters took a case to Chancery. Their case was based on a settlement made in 1741 that distributed one-third of the Blundell estate to each of the late Viscount's three daughters in failure of male issue. By 1766 William Macartney, a tenant farmer on the estate, owed the sisters £2,010. The three women obtained an order in August 1765 to bring about his ejectment for non-payment of rent and refused to renew his lease, stating that they were not bound by the previous practice of their father, as he was 'bare tenant for life'.[16] Not only were these women able to take a case to Chancery, but they did not regard themselves as bound by the practice of their father in estate management.

The income of single women

When land was bequeathed to unmarried daughters it may not have been a major source of income, and may have been used to provide for several daughters. In 1842, by the terms of their father's will, the six unmarried daughters of Henry Boyle, third Earl of Shannon (1771–1842), and his wife Sarah Hyde (d. 1820) were bequeathed an estate of land in Courtmacsherry, Bandon, County Cork. The daughters of Lord Shannon were, in order of birth, Charlotte (d. 1880s?), Sarah (d. 1884), Louisa Grace (d.1856), Jane (d. 1876), Elizabeth (d. 1886) and Katherine Boyle (d. 1867). The Courtmacsherry estate was devised to all the daughters during their respective lives as joint tenants, with the right of survivorship. The estate could not therefore be devised to any other person, and may have returned to the Shannon estate after the death of the last surviving sister.[17] The house and household contents at Courtmacsherry also appear to have been held as a joint tenancy.[18] Therefore, when one sister died, her share of the property was divided between her remaining sisters.[19] The sisters had also been 'entitled to a proportionate share of a mill in Ireland on a lease for lives', although in 1853 no rent had been received from this property for a number of years.[20]

The land bequeathed to the Boyle sisters had been held in fee simple by Lord Shannon, was valued at £4,048 in 1858, and took an annual gross rental of £4,089.16.6.[21] At least one of the daughters also inherited land from other sources. On her death in 1837, Katherine Boyle bequeathed an estate in the Barony of Duhallow in County Cork, 'commonly called or known by the name of "Dickson's estate"' unto two trustees for the use of her sister, Sarah, during her life. The land was to pass to Katherine's brother, Robert Francis Boyle, on Sarah's death. Only on Sarah's death was this property to go to her other sisters. On the death of 'the longest liver' the property was bequeathed to 'the Society for the Promotion of the Gospel in Foreign Parts'.[22]

It was common among the families surveyed here for income to be based either solely, or in addition to land, on investments in government stock. On her death in 1852, Lady Louisa Boyle's income from the Courtmacsherry estate was £770, and along with mortgage and interest payments due in 1852, she was owed £1,519 at the time of her death. Lady Boyle also owned a significant amount of capital in government 3 per cent stocks, valued at £5,820 on a principal sum of £5,350.[23] Her entire property was valued at £6,361.10.9, the bulk of which was made up from her stocks, but which also included cash in the house, cash in the bank, furniture, jewellery, plate, china and books.[24] All the Boyle sisters appear to have lived within a similar financial structure.

Lady Jane Boyle, for example, owned a principal sum of £4,682 in government 3 per cent stocks, with dividends of £77 payable at her death in 1876.[25]

For some women such investments would have created a substantial income. In terms of daily living, the ownership of a large principal sum held in stocks provided financial independence comparable to the holding of a piece of land. At the time of her death in 1852, Lady Elizabeth Alexander's investments and items of personal property converted into cash totalled £32,489. The total still in stocks on her death was £6,306.[26] She was therefore very well provided for, although she did not own an estate in land. However, not all daughters owned the principal sum. Meliora Creighton (d. 1795), the sister of John Creighton, first Earl of Erne (1731–1828), enjoyed the interest of a sum of £2,000, held for her use for life by trustees, which went to her brother Abraham Creighton (d. 1819) on her death.[27] Also, for other women the income derived from investments was much less, although in such cases several types of income provision may have been employed. For example, owing to an arrangement made in their father's will, from 1801 the two daughters of Richard Wingfield, Viscount Powerscourt (1730–88), received the interest of £7,500, divided equally between them. From this interest each daughter received an annual annuity of £374 which was paid in two instalments of £187.[28]

Disposal of property

Access to cash that could be spared meant that single women, like wealthy married women and widows, could be part of family lending networks. In May 1821 Elizabeth Alexander lent £20,000 to Arthur Hill-Trevor, Lord Dungannon, at 6 per cent interest, for which he mortgaged his estate in County Down to secure the debt before it was repaid in June 1824.[29] Such mortgages were regarded as assets and as such could be bequeathed by last will and testament. On her death Cadwallader, Lord Blayney, owed Elizabeth Alexander's executors £4,000 as a mortgage payment.[30] The last will and testament of Meliora Creighton makes provision for the repayment of a debt of £1,500 'which is due to me by the bond of John King esq of Ballyin' and £500 which a Gilbert King, brother of Rebecca King, owed her 'by his bond'.[31]

Interest received on loans was potentially a significant source of income for women. For example, if we consider that upon her death in 1852 Elizabeth Alexander's assets totalled nearly £40,000, the interest on this loan over the three years was 9.3 per cent of her personal estate – from one loan transaction. And this was not the only loan Elizabeth

Alexander undertook, as on her death she was owed a further £4,000 from a loan to Lord Blayney.

The last wills and testaments of single women provide a useful insight into the type of property they owned, and had power to dispose of, during their lifetimes, as well as information on their social and family networks. The types of bequests made by single women in these families tended to be legacies of cash and the bequest of personal property, such as jewellery, books, furniture and clothing. These were made to immediate family and extended kin, friends, servants and charity. Louisa Boyle bequeathed a legacy of £1,000 in bank annuities to her brother Robert Francis Boyle, as well as six legacies to servants and four legacies to charitable institutions. She also stated that her brother, the Earl of Shannon, and his wife the Countess of Shannon and two of her sisters, Ladies Katherine and Sarah Boyle, were to select 'any article that they severally may like to have in remembrance of me and as a mark of my sisterly affection'.[32]

Louisa Boyle's will is not much different from later wills of the other Boyle women, which demonstrate a similar concern with legacies to servants, family members and charity. All six of the annuities in Jane Boyle's last will and testament of 1876 were bequeathed to servants, while several family members were to select a memento from her books or other personal effects 'as a mark of my sisterly affection'.[33] Of the nine legacies noted in Sarah Boyle's 1885 will, one was for a family member, her brother Lord Shannon, four were for servants and four for charitable institutions.[34] The three legacies in Elizabeth Boyle's 1886 will were all to servants.[35] Katherine Boyle's will is exceptional in the range of beneficiaries it names, as she bequeathed all her property, which included cash, stocks and items such as books, plate and jewellery, to her sister Sarah. Katherine's will is also unusual as she names only one charity, which was to ultimately receive the remainder of her estate, and one beneficiary, with the rest of the family mentioned only as beneficiaries by default.[36]

If we compare the wills of the Boyle sisters with that of Elizabeth Alexander, also proved in 1852, we can see a similar concern to provide for family members, servants and charitable institutions. Out of a total of twenty legacies, Elizabeth's sister, Lady Blayney, was her principal beneficiary with a legacy of £3,000, her house in Fitzwilliam Square in Dublin along with the contents of the house and the remainder of the estate as residuary legatee. Elizabeth also bequeathed legacies to one nephew and two nieces, one great-niece, four servants and six people who were not blood relations, and left four legacies for charitable causes.[37]

In the will of Meliora Creighton, four bequests were made to her two brothers, two to her nephew, one to her niece and one bequest of £30 to her maid, Margaret Morris. Nothing was bequeathed to charity. The remaining five bequests were to friends. For example, she bequeathed 'to my dear friend' Lady Erne 'my gold watch as a token of my esteem and regard' and twenty guineas each 'as tokens of regard and affection' to her two brothers, her sister and her 'worthy friend James King of Eccles St Dublin', which, she requested, 'they may layout same in rings or some other tokens of remembrance for me'.

The main beneficiaries of Meliora Creighton's will were her nephew and niece. She bequeathed £1,900, 'which I have as change now lying in my brother Lord Erne's estate' to her nephew John Creighton plus a further legacy of £1,000 sterling, payable out of money and securities she had at the time of her death. Her nephew John Creighton was also her residuary legatee. To her niece Lady Catherine Creighton, she bequeathed her interest in the house 'where I now live' in Temple Street, Dublin, including all household furniture and utensils except plate, which was bequeathed for her life only and on her death was to go to her nephew John Creighton and his heirs. Another major beneficiary of her will was a widowed friend, Mrs Rebecca King, to whom she bequeathed £1,500 owed to Meliora by Mrs King's brother-in-law. The money was to be held in trust for Mrs King, for her to divide among her children 'in such shares and proportions as they shall require and merit from her'.[38]

A further example of the importance of extended family and friends in the wills of spinsters of this class is the will of Lady Harriet Seymour-Conway, described in her will as 'of Chichester, Co Sussex', daughter of Francis Seymour-Conway (1679–1731), the first Lord Conway and sister of Francis Seymour-Conway (b. 1718), second Lord Conway and first Marquess of Hertford. The main beneficiaries of her will were her extended family, the children of her half-sister Mary (d. 1728), who married Nicholas Price of Saintfield, County Down.

There are forty separate bequests to thirty-five different people in Lady Harriet's will, nine of which are to people related to her by blood, including great-nieces and nephews, and two more of which were to the wives of her two brothers. Six bequests were made to servants and two to charity, which means that sixteen of the beneficiaries who were not employees were either friends or acquaintances. It is clear that Harriet was concerned to provide for members of her extended family and for non-family members rather than for her immediate family. Her nephew Francis Price was her sole executor and the main beneficiary of the will. He was to receive all her 'stock in the public funds and all my moiet[ies] and securities for moneys and all other my goods, chattels and personal estate whatsoever'. On his death, £2,000 was to be raised from this property and given to his eldest daughter, her great niece, 'on the day of her marriage or aged eighteen'. Harriet made clear that this sum was to be in addition to the portion her parents might give her on marriage. If this niece died, the same was to be given to the second great-niece or nephew. Meanwhile, the residue of this stock was bequeathed to her great-nephew Nicholas Price, the son of Francis Price. Two further legacies, of £50 and £100, were also bequeathed to a Miss Letitia Waring, eldest daughter of Mr Waring, who does not appear to have been a blood relation.

Harriet also provided for her servants. A further five legacies of varying amounts were bequeathed to particular servants; her maid Catherine Wilkes, for example, was bequeathed £20 while another maid was bequeathed £10. In addition, all servants who had lived with her for three years or more were to receive one year's wages within six months of her death, as well as 'wages and board wages owing to them until they are discharged'. Non-family members were also beneficiaries of the will. Her 'worthy friend and old companion' Mrs Hellena Pelham was bequeathed one annuity of £100 charged on her personal estate and to be paid quarterly on 'usual feast days' by her executor. If this payment was delayed by one month it was subject to £5 penalty, and if delayed by one year it was subject to a £20 penalty. Alongside this, she was also bequeathed, 'for her sole use and benefit', bedroom and 'best parlour' furniture not otherwise bequeathed, including 'china dishes, cups, saucers and stoneware', as well as 'the table in the hall and one round wainscot table', various pots and pans, 'my warming pan, my copper coffee pot, chocolate pot and tea kettle, my scales and weights my two silver candlesticks engraved with my arms, also six silver table spoons and six tea spoons, strainer and tongs silver' and 'her choice of all my nightgowns, quilted petticoats underpetticoats, cotton stockings, lace caps . . . pocket handkerchiefs, fine aprons and cloaks' as well as 'sheets, towels, napkins . . . and ribbons'. Hellena Pelham therefore was to have her choice of most of Harriet Conway's personal belongings and household utensils. Whatever she chose not to take was to go to Harriet Conway's 'own maid' to give to two other servants living with her.

Through her detailed bequests Harriet Conway indicated that she took care to bequeath as much of her personal property as possible to specific people. The largest part of the will is taken up with mementoes: twenty-seven bequests fall into this category, ranging from a snuff box worth five guineas, bequeathed to a Mr Walter Bowman, to 'my antique cameo set in gold also my small trinket containing The Lord's Prayer', bequeathed to the Countess of Plymouth.[39] The testamentary practice of these single women indicates a concern to provide for extended family and friends, according to the perceived need of their beneficiaries and a desire to account for all their personal property, from legacies to mementoes. Because of the place of single women outside the main family estate, this extended network of kin and non-kin may have been a more significant factor in their lives than in the lives of their married or widowed contemporaries. A further possible reason for the careful, detailed bequests may also have been the lack of any obvious beneficiary in the event of a single woman dying intestate.

Records of single women's charitable contributions during their lives are sparse among the sample families. There is no record of what the Boyle sisters contributed to charity during their lives, although it can be assumed that they did contribute to various causes. When information does exist, it indicates that the charitable contributions of these women, their concern for the local, 'deserving' poor and their adherence to the ideals of the self-improvement of the poor were in accordance with the general trend of women's involvement in private rather than institutional charity at this time.

Elizabeth Alexander contributed an annual subscription of £3.10.10 to the Mendicity Society, founded in 1829 by her brother Du Pre Alexander, Earl of Caledon, and his wife Catherine Alexander, Countess of Caledon. This increased to £5 in 1833 and to £10 in 1837.[40] The Mendicity Society was founded for the relief of the poor in the neighbourhood of the Caledon estate. The aim of the society was to consider applications for financial assistance from the poor, which would be assessed according to perceived need. A weekly allowance would then be granted to petitioners. The personal morality of claimants was an important aspect of the Society. There was disapproval of the 'undeserving poor', such as 'Pat Ryan's wife', who was in receipt of an allowance from the society and was 'in the habit of having a dance every Friday night at which many young persons meet and are in the habit of drinking much even to intoxication. It is also said Ryan's wife is in the habit of stealing fowl.'[41]

Sophia Ward, one of the younger daughters of Bernard Ward, Lord Bangor, never married, and made provision, in an indenture, for the erection of 'a house for the residence of four poor women of the age of 60 y[ea]rs [and] upwards' and the maintenance and support of them. She paid £1,000 to her nephew Edward Ward, and £40 per annum was to be paid to the Reverend Henry Ward and Reverend Charles Wolesley for the foundation of this charitable institution.[42]

Testamentary bequests to charity among single women from the sample families were also in accordance with the general trend. Elizabeth Alexander bequeathed a total of £120 in five legacies to charitable causes, from £10 to 'the blind man of Castle Blayney' to £30 to the Dublin Mendicity Institution.[43] Harriet Conway bequeathed a legacy of £100 'to the poor of the parish of Lisburn', and £10 was to be distributed to the 'honest, industrious poor housekeepers of the city of Chichester . . . at the discretion of Reverend Mr Clarke'.[44] Louisa Boyle's legacies were larger. She contributed a total of £200 in four charitable legacies that ranged in amounts from £100 for the Church Educational Schools, County Cork, down to £25 to the London City Mission. Louisa's legacies were however much smaller than those made later in the century by her sister Sarah Boyle, who bequeathed a total of £1,400 to four charitable causes ranging from £500 to the Irish Church Mission down to £200 to the Female Hibernian Society.[45] The difference in the amount bequeathed can possibly be accounted for by the different income of the two sisters, as later in the century Sarah Boyle would not only have been more wealthy, but would have been a beneficiary of encumbered estates legislation. However, the amount spent on charity is significant.

There was a particular emphasis on religion in bequests by the Boyle sisters. The causes that they supported included the Church Educational Schools in Cork, the John Street Chapel Schools in London, an orphan nursery in Connemara and the London City Mission. In 1885, Sarah Boyle bequeathed a legacy to the Church Missionary Society, whose activities included 'sending the gospel to those who are still in heathen darkness'.[46] The contributions made to charitable causes by these women offers us some insight into their personal religion and morality. For Elizabeth Alexander and the Boyle sisters, religion and charity played an integral part in their social life. The rental of pews by a 'Lady Boyle' illustrated the integration of wealth, status and church attendance.[47] In their concern for the local 'deserving' poor, and the promotion of temperance and religious salvation for those at home and abroad, these women displayed their adherence to values inherent in eighteenth- and nineteenth-century philanthropy.

Living arrangements

The life-choices available to single women from the wealthy landed class who were without an independent fortune were limited. Caroline Hamilton's description of two spinsters living at the Tighe family home in Rossana, County Wicklow, at the time of her parent's marriage in the mid-eighteenth century is an example of how economic dependence was interlinked with the negative stereotype of the spinster. One of the spinsters, Miss Chloe Lovet, was 'an old maid dressed like a little nun, whose hair had grown grey in a single night when she was young, from her lover having deserted her, and carried off all her fortune on the eve of their marriage'. The other was Betty Toole, 'whose nose met her chin'.[48] A spinster with inadequate resources was left with little option but to stay at home and act as a housekeeper or governess. Caroline Norton, the sister of Helen Blackwood, Lady Dufferin, referred to an unmarried aunt who lived with her other aunt, Lady Graham, as 'a kind, good soul, who was like a second mother and governess to Lady G[raham]'s children'.[49]

The living arrangements of an unmarried daughter may have been determined by the last will and testament of her father. In the will of John Blackwood of Ballyleidy, County Down, for example, it was stated that his daughters could have the use of the Blackwood house at Killyleagh while they remained unmarried and lived there with their mother Dorcas, the future Baroness Dufferin and Clandeboye.[50] However, while living in the family home was necessary for young women, for reasons of propriety as well as finance, adult single women were more likely to live in their own establishments, either owned or rented. In her last will and testament Elizabeth Alexander was described as of Bath. She also owned at this time a house in Dublin.[51] Meliora Creighton also owned the 'interest' in a house in Temple Street in Dublin, which it was in her power to bequeath.[52] Presumably the woman gained this right when she was a confirmed spinster, around thirty years old.

Spinsters may have shared establishments with each other at particular times. In March 1813 the affairs of Anne Catherine Ward, one of the daughters of the late Bernard Ward, Lord Bangor, were in a 'very unsettled state'. She had been living with her sister Sophie Ward in Clifden, England, 'at *free cost* [emphasis in original]' from January 1813. This arrangement changed, according to Anne Catherine, because Sophia 'said she could not afford the expense of my being with her', although Anne Catherine noted in a letter to her sister-in-law Arabella Ward: 'when I left her she settled an establishment, which cost her full as much, without her having the convenience of my horses, and carriage, or my society'.[53] One month later, in April 1813, Anne Catherine was renting her own house in Kenton, England, before returning to Castle Ward to live as the part of the committee of her insane brother, Nicholas Ward, Lord Bangor.[54]

The Boyle sisters, who all appear to have lived in London at least until later in the century, possibly shared accommodation with each other at particular times. Louisa Boyle rented a house 'from year to year' at 69 Cambridge Terrace, London.[55] Receipts signed by her for sewage tax, water tax and property tax indicate that she lived there until her death in 1852. Property tax receipts also indicate the size of her establishment:

between 1845 and 1852 she was taxed for one male servant, between twenty-four and twenty-eight windows and three dogs.[56] The sisters may have shared homes with each other, with one sister being the primary occupant. Receipts for household items and jewellery, as well as occasional property tax receipts, were directed to either Louisa Boyle or to 'the Ladies Boyle', and the rent of the house at Cambridge Terrace was paid by the remaining sisters after Louisa's death in 1852. In 1837 Katherine Boyle described herself in her last will and testament as 'of No 7 Connaught Place' in London.[57] In 1860, Jane Boyle in her will described herself as 'heretofore of Connaught Place and afterwards of Cambridge Terrace . . . and now of Courtmacsherry House, Bandon in Ireland'.[58] She therefore evidently shared accommodation with her sister Katherine before moving to Cambridge Terrace, either to share with her sister Louisa or live there after her death, before moving to Ireland to live on her estate in Bandon.

Conclusion

When studying the experience of single women and property in this class, it is useful to consider the boundaries within which they operated. Spinsters, like widows, were legally regarded as *feme soles*, and had the right to own and control their own property. Otherwise, their situation differed from that of their widowed contemporaries. The financial life of a spinster was influenced primarily by family settlements, in particular the last will and testament of her father. It is clear that some single women among the core families were well provided for. Some women enjoyed an income from landed property. In other cases, substantial sums invested in stocks could provide wealth and financial independence for a spinster, which, in terms of daily life, was comparable to an income based on land. However, the trend at this time for not settling land on daughters or younger sons must have had an impact on other unmarried daughters in these families, increasing their financial dependence on the head of the family.

Economically independent single women were active members of loan networks with family members and friends. Charitable contributions by spinsters were also in accordance with prevailing trends in this period to provide for the local 'deserving' poor. Testamentary bequests reveal a more complex picture, however. The importance of religion in the lives of the Boyle sisters is discernible. Bequests to extended kin and especially to non-kin suggest that as well as making bequests in accordance with perceived need, spinsters valued wider kin and non-kin networks more highly than did their married or widowed contemporaries.

Notes

1 Amy M. Froide, 'Marital status as a category of difference: singlewomen and widows in early modern England' in Judith M. Bennett and Amy M. Froide (eds), *Singlewomen in the European past, 1250–1800* (Philadelphia: University of Pennsylvania Press, 1999), p. 236.

2 Bridget Hill, *Women alone: spinsters in England 1660–1850* (New Haven and London: Yale University Press, 2001), p. 3.

3 Susan S. Lanser, 'Singular politics: the rise of the British nation and the production of the old maid' in Bennett and Froide (eds), *Singlewomen*, p. 316.

4 Herbert, *Retrospections of Dorothea Herbert*.

5 Hill, *Women alone*, p. 8.

6 Blackstone, *Commentaries*, pp. 446–54.

7 PRONI, Caledon papers, D/2433/A/1/127/5, copy of the last will and testament and four codicils and probate of James Alexander, Earl of Caledon, extracted from the Court of Prerogative in Ireland, will dated 30 January 1799, probate granted 19 May 1802.

8 PRONI, Caledon papers, D/2433/A/2/9/5, copy of the legal opinion of William Saurin in the Case between Lord Caledon and Lady Elizabeth Alexander, 1803.

9 PRONI, Caledon papers, D/2433/A/2/9/5, copy of the legal opinion of William Saurin in the Case between Lord Caledon and Lady Elizabeth Alexander, 1803.

10 See appendix F.

11 *Ibid.*

12 PRONI, Foster/Massereene papers, D/562/2736, Alan Waring to Anne Skeffington, Countess of Massereene, 9 October 1762.

13 PRONI, Londonderry Estate Office papers, D/654/F1/15, marriage settlement of Louisa Symes and Robert Ward, 17 May 1797.

14 PRONI, Farrer and Co. Solicitors papers, D/585/55, last will and testament and probate of Robert Ward, will dated 7 November 1828, three codicils dated 10 November 1828 and 30 March 1829, probate granted 6 June 1831.

15 Jill Liddington, *Female fortune, land gender and authority: the Anne Lister diaries and other writings, 1833–36* (London: Rivers Oram, 1998), p. xviii.

16 PRONI, Downshire papers, D/671/D6/1/33, printed copy of a case in the Irish Court of Chancery between William Macartney and Anna Maria Blundell and others, 24 April 1789.

17 There are no deeds relating to the fate of the Courmacsherry estate extant in the Shannon papers held at PRONI. However, in the absence of evidence that the land was ultimately bequeathed by the last surviving Boyle sister, it can be assumed that the sisters held the land as a life interest only, with no powers of bequest, and that the estate passed back to the Shannon estate after their death.

18 PRONI, Shannon papers, D/2707/B17/328–348, Edward Green Foley to W. B. Leslie, 8 July 1886.

19 PRONI, Shannon papers, D/2707/B17/349–366, Inland Revenue, account of the succession on real property of Lady Jane Boyle, 1867.

20 PRONI, Shannon papers, D/2707/B17/217–230, Inland Revenue, residuary account of the property of Lady Louisa Boyle, 1853.

21 PRO, PROB/11/1963, last will and testament and four codicils of Henry Boyle, Earl of Shannon, extracted from the will registers of the Prerogative Court of Canterbury, will dated 27 August 1841, probate granted 26 May 1842; PRONI, Shannon papers, D/27007/B17/1, detail book of the Ladies Boyle, Countmacsherry estate, with the tenure and ordnance valuation of each holding, 30 August 1858.

22 PRONI, Shannon papers, D/2707/B17/349–366, copy of the last will and testament of Lady Katherine Boyle, dated 19 April 1837.

23 *Ibid.*

24 *Ibid.*

25 PRONI, Shannon papers, D/2707/B17/367–397, Inland Revenue, residuary account of the property of Lady Jane Boyle, 1876.

26 PRONI, Caledon papers, D/2433/B/22/1, account of the property of Lady Elizabeth Alexander made by her executors, undated [1854].

27 PRONI, Erne papers, D/1939/25/1/8a&b, copy of the last will and testament of Meliora Creighton, dated March 1795.

28 PRONI, Verner-Wingfield papers, D/2538/C/14, Emily Wingfield to Henry Stewart, 19 June 1805.

29 PRONI, Caledon papers, D/2433/A/1/423/1, reconveyance of a mortgage from Lady Elizabeth Alexander to Arthur, Lord Dungannon, 10 June 1824.

30 PRONI, Caledon papers, D/2433/B/22/1, account of the property of Lady Elizabeth Alexander made by her executors, undated [1854].

31 PRONI, Erne papers, D/1939/25/1/8a&b, copy of the last will and testament of Meliora Creighton, dated March 1795.

32 PRONI, Shannon papers, D/2707/B17/236–327, copy of the last will and testament, and probate, of Lady Louisa Boyle, probate granted 7 December 1852; Inland Revenue, residuary account of debts and legacies of Lady Louisa Boyle, 1852.

33 PRONI, Shannon papers, D/2707/B17/367–397, copy of the last will and testament of Lady Jane Boyle, dated 27 February 1860.

34 PRONI, Shannon papers, D/2707/B17/398–413, list of pecuniary legacies from the last will and testament of Lady Sarah Boyle, prepared by solicitors Edward Green Foley, Lower Sackville Street, Dublin, 1885; receipts from legatees, dated August 1885.

35 PRONI, Shannon papers, D/2707/B17/328–348, Edward Green Foley to W. B. Leslie, 8 July 1886.

36 PRONI, Shannon papers, D/2707/B17/349–366, copy of the last will and testament of Lady Katherine Boyle, dated 19 April 1837.

37 PRONI, Caledon papers, D/2433/B/22/1, last will and testament and two codicils of Lady Elizabeth Alexander, will dated 19 February 1852.

38 PRONI, Erne papers, D/1939/25/1/8a&b, copy of the last will and testament of Meliora Creighton, dated March 1795.

39 PRONI, Perceval–Price papers, D/993/2/30, copy of the last will and testament and probate of Harriet Seymour Conway, probate granted 7 June 1770.

40 PRONI, Caledon papers, D/2433/A/11/1, account book of the Mendicity Society in Caledon, 1829–69.

41 *Ibid.*

42 PRONI, Ward papers, D/2092/12/4, indenture between Sophie Ward and Edward Southwell Ward, Viscount Bangor, undated [1830s].

43 PRONI, Caledon papers, D/2433/B/22/1, last will and testament and two codicils of Elizabeth Alexander, will dated 19 February 1852.

44 PRONI, Perceval–Price papers, D/993/2/30, copy of the last will and testament and probate of Harriet Seymour Conway, probate dated 7 June 1770.

45 PRONI, Shannon papers, D/2707/B17/398–413, list of pecuniary legacies from the last will and testament of Lady Sarah Boyle, prepared by solicitors Edward Green Foley, Lower Sackville Street, Dublin, 1885; receipts from legatees, dated August 1885.

46 PRONI, Shannon papers, D/2707/C4/2, Church Missionary Paper, for the use of weekly and monthly contributors, Christmas 1835.

47 PRONI, Shannon papers, D/2707/B17/1–64; D/2707/B17/65–160, miscellaneous receipts for 'the Ladies Boyle' and Louisa Boyle, dated 1840s and 1850s.

48 NLI, Wicklow papers, MS 4811, the reminiscences of Mrs Caroline Hamilton; Bell (ed.), *The Hamwood papers*, p. 11.

49 PRONI, Dufferin and Ava papers, D/1071/F/E2/1, Caroline Norton to Edward Ellice, [1839].

50 PRONI, Dufferin and Ava papers, D/1071/A/N3/3b, copy of the will of John Blackwood, 31 December 1781.

51 PRONI, Caledon papers, D/2433/A/1/423/1, reconveyance of a mortgage from Lady Elizabeth Alexander to Arthur, Lord Dungannon, 10 June 1824.

52 PRONI, Erne papers, D/1939/25/1/8a&b, copy of the last will and testament of Meliora Creighton, dated March 1795.

53 PRONI, Ward papers, D/2092/1/11/56, Anne Catherine Ward to Arabella Ward, 11 March [1813].

54 PRONI, Ward papers, D/2092/1/11/68, Anne Catherine Ward to Arabella Ward, 8 April [1813].

55 PRONI, Shannon papers, D/2707/B17/217–230, Inland Revenue, residuary account of the property of Lady Louisa Boyle, 1853.

56 PRONI, Shannon papers, D/2707/B17/1–64; D/2707/B17/65–160, miscellaneous receipts for 'the Ladies Boyle' and Lady Louisa Boyle, dated 1840s and 1850s.

57 PRONI, Shannon papers, D/2707/B17/328–348, copy of the last will and testament of Lady Katherine Boyle, dated 1 February 1837.

58 PRONI, Shannon papers, D/2707/B17/367–397, copy of the last will and testament of Lady Jane Boyle, dated 27 February 1860, probate dated 1 May 1876.

5

Married women and property

Before the introduction of the Married Women's Property Acts in 1870 and 1882, a married woman's income was either arranged by the settlement of her separate property in equity or subject to the goodwill of her husband.[1] The married woman's experience of property was therefore, to an extent, arbitrary: some women had access to substantial incomes from separate property arrangements, while other women were dependent on their husbands for income during marriage. In addition, a married woman's income may have been affected by particular family circumstances such as family wealth, relationships and the presence or absence of male heirs.

Under the English common law doctrine of coverture the legal identity of a married woman was merged with that of her husband. Husband and wife were one person in law, and that person was the husband. A married woman could not acquire, hold or alienate property, either real or chattel, or enter into contracts. Her husband acquired a freehold interest in her estates of inheritance and life interest. Money and personal chattels used by a woman during her marriage legally belonged to her husband. It was however possible to circumvent the legal disabilities inherent in coverture by the use of trusts in equity. Separate property arrangements could be made guaranteeing a married woman access to an income, independent of her husband. Such settlements were a common feature in Irish wealthy landed families, and provide another perspective on family property interests: the interests of the bride and her representatives as opposed to the interests of the bridegroom and his family.[2]

There were three types of property that married women 'owned' in this period: paraphernalia, pin money and separate estate. A woman's right to own her paraphernalia, such as clothes and dressing room furniture, was ambiguous. Although a man was able by law to alienate his wife's paraphernalia during the marriage, as it was legally his, he could not bequeath it to another person. As Staves notes: 'if he predeceases her, unlike her other chattels, which go to his representatives,

Table 5.1 Amounts received as pin money, 1761–1845

Name	Year of marriage	Pin money
Ann Hamilton	1761	£500
Sarah Stewart	1766	£300
Frances Stewart	1773	£300
Charlotte Browne	1777	£300
Mary Browne	1783	£300
Mary Hill	1786	£1,200
Amelia Stewart	1794	£1,600
Anna Blackwood	1801	£500
Catherine Alexander	1811	£500
Frances Anne Vane	1819	£2,000
Augusta Westenra	1819	£500
Mary Brownlow	1822	£400
Helen Blackwood	1825	£133
Louisa Hamilton	1832	£1,000
Augusta Dawson	1841	£500
Jane Alexander	1845	£400

Sources: See appendix D.

her paraphernalia goes to her, subject to the rights of his creditors'.[3] However, it is questionable if this was assumed to be the case among Irish landed families, as there is at least one example in this period, in the 1836 last will and testament of James Blackwood, Lord Dufferin, of a husband bequeathing his wife her paraphernalia, which suggests that her owner-ship of this property was not considered secure.[4]

Table 5.1 outlines the available information on pin money for sixteen women from the sample families, all of whom married the heir to the family estate. Pin money arrangements were based, to a certain degree, upon portion brought by the bride to the marriage. Although, as noted in chapter 2, the percentage of pin money to portion varied in the sample families between 4 and 10 per cent, portion was a crucial factor in such arrangements, and the amount of income received by women as pin money varied accordingly. Frances Anne Vane-Tempest Stewart, Lady Londonderry, who brought a landed estate in England and Ireland as well as a marriage portion of £10,000, received £2,000 a year. Helen Blackwood, Lady Dufferin, who brought no portion and whose husband raised £10,000 upon which to base her provisions, appears to have received the annual sum of £133.[5] Pin money was not essential to bar dower, so it could be settled at a later date, or in a separate document at the time of marriage if necessary. There is such variety in the amount of pin money settled that it is likely that less formal arrangements were made to provide additional sums to the women in this sample.

It was unusual among the sample families for separate estate to be settled at the same time as jointure, and separate property arrangements are largely absent from family papers. As in the case of pin money, this may have been due to the fact that the arrangement of separate estate did not have a legal impact on the family estate, and so could be arranged separately from the main marriage settlement. There is information on separate estate arrangements made for eight women in these families. In three cases separate estate was in the form of investments, and in five cases separate property was in the form of land. Separate estates in the form of investments were, on two occasions, settled by the bride's husband either before or during marriage. James Stevenson Blackwood, Lord Dufferin, arranged, as part of his marriage settlement, for £3,000 to be invested in government securities. When the sum reached £10,000, Anna, Lady Dufferin, was to receive the interest for her life. Lady Dufferin also had the power to appoint the fund if she survived her husband.[6] Prior to his marriage to Augusta Charteris (d. 1840) in 1819, William Westenra, Lord Rossmore (1765–1842), conveyed the principal sum of £4,500, in a mortgage deed, and a further sum of £2,000, to trustees to be invested in government stock. Lady Rossmore was to receive the interest and dividends on both sums during her marriage. The capital sums came into her possession on the death of her husband.[7] Anne Willoughby Cole, Viscountess Enniskillen, was also entitled to the interest and dividends on £2,000 and on the principal sum, which had been invested for her use, by her husband, during their marriage.[8] The five women in this sample who had access to separate property in the form of land were Theodosia, Countess of Clanwilliam, Anne Katherine, Countess of Antrim, Charlotte Kerr, Mary, Marchioness of Downshire, and Frances Anne, Marchioness of Londonderry.[9] All five women inherited these interests from their family of origin. Although separate estate was distinct from the inheritance of a life interest in the family estate, both types of property interest were interconnected, as all five women were also life tenants of their family estates in default of male heirs.

Another possible source of income for married women in this class was a life interest, in rental or investment, settled to their separate use. Like other separate property arrangements, life interests as income interests were arranged through trusts. For example, it was acceptable testamentary practice for women to settle separate income interests for the benefit of their daughters. Letitia MacDonnell, Marchioness of Antrim, subjected the land she had inherited from her brother Lord Viscount Mount Morres to the charge of £10,000, which he was to invest, 'within five years' of her death, in government securities in Ireland or England and pay the dividends and interest to her daughter Lady Charlotte Kerr, for her own use during her life. On Charlotte's death this sum was to be divided among her younger children.[10]

Although trusts were a useful instrument in securing income for women during marriage, their use highlights the alienation of women from landed property. The concept of a married woman owning property was problematic, as it contradicted the traditional authority of the husband over family property, and married women's separate property ownership developed several characteristics that reflected this anomalous position. No arrears of pin money could be claimed after a period specified in the marriage settlement, usually one year. It was therefore necessary for a married woman to ensure she received her payments on time, and, if necessary, initiate a suit in Chancery against her husband within the specified period.[11] Also, the extent to which a married woman 'owned' chattel or real property bought with her pin money or income from her separate estate was questionable.[12] Susan Staves notes that in late seventeenth-century England, marriage settlements made explicit the bride's right to bequeath any property purchased with savings from her pin money if she predeceased her husband, and that they would pass into her ownership if she survived her husband. However, no such arrangements were made in the marriage settlements in this study.[13]

The legal status of separate estate arrangements was ambivalent. Regarding the control exercised by a woman over her separate estate, there was a distinction between real and chattel property. Both real and chattel property would pass to the husband if his wife pre-deceased him, if she did not devise the property by last will and testament.[14] A married woman's right to devise her chattel property was assumed. However, her right to dispose of her real estate appears to have been open to debate. There was some disagreement among contemporary legal commentators about this issue. Samuel Roper argued that a married woman had no power to dispose of real estate in law 'otherwise by fine and recovery'.[15] However, John Fraser MacQueen argued that 'according to the principle of modern cases, the heir would be treated as a trustee' and 'the inclination of the Courts in the present day is to give effect to the wife's disposition of her separate estate, exactly as if she were sole'.[16]

As with all trusts, the key element of such arrangements was the clear expression of intention. Although a married woman's right to dispose of her personal property and reversionary interests in chattels real was assumed in this period, unless the boundaries of a married woman's ownership were clearly expressed, there was a danger that her rights over the separate estate could be curtailed.[17] When Letitia MacDonnell, Marchioness of Antrim, bequeathed 'all my trinkets, lace and jewels and cloth[e]s' to her daughter Lady Charlotte Kerr, she did not include any wording marking this property out for her 'sole and separate use'. However, when bequeathing Lady Charlotte £500 out of the rents from Lady Antrim's Castle Morres estate, as well as her arrears of jointure, these were specifically noted to be for her 'sole and separate use on her receipt alone . . . notwithstanding her coverture'.[18]

The legal establishment's ambivalence to the issue of married women's separate property is highlighted by the fact that statutory measures were introduced in an attempt to secure a degree of protection for married women from feckless or bullying husbands, while at the same time ensuring that the traditional authority of a husband over his wife's person and property remained intact. A married woman did not have the power to alienate her own property during marriage after the introduction in England of 'restraint upon anticipation' by Lord Thurlow in 1798. This measure was introduced according to the principle that women needed to be protected from the possibility that bullying husbands might force them to alienate estates intended for their protection.[19] The control that a married woman exerted over her property was therefore curtailed, and the perception of the legal establishment was that this was in her own interests. One example of this in Ireland was the legislation to abolish fines and recoveries, introduced in 1834. This statute was almost identical to the Act passed in England one year earlier. The Act made provision for a married woman to devise property without the consent of her husband if the husband had been declared insane or was in prison, overseas or separated or divorced from her, by applying to the Court of Common Pleas in Dublin. However, it also stated that such rights were to be 'without prejudice to the rights of the husband as then existing independently of this Act'.[20] One mid-nineteenth-century legal commentator foresaw potential problems with this apparent contradiction, arguing that it was 'not easy to comprehend how his rights can escape "prejudice" if the wife, without his concurrence, (and it may be without his knowledge), shall have power to settle the property, giving the purchaser a good and absolute title, with a sufficient discharge for the purchase'.[21]

Such legal ambiguity increased the dependence of married women on the reliability and legal knowledge of the framers of the private settlements and testamentary documents that settled their separate estate. The consequences for women of careless wording in testamentary documents are illustrated by the litigation caused by the last will and testament of Randall MacDonnell, Marquess of Antrim. Lord Antrim had died without male issue in 1791 and had bequeathed his estate in County Antrim to his three daughters, Anne Katherine, Letitia and Charlotte MacDonnell. Anne Katherine married Henry Vane-Tempest (d. 1813) in 1799. The only child of the marriage was Frances Anne Vane-Tempest, the future Marchioness of Londonderry. The second daughter, Letitia, died unmarried; the youngest daughter, Lady Charlotte, married Lord Mark Kerr in 1799, and four sons and six daughters were born of this marriage.

Lord Antrim's last will and testament was contested in the Court of Chancery in Ireland by various family members until the 1830s. The problems at the centre of the litigation were inconsistencies in the will regarding the title and entail of the Antrim estate, which, following the payment of the late Lord Antrim's debts, brought a much reduced annual income of approximately £15,000.[22] In his will, Lord Antrim had settled the estate on his three daughters, to be divided equally among them as tenants in common, and because of the lack of male heirs, he had arranged for the Antrim earldom to be specially remaindered on his daughters and their male heirs.[23] The title to the estate and the division of the property were the subject of much dispute, and the estate was not divided between the two surviving sisters until 1814. At that time, both sisters each inherited one-third of the estate that remained, plus an equal half share in the property of their deceased sister.[24] The title passed to the eldest daughter, Anne Katherine, who assumed the title Countess of Antrim, and passed on Anne Katherine's death in 1834 to Lady Charlotte Kerr.[25]

The entail of the estate was also a matter of contention, as Lord Antrim had limited the estate both to 'heirs general of the bodies' of his daughters and, in a later part of the will, to 'heirs male'. This led to dispute among the sisters, as the latter interpretation would have disinherited Anne Katherine's daughter, Frances Anne, in favour of the eldest son of Charlotte Kerr. The future of the estate was not decided until the death of Anne Katherine, Countess of Antrim, in 1834; at this time Charlotte Kerr's eldest son was the heir to the earldom and the shares of both Charlotte and Anne Katherine in the Antrim estate, with the exception of the latter's half of their deceased sister's part of the estate, which was devised to her daughter, Frances Anne, as separate estate.[26]

Disagreement over the last will and testament of Lord Antrim extended to the next generation of beneficiaries. Frances Anne married Charles Stewart, the future Marquess of Londonderry (1778–1854), in 1819. At the time of her marriage she was the heiress to the estates and collieries owned by her late father, Henry Vane-Tempest, in County Durham, which were entailed on her male heirs and settled on her husband for his life. The collieries at Seaham, as well as other mining interests in the region, were profitable interests for the Londonderrys, who were active in their development, opening a new extended harbour in January 1845; this led to significant increases in the export of coal, which brought an annual profit of £5,000.[27] Lady Londonderry's County

Antrim estate was situated around the fishing village of Carnlough in the parish of Ardclinis, the only town in the parish. It was considered a small town, 'the houses bad and the inhabitants poor', with most being small farmers or fishermen in the 1830s. The principal commodity at this time was coal imported from Scotland, 'together with some trifling merchandise from Belfast', and potatoes, grain and limestone were the principal exports from the region.[28]

In the 1840s Lady Londonderry was interested in developing her potentially lucrative and under-exploited fishery rights off the coast of Carnlough, and this brought her into conflict with the competing interests of Edmund MacDonnell (d. 1852), the widower of her mother, Anne Katherine, Countess of Antrim, and Hugh MacDonnell, Earl of Antrim (1813–55), both of whom had established fisheries adjacent to land they had each inherited from Anne Katherine and Charlotte Kerr respectively. The issue was brought to the Court of Chancery in 1845. The case rested on the questionable rights of ownership that Lady Londonderry had to '*certain lands* [emphasis in original]' in the area, and the will of the late Marquess of Antrim was again brought under scrutiny.[29] The outcome of the dispute is unclear but it appears to have continued for at least another two years. In 1847 Lady Londonderry's County Antrim agent John Lanktree was still taking advice on fishery rights, while relations between Edmund MacDonnell and Lady Londonderry remained acrimonious.[30] In 1847, for example, John Lanktree informed Edmund MacDonnell's agent that Edmund was 'not to shoot anymore on your ladyship's lands'[31] and was also forbidden to use Lady Londonderry's land for fastening the ropes of fishing nets. [32]

The inheritance of the Countesses of Antrim was an exception to more commonly made arrangements for separate estate, and the last will and testament of Randall MacDonnell, Marquess of Antrim, is possibly a unique case in the level of confusion and antagonism it caused over at least two generations. As one lawyer noted, when considering the fishery rights of Lady Londonderry in 1834, the will was 'singularly expressed, and it is not easy, if indeed possible, to understand the cause of the inconsistencies in apparent parts of it'.[33] The substantial inheritance that Anne Katherine, Countess of Antrim, and Lady Charlotte Kerr eventually received was delayed for fifteen years through inconsistencies in their father's last will and testament, and Lady Londonderry's property rights were, to a large extent, dependent on the later interpretation of the will by the Irish Court of Chancery.[34] The confusion and acrimony that surrounded the will however offers a perspective on the potential problems that could occur when substantial estates were settled on daughters, and were therefore dependent on testamentary clarity.

Separation and divorce

Ambiguity surrounding women's separate estate and the importance of clarity in settlements is further illustrated in deeds of separation. Separation was a viable alternative to divorce, as the only means by which a marriage could be legally dissolved in this period was by a private Act of Parliament. The expense involved in parliamentary divorce procedures limited their availability to all but the very wealthy and it was a laborious process that was available to petitioners only on particular grounds. For example, a man could divorce his wife on the grounds of adultery. Before initiating a bill in parliament he had first to take a case to the ecclesiastical courts for a judicial separation, and another case to the common law courts, also known as 'criminal conversation', to sue the person with whom his wife had committed adultery for damages.[35]

The different requirements for men and women reflect the concern of the legal establishment regarding the protection of landed interests. The one example of divorce among the families surveyed here was that of John James Hamilton, Marquess of Abercorn (1756–1818), from his second wife, Lady Cecil Hamilton (b. 1770), whom he had married in 1792. The divorce was obtained by the Marquess of Abercorn in 1799 on the grounds of Lady Cecil's adultery. The House of Lords noted the legitimacy of his claim as due to the fact that Lady Cecil 'hath by her adulterous behaviour dissolved the bonds of marriage on her part and [the Marquess of Abercorn] stands deprived of the comforts of matrimony, and may be liable to have a spurious issue imposed on him to succeed to his titles, honour, estate and fortune'.[36]

Criminal conversation cases could be particularly damaging for the social reputation of an accused wife, even if adultery was not proven. It was common practice to summon family servants to testify in court about their mistresses' behaviour, and cases were widely reported in newspapers. As a married woman, the accused could not defend herself in a common law court. However, the advantage of parliamentary divorce was that it was the only means to dissolve a marriage and leave both parties free to remarry.[37] Lady Cecil went on to marry Captain Joseph Copely, with whom she had been accused of committing adultery.[38]

Another option was to take a case to the ecclesiastical courts for a judicial separation from bed and board. Again, there was a distinction between procedures for men and women in the court. A woman could obtain a legal separation from her husband only on the grounds of adultery and cruelty. A husband could obtain a legal separation from his wife on the grounds of her adultery alone.[39]

The final means to end a marriage, by private agreement, was the one most widely used by landed families in this period in England. By the second half of the eighteenth century, a private separation agreement was essentially a means to arrange maintenance payments between husband and wife and deal with the consequences of coverture on the wife after separation.[40]

The one example of a separation among these families is that of Bernard Ward, Lord Bangor, and Anne, Lady Bangor (d. 1789), who separated in 1766. In the absence of a deed of separation among the Ward papers, the only reference to the details of separate property arrangements made for Lady Bangor is the confirmation by Lord Bangor, in his last will and testament, that Lady Bangor was to have possession of 'all the jewels she usually wore', which suggests his belief that her ownership of these items was not already legally secure.[41] As coverture remained legally in place during a separation, the function of a separate maintenance agreement was to state a married woman's rights to her property and independence of her person. Aside from maintenance, important aspects of such agreements were assurances that economically and physically, a married woman would be enabled to act as a single woman, make contracts, sue and be sued, and live where she chose and with whom she chose, without fearing further litigation from her husband.[42]

As there is no separation agreement extant among the Ward papers, it is useful here to consider a similar arrangement made by another family. The form that separation agreements took, and typical terms agreed, are illustrated by the settlement made upon the separation of the Earl and Countess of Kilmorey. Francis Jack Needham, Earl of Kilmorey (1787–1880), married Jane Gun-Cunningham (d. 1867) in 1814 and they separated in 1835. The deed began with an acknowledgement that '[w]heras unhappy differences have arisen and still subsist between Francis Jack Earl of Kilmorey and Jane Countess of Kilmorey . . . and in consequence thereof they have agreed to live separate and apart from each other'. The first section of the agreement was concerned with undoing the financial arrangements made on the marriage of the Earl and Countess. The Countess's jointure was £1,200, charged on his estates in Chester and Shropshire, and her separate estate was the right to interest and dividends of a principal sum of £5,000. The Countess was to give up her interest in this separate trust in return for an annuity of £2,000.

The second section of the separation agreement dealt with the rights of the Earl of Kilmorey to the person of his wife and listed assurances that he would not exert his rights under coverture. In contradiction to coverture, the deed asserted the right of the Countess of Kilmorey to 'live separate and apart' from her husband 'in such place or places and with such persons as she shall think proper as freely to all intents and purposes as if she were sole and unmarried'. The Earl of Kilmorey agreed not to seek the restitution of his conjugal rights by forcing her to co-habit with him, and she was to be 'freed and discharged from the restraint molestation authority and government' of her husband. Furthermore, her husband agreed not to sue or prosecute anyone 'harbouring protecting or assisting' the Countess and not to 'molest interrupt or disturb her in her place or mode of living'.

The third and final section of the agreement dealt with the property rights of the Countess, settling her personal property 'to her own separate and absolute use notwithstanding her coverture'. This personal property consisted of 'all such jewels, personal ornaments, plate, furniture, clothes, linen, wearing apparel articles, and things whatsoever as now are or at any time or times hereafter shall be in her personal use or in her possession or control as her own or as her reputed property or which she shall save from or acquire with the savings of any property hereby or otherwise limited to her separate use'. The Countess's right to alienate such property by deed or last will and testament was asserted, and the Earl was to permit the probating of any such last will and testament.[43]

Separation agreements in Ireland therefore followed practice in England, and can be regarded as a comprehensive overturning of the effect of coverture on a married woman's person and her property, declaring lawful that which in fact was not lawful and establishing the legal right of a married woman to act as a *feme sole* in such matters. Consequently, the shortcomings of English separations also applied in Ireland. The effectiveness of such arrangements is questionable. Lawrence Stone notes that maintenance payments were not guaranteed in the event of any apparent sexual misconduct on the part of the wife, as a husband could then stop maintenance payments on these grounds, while he could freely keep a mistress.[44] Regarding the assurance of no further litigation, Stone also notes that as such agreements were not recognised by the ecclesiastical courts, they could not prevent a husband suing his wife for adultery or for the restitution of conjugal rights.[45] Also, the legality of asserting the wife's right to her personal property is open to debate. From the perspective of a married woman, therefore, much depended upon the personalities of the people involved, and their financial and physical vulnerability.

Married women and family finances

The centrality of the landed estate to aristocratic families meant that it was a natural part of family business for women to take part in estate management. For example, Margaret Hamilton, Countess of Orrery, 'took an active part in the management of the Caledon estate in County Tyrone, a very necessary proceeding on account of the frequent absences of her husband'.[46] In 1749 the Countess took care of the roads on the estate in the absence of the Earl, who was responsible for their upkeep as director and overseer of roads in Caledon manor.[47]

Some married women acted in their own capacity, and in their own interests, as landowners. Women such as Anne Skeffington, Countess of Massereene, Theodosia Meade, Countess of Clanwilliam, and Mary Hill, Marchioness of Downshire, were responsible for the management of their own property, hired and fired their own agents and settled their own financial disputes. However, the roles taken in family financial business by most women in this sample were determined by the personal relationships of family members, and by what was perceived as acceptable authority for women.

Housekeeping was an acceptable activity for women of all classes. The domestic economy of wealthy landed households involved the hiring and organisation of servants and the upkeep of household supplies. Letitia MacDonnell, Countess of Antrim, received the annual sum of £1,000 'for housekeeping'.[48] This was for a household of forty-four people, including servants.[49] The accounts kept by Louisa Conolly also involved substantial sums of money. In a randomly chosen year, 1772, household bills, tradesmen's accounts and servants' wages for the Conolly seat at Castletown totalled £2,255.2.3.[50] Louisa Conolly also organised decoration and renovations at Castletown, and assisted her sister, Emily, Duchess of Leinster, in similar work at the Fitzgerald house at Carton, County Kildare.[51] When the Duchess of Leinster was planning renovations to her house at Blackrock, Louisa oversaw the work of the builder and informed Emily of the accumulating cost of the work, which had reached over £1,300 in September 1775, and Louisa imagined that the builder 'must have about £500 more before it's done. He does go on, but not as fast as I could wish'.[52] Louisa also took inventories of household items when Emily was abroad, and checked on them.[53] When Emily required new servants, Louisa was 'determined to look out for somebody for you while I am in England'.[54]

The role taken by these women in household management contrasts with the more curtailed experience of Helen Blackwood, Lady Dufferin, during her first marriage to Price Blackwood, Lord Dufferin. Helen exercised significant control over household decisions and finances only during her husband's long absences at sea. This may have been due to the straitened financial situation that the Blackwoods were in during the period before Price Blackwood inherited the Dufferin title and estates in

1839. The level of involvement that a woman had in the household may therefore have been determined by the financial situation of her husband and her relationships with other family members.

The financial circumstances of the Blackwoods varied greatly between their marriage in 1825 and Price Blackwood's inheritance in 1839. When they married in 1825 Helen had no portion and Price, as a younger son, had no income except for his half pay as an unemployed naval officer and a small annuity from the Dufferin estate. In order to save money, and to allow the Blackwoods' disapproval of the financially disadvantageous marriage to dissipate, Helen and her husband moved soon after their marriage to Italy, where their only child, Frederick, was born.[55] Several years after returning to England, in 1831, Price did get a ship, the *Imogene*, and from 1831 until 1835 he was abroad, in India, Australia and the China Seas. Helen and her son Frederick lived in the 'grace and favour' apartments at Hampton Court Palace occupied by her mother, Henrietta Sheridan, a move intended to save money. While abroad, Price's financial position improved when the death of his uncle the Reverend John Blackwood in 1832 entitled him to an annuity of £250 from the Dufferin estate.[56] However, his financial problems continued, and in January 1834 Price wrote to Helen that '[t]he dread of debt confines me, and unless absolutely necessary I shudder at the thought of returning to England on the wrong side of [his agent] Halford's books'.[57] Price's situation appears to have improved later in 1834, as he projected receiving an annual income of £850 'which will keep our heads above water for the present'.[58] However, the most significant improvement to his income came only in 1836 on the death of James Blackwood, Lord Dufferin. At this point Price's father, Hans Blackwood, inherited the Dufferin title and estate, and as his eldest surviving son Price became heir, with an entitlement to an annuity of £2,000 from the Dufferin estate.[59] In 1839 he inherited the estate and title on the death of his father, and he died two years later in 1841.

Helen's financial situation was characterised by economy, prudence and dependence on her husband. Price Blackwood made all household decisions and kept all household accounts, while Helen assisted him, undertaking tasks that he chose. For example, when the Blackwoods moved house in 1841, Price left furniture for Helen to choose from, while he organised the sale of cows, pigs and poultry and terminated the employment of two gardeners and a housemaid.[60]

The economic control exercised by Price Blackwood had an impact on other areas of Helen's life. In 1837 Helen's January allowance was £31.5.0, which if paid quarterly would have given her an annual allowance of £125.[61] When Price's income improved he increased her annuity to £350. This was a temporarily inflated amount, owing to Price's absence, although it was possible for Helen to survive on this amount in London society only because she lived with her mother at Hampton Court during her husband's absence.[62] Helen also received other, sporadic, income from the publication of her songs. In 1830, for example, she hoped to ask £200 'for a collection', while in 1832 she received £56 for three she had sold.[63] However, by the standards of her class she was not wealthy and these years were characterised by her 'prudence' and restraint in London society.[64]

Price did not approve of Helen publishing her songs, and although she did publish some songs in this period, she did curtail this activity. In October 1833 Price thanked Helen for her 'mark of affection in yielding, perhaps your own opinions to my wishes' by no longer publishing her songs.[65] However, four months later, in February 1834, he remarked on Helen's contributions to *The Court Magazine*, edited by Helen's sister Caroline Norton: 'I see Caroline has got your name on the outside of her magazine as one of the contributors. I shall be very glad to see it removed.'[66] The economic constraints of Helen Blackwood's marriage had repercussions for her freedom in other aspects of her life. For example, Price objected to her wish to have her portrait painted free of charge, although 'several' portrait painters had requested to paint it, and Helen did not have enough money to have it done 'out of my own pocket'.[67] In view of Helen's relatively small income from her husband, the small, irregular payments she received for her songs can be regarded as essential supplements to her income. The desire of her husband to prevent her publishing her songs therefore had economic implications, as her already dependent relationship with her husband would be increased by the removal of another, albeit small, source of income.

Despite the overall control of family finances assumed by Price Blackwood, it was possible for Helen to assume a more active role at particular times. The longest such period was between 1831 and 1835 when Price was abroad; during these years Helen assumed more control over her own expenditure, for example being in charge of her carriage for the first time.[68] Helen also took a more direct role in Blackwood family affairs, as intermediary between her husband and his family. The death of the Reverend John Blackwood in 1832 and the consequent rearrangement of family finances that entitled Price Blackwood to an increased annuity of £250 was accompanied by correspondence between James Blackwood, Lord Dufferin, and Helen regarding the best way to deal with the £250. While continuing to acknowledge her husband's 'superior judgement' in financial matters, Helen wrote to Lord Dufferin advising that 'I should like it, if possible to be invested advantageously, in stock or otherwise, as he thinks best, so as to accumulate into a little sum to help us to begin house-keeping again.'[69]

As the varying income of Price Blackwood indicates, the position of younger sons in families led to diverse levels of wealth within the same family, which might change as other family members died. The required absence of a husband due to financial need might place a wife in a situation where she was negotiating with her husband's family over his income from the estate. Therefore, Helen Blackwood, of necessity, assumed a more active role in the informal financial management decisions than she might otherwise have experienced.

Women's role as intermediaries in the financial affairs of younger sons was facilitated by the structure of property relations in the wealthy landed class. Control over family wealth was exerted to a significant degree by the head of the family, placing younger sons and daughters in a financially dependent position. It was also in accordance with contemporary views on acceptable feminine behaviour for women to act as supporters and intermediaries. It appears to have been normal practice to discuss property and money matters in correspondence between members of extended family networks and friends as well as immediate family members. In 1821, for example, Emily Stratton wrote to her sister, Harriet Skeffington, Countess of Massereene, when her brother's son, Lord Roden, stopped the annual allowance which he had promised her. Women were often well placed to intercede in such matters; in this instance Emily asked her sister to explain the situation to Percy Jocelyn, Bishop of Clogher, in order to gain his support.[70]

Furthermore, the position occupied by women in the family and the cultural ideals of feminine virtue and Christian humanity made women an obvious target for assistance in appeals to the male head of the family. During a protracted legal dispute in 1783 between Edward Stratford, Earl of Aldborough, and his agent, Annesley Devezney, Anne Elizabeth, Countess of Aldborough, received letters from Devezney's wife, Sarah. The letters appealed for the Countess's intervention to prevent the 'shocking distresses' suffered by Sarah Devezney, her husband and their eight children, on the grounds of the 'well known Christian humanity and benevolence' of the Countess, who was 'ever a friend to [the] unfortunate and distressed'.[71]

Charity

The role of married women in charity cannot be distinguished from that of single and widowed women. The only possible distinction would be the likelihood of greater access to property and time to spend on charitable causes, two variables that make any generalisations impossible. Married women were just as active in local poor relief and the support of charitable institutions as their single and widowed contemporaries. Lady Bangor and the Countess of Kildare, for example, each paid £10 to the County Down infirmary in 1772.[72] In 1794 Lady Louisa Conolly was in Dublin to 'attend and collect at the annual sermon for the poor little female orphans' of the Female Orphan House.[73] In 1847, Frances Anne, Marchioness of Londonderry, helped organise a bazaar for famine relief.[74] The Marchioness of Sligo's 'casual donations' to the poor in the Barony of Murrisk, County Mayo, in 1802 were 'constant, abundant and extensive'.[75]

It was also common for husbands and wives to be active in support of education and various charitable causes in their locality. In the town of Caledon, County Tyrone, the Earl of Caledon gave an annuity of £8 to a parochial school and founded a mendicity society to which he also subscribed £100 a year. The Countess of Caledon 'built and supported' a girls' school 'in which [forty] girls are clothed and educated'.[76] Other examples from outside the sample families include the Earl and Countess of Dunraven, who both supported schools in their locality. In Adare, a town in County Limerick, the Earl of Dunraven supported the parochial school, in which there were approximately eighty boys and fifty girls, while the Countess of Dunraven restored a Franciscan abbey in 1815 to be used as a school for 300 children, which she 'wholly supported'.[77] In the town of Abbeyleix, County Kilkenny, Lord de Vesci erected a parochial school, while Lady de Vesci 'maintained' an almshouse for poor widows.[78]

In 1831 the government attempted to create a state-funded elementary education system by establishing the Board of Commissioners for National Education. The aim of the national schools system was to provide non-denominational education on the basis of local initiatives. Landowners would establish schools in their locality, and the national schools board would provide two-thirds of the costs of school buildings, equipment and teachers' salaries from public funds.[79] The piecemeal poor-relief measures of the government during the Great Famine and the national schools initiative were both unsuccessful in their respective aims. However, they were significant as the first large-scale state intervention in Ireland.

Until the introduction of the Irish poor law in 1838, the government response to the problem of the poor in Ireland was to subsidise public works and encourage local health services.[80] The ideology underlying welfare provision at this time was that it should be locally based and commonly administered by local landowners, on a voluntary basis. It is the lack of local infrastructure that partly accounts for the lack of any comprehensive poor relief in Ireland until the 1830s.[81] Charity and estate management operated together when a woman was a landowner in her own right, and on such occasions government policy may have affected charitable behaviour as much as contemporary assumptions surrounding gender and class.

The Irish poor law was the first step towards increasing government intervention to address the problem of the poor in Ireland. This Act was modelled on the 1834 English Act, and offered strictly workhouse-based relief. When the established system failed to meet increasing demand for relief during the Great Famine, this led to the introduction of further statutory temporary relief measures from 1845 until the poor law was amended in 1847. In 1845 local relief committees distributed £100,000 worth of maize, or Indian corn, imported by the government from the United States. Public works were established to enable the destitute to earn money to buy food. When it became evident that these relief measures were inadequate, the 'soup kitchens act' was introduced in 1847 to provide free, cheap food to the destitute.[82]

One consequence of these measures was to render landlords increasingly responsible for the poor on their estates. Landlords were liable for the poor rate on all holdings under £4, and if rent was not paid, poor rates could exceed income.[83] Local landowners were regarded as essential components to both schemes, owing to the concern that such measures should be locally based. Regarding poor relief, it was believed that landowners were in an ideal position to guard against fraudulent applications. Landowners were also believed to have a duty to help relieve poverty on their estates, summed up in the principle that 'Irish property must support Irish poverty'.[84]

The effect that government intervention had on estate management, and particularly charity on the estate, can be explored by considering the estate management of Frances Anne, Marchioness of Londonderry, on her County Antrim estate in the 1840s. The relationship between Lady Londonderry and her tenants was distant but benevolent, and was characterised by her occasional visits to the tenants.[85] For a female landowner at this time, several interconnecting ideologies were at work. There was no apparent contradiction between Lady Londonderry's roles as landowner and morally virtuous woman. She was represented as 'the distinguished benefactor of a long neglected people' while also being noted for the 'fostering care' which had 'enobled your name in Ireland'.[86] The public image that Lady Londonderry was keen to promote is suggested by the Great Famine memorial at Garron Point, set into the wall of the North Antrim coast road, which records the benevolence shown by her towards her tenants. Garron Tower, erected in 1848, was also built during the worst years of the Famine in Ireland, in a particularly poor barony. The brass plate at the entrance stated the wish of Lady Londonderry to live there 'in the affections of a devoted and loyal tenantry'.[87]

In 1843, on the eve of the Great Famine, the tenants on Lady Londonderry's estate numbered approximately 1,200 individuals, who made up 200 families of, on average, five members each. By 1844, her agent, John Lanktree, was already writing accounts of increasing destitution and sickness among the tenants, and he estimated that a total of 170 were destitute in July 1844.[88] At the beginning of March 1846 Lanktree reported that the potato blight was 'acutely felt' on the estate.[89] By the end of March he noted that fever had 'begun here to result from the privation of the poor'.[90] By April 1846 Lanktree wrote that in Glenarm, destitution exceeded his expectations.[91]

In response to the increasing destitution on her estate and in accordance with general philanthropic practice among this class in Ireland, Lady Londonderry subscribed to local relief schemes such as a dispensary at Clogher, and donated money to the local poor. The tenants at Drumcrow, for example, one of the worst affected areas on the estate, were given an allowance totalling £24 in 1844.[92] The remainder of Lady Londonderry's charity in 1844 was directed towards the provision of blankets and soup for the poorest tenants, a subscription to a farming society, a sum of money to 'Widow Wright' and 'various relief as necessary'.[93] Lady Londonderry also received petitions from particular individuals, such as 'Widow Mulvenna', otherwise known as Alice MacDonnell, who claimed to be a blood relative of the MacDonnells and to whom her mother, the Countess of Antrim, had also given money.[94]

There were three primary motivations underlying this charity. The first was the need of the impoverished tenantry. Dispensaries, for example, were supported because, as John Lanktree noted, 'in a country like this, thickly inhabited and very poor – no medicinal man would settle if it were not for dispensaries and the people would perish'.[95] While conditions on the estate were deteriorating because of the potato blight, and assistance to tenants was crucial, it was felt that it was equally important to ensure that only the 'most indigent' should avail themselves of such provision.[96] Secondly, private virtues were an integral part of Lady Londonderry's philanthropic activities. In 1844, blankets were distributed to 100 people on the estate, and in 1845, eighty-five people received blankets, quilts or petticoats.[97] The idea behind such charity was to encourage the poor to undertake different habits of housekeeping. Petticoats and quilts were given to poor tenants 'with a view to encourage them to endeavour after greater cleanliness and comfort in their own houses'.[98] This desire to improve the habits of the poor was reinforced by the 'lady visitors' on the estate, who visited the poorest tenants with a view to promoting cleanliness and consequent moral improvement.[99]

Thirdly, alongside the development of habits of cleanliness and domestic virtue, self-reliance and industry were also virtues that the Londonderrys hoped to instil in the poor on the Antrim estate. A scheme to distribute oatmeal to each family daily from March until October 1846 was considered impossible owing to the cost, which would amount to £1,105, and the concern that it would also potentially 'have the effect of causing the tenants to depend too little on their own resources'.[100] Agricultural information was distributed to landlords by the Poor Law Commission with a view to promoting assistance to tenants.[101] Financial assistance was given to tenants for the slating of their houses and for the erection of pigsties, in the belief that this would render the poor 'eventually independent of assistance'.[102]

Lady Londonderry also participated in government schemes for the provision of grain to the poor, public works and education. The central principles of these schemes continued to be the encouragement of self-reliance and industry among the poor, and this included paying for subsidised relief. Lady Londonderry was involved in the distribution of grain and the organisation of public works. In 1845 and 1846, maize was purchased by the government from the United States and distributed to local relief committees, who sold it to landowners, who in turn sold it to the poor of their estates.[103] In 1847 £114.13.6 was spent on grain to be distributed to tenants, who would undertake to repay the cost at 8½ per cent interest. A further £100.8.5 was spent in 1847 on the distribution of 'seed' to poor tenants, half of which was expected to be repaid. Public works were also established, in order to enable the local poor to earn money. Land drainage schemes were established by the 1846 Relief and Drainage Acts 'by which', Lanktree informed Lady Londonderry, 'provision is made for the outlay of public money in providing employment for the destitute'.[104] In 1847, after gaining the approval of the Board of Works, Lady Londonderry also arranged for the establishment of a lime works at Carnlough, at a total cost of £188.8.5, and it was expected that the entire sum would be 'more than repaid'.[105]

Schoolhouses built on Lady Londonderry's estate were subject to the approval, and partial funding, of the National Schools Commission.[106] In 1847, for example, £83.8.9 was spent on the completion of the Garren Point schoolhouse, of which £55.12.6 was expected to be repaid by the commission for national schools.[107] The school officially opened in May

Married women and property

145

1849, after the receipt from the National Schools Commission of 'the official satisfaction from headquarters of the register of your ladyship's patronage'. Once opened, a teacher, Mr Dorcey, was installed in the school of thirty-four children.[108] As well as the building of schools, teachers' salaries had to be considered. Dealings with the Commission meant that, according to Lanktree, it was necessary that Lady Londonderry should state whether she would contribute an annual sum as a grant to fund teachers' salaries.[109]

The example of one teacher, Mary Magee, further illustrates the interconnectedness of ideas of philanthropy with public policy on funding schools. Mary Magee opened a school at Ballymacaldrick in April 1847, with an initial attendance of twenty children, which rose to a school population of fifteen boys and forty-four girls. She taught English grammar, geography, plain needlework and 'fancy needlework'. In 1847 grants of clothing were made to children at the school. Also in 1847 an application was made to have the school placed under the national board.[110] Lady Londonderry paid Mary Magee £1 per quarter, later raised to £1 per month, 'to encourage her to make a good beginning'.[111]

The impact of government intervention in poor relief in the 1840s on the estate management and charitable expenditure of Lady Londonderry can be further explored by considering the proportions of private charity to government-sponsored poor-relief measures. Table 5.2 outlines Lady Londonderry's expenditure on private charity, poor rates and government-sponsored poor-relief schemes from 1844 to 1847. As poor rates were a compulsory payment I have separated poor rates from government poor-relief measures. In 1844, Lady Londonderry's expected income from her estate, inclusive of arrears, was £3,400. As Table 5.2 indicates, the income received from her estate fell from 1844 onwards, reaching its lowest point in 1846, before rising slightly in 1847. There were also fluctuations in spending between 1844 and 1847. Spending on private charity was £46.2.0 in 1844, rising to £123.5.9 in 1845, falling to £56.16.11 in 1846, and rising to £252.8.1 in 1847.

The fluctuations in Lady Londonderry's spending on private charity can be explained by her spending on poor rates and government-sponsored schemes. As we can see from Table 5.3, Lady Londonderry's expenditure on the Antrim estate that was connected with government schemes rose over the period 1844–47, peaking in 1847, although she actually spent a higher percentage of her income in 1846.

As Table 5.3 demonstrates, if this subsidised charity is included in the total amount spent by Lady Londonderry to alleviate distress on the Antrim estate, government-subsidised charity is shown to have had a significant impact on the total amount spent, which was only 4 per cent of

Table 5.2   Lady Londonderry's expenditure on Antrim estate poor relief, 1844–47 (£)

Year	Private charity	Subsidised charity	Poor rates	Total charity	Total Antrim estate income
1844	46.2.0	25.7.3	38.19.4	110.8.7	2877.5.8
1845	123.5.9	30.0.0	25.10/10½	178.6.7½	3045.2.10½
1846	56.16.11	192.13.13½	16.3.5½	265.14.6	1237.10.7
1847	252.8.1	486.8.10	25.5.10½	764.2.9½	2280.12.6½
Total	478.12.9	734.10.2	105.19.6½	1318.12.6	9441.1.7

Sources: PRONI, Earl of Antrim papers, D/2977/5/1/8/4/8, memorandum of Antrim estate accounts, 1 October 1844; PRONI, Earl of Antrim papers, D/2977/5/1/8/5/4, *Ibid.*, 30 September 1845; PRONI, Earl of Antrim papers, D/2977/5/1/8/8/28, *Ibid.*, 1 October 1846 to 31 May 1847; PRONI, Earl of Antrim papers, D/2977/5/1/8/8/38, *Ibid.*, 30 September 1847.

Lady Londonderry's total Antrim estate income in 1844, and 33 per cent in 1847. Also, in the years in which Lady Londonderry spent most on state-subsidised poor relief, the amount she spent on other charity actually fell between 1845 and 1847. The main conclusion that can be drawn from this is that Lady Londonderry regarded the role of state-subsidised projects as a replacement for other forms of relief, although private charity also increased in response to poverty on the estate. In February 1847, for example, Lady Londonderry paid £10 for relief of the poor at Ardclines, and one month later, in March 1847, she paid £20 for the relief of the poor at Glencary.[112] However, she disapproved of the rise in expenditure in 1847 to the extent that her concerns were relayed via Lord Londonderry's agent to John Lanktree. Lanktree was informed that she was 'very much dissatisfied' with the 1847 accounts, and that unless he undertook a more 'economical management', she 'seemed quite determined to look out for another agent.' It was further noted that 'Mr Lanktree sh[oul]d learn in other's affairs, as Lord L[ondonderry] suspects he knows in his own: there is a charity sh[oul]d be at home as well as elsewhere'.[113]

As this case illustrates, a variety of factors influenced Lady Londonderry's management of her County Antrim estates. The impact of the Great Famine in the 1840s and the consequent necessity of providing for the poor on the estate highlights the ideology underpinning charity and estate improvement at this time. The balance between assisting the poor and encouraging their improvement by cleanliness and moral development was constantly sought. Lady Londonderry, in common with other landlords in the north-east of Ireland, was not financially ruined by

Table 5.3 **Percentages of Lady Londonderry's expenditure on Antrim estate poor relief, 1844–47**

Year	Private charity %	Subsidised charity %	Poor rates %	Total Antrim estate income %
1844	42	23	35	4
1845	69	17	14	6
1846	21	72	6	26
1847	32	64	3	33
Total	36	56	8	14

Sources: See Table 5.2.

the Great Famine, as she managed to collect a significant proportion of her expected rental during these years, and this may explain the absence of large-scale evictions on her estate.[114] Increasing state involvement in Irish life, illustrated by the Poor Law Commissioners and the national board for schools, meant that the improvements made by landowners were influenced by government policy in a new way. Lady Londonderry's approach to estate management was necessarily influenced therefore by both the old, aristocratic, autonomous approach, whereby she was the patron of her people at her own discretion, and the new opportunities afforded to landowners by grant aid from government bodies.

Conclusion

The property experience of married women in the wealthy landed class in Ireland was based upon private settlements and determined by a variety of factors such as individual wealth, the type of property they owned, their family relationships and particular circumstances. Married women's power within families was determined by their financial situation. The use of trusts in equity enabled some women to have access to substantial separate estates and therefore ensured them a degree of economic independence during marriage. The experience that married women in the wealthy landed class had of property was however legally ambiguous, and diverse. The types of arrangement made for women varied significantly between families, and some women were entirely financially dependent on their husbands.

Married women's relationship to family property was also influenced by factors other than wealth: acceptable female roles, family relationships and circumstances all played a part. In landed families there was also the possibility that a situation could enable a woman to take a more prominent role in financial management, such as when her husband was dependent on the family estate and was absent for long periods. In such situations she could act as intermediary between her husband and his family.

The roles of intermediary and deputy to their husbands were in accordance with contemporary views on acceptable female behaviour, positioning women directly in a subordinate relationship to the men in the family. In a similar vein, married women were just as prominent in private, local charity as their single and widowed contemporaries. Charitable activity was in accordance with the idealised attributes of benevolence and maternal concern for the health and moral welfare of the poor. At the same time, women were also landowners in their own right, acting in their own interests. The role of landowner existed alongside traditional ideals of female behaviour. Additionally, as we have seen in the case of Lady Londonderry, private charity co-existed with the introduction of government intervention in poor relief.

Notes

1 Erickson, *Women and property*, p. 110.
2 *Ibid.*, p. 101.
3 Staves, *Married women's separate property*, p. 148.
4 PRONI, Dufferin and Ava papers, D/1071/A/N/3/1, copy of the last will and testament and probate of James Stevenson Blackwood, dated 5 March 1836.
5 PRONI, Dufferin and Ava papers, D/1071/F/B4/4, account book and diary of Helen Blackwood, 1837.
6 PRONI, Dufferin and Ava papers, D/1071/A/N3/7, copy of the marriage settlement of James Stevenson Blackwood and Anna Foster, dated November 1801.
7 PRO, PROB/11/1947, last will and testament of Augusta Westenra, Lady Rossmore, extracted from the will registers of the Prerogative Court of Canterbury, will dated 1 July 1840, probate granted 8 June 1841.
8 PRONI, Enniskillen papers, D/1702/1/27/3a, last will and testament of Anne Lowry, Viscountess Enniskillen, dated 1793.
9 PRONI, Clanwilliam/Meade papers, D/3044/D/1/20, fragment of a declaration by Theodosia Hawkins-Magill, Countess of Clanwilliam, undated; PRONI, Clanwilliam papers, D/3044/D/1/51, photocopy of a letter from Theodosia, Countess of Clanwilliam to Robert Meade, 21 October 1808; PRONI, Downshire papers, D/671/D14/2/221&b, last will and testament of Mary Hill, Marchioness of Downshire, 3 May 1832, probate granted September 1836; PRONI, Earl of Antrim papers, D/2977/2/1/24/1&2, state of the title to the Antrim lands sold under the decree of the Court of Chancery of Ireland, 23 December 1803; PRONI, Earl of Antrim papers,

D/2977/2/1/23/14, rental of the estate of Anne Katherine MacDonnell, Countess of Antrim, 1815; PRONI, Earl of Antrim papers, D/2977/2/1/ 23/9, legal opinion of the estate of Anne Katherine MacDonnell, Countess of Antrim, 1815; PRONI, Earl of Antrim papers, D/2977/2/4/3/13, the opinions of counsel on the right of [Frances Anne Vane-Tempest-Stewart, Marchioness of] Londonderry to the estates of her mother the late [Anne Katherine MacDonnell] Countess of Antrim, on the harbour of Carnlough, 1834.

10 PRONI, Earl of Antrim papers, D/2977/1/2/4, last will and testament of Letitia MacDonnell, Marchioness of Antrim, 31 July 1799, probate dated 10 February 1802.

11 Staves, *Married women's separate property*, p. 142.

12 *Ibid.*, p. 147.

13 *Ibid.*, pp. 147–8.

14 MacQueen, *The rights and liabilities*, p. 285.

15 Samuel Roper, *Husband and wife*, quoted in MacQueen, *The rights and liabilities*, p. 296.

16 MacQueen, *The rights and liabilities*, p. 296.

17 *Ibid.*, pp. 294–5.

18 PRONI, Earl of Antrim papers, D/2977/1/2/4, copy of the last will and testament of Letitia MacDonnell, Marchioness of Antrim, dated 31 July 1799, probate granted 10 February 1802.

19 Staves, *Married women's separate property*, p. 153.

20 4 & 5 George IV, c. 92 (Ireland).

21 MacQueen, *The rights and liabilities*, p. 295.

22 Malcomson, *The pursuit of the heiress*, p. 27.

23 PRONI, Earl of Antrim papers, D/2977/1/2/2, last will and testament of Randall MacDonnell, Marquess of Antrim, 14 August 1790, probate granted 15 August 1791.

24 PRONI, Earl of Antrim papers, D/2977/2/1/24/1&2, state of the title to the Antrim lands sold under the decree of the Court of Chancery of Ireland, 23 December 1803; PRONI, Earl of Antrim papers, D/2977/2/1/23/14, rental of the estate of Anne Katherine MacDonnell, Countess of Antrim, 1815; PRONI, Earl of Antrim papers, D/2977/2/1/23/9, legal opinion of the estate of Anne Katherine MacDonnell, Countess of Antrim, 1815; Malcomson, *The pursuit of the heiress*, pp. 26–30.

25 Malcomson, *The pursuit of the heiress*, p. 26.

26 PRONI, Earl of Antrim papers, D/2977/2/4/3/13, the opinions of counsel on the right of [Frances Anne Vane-Tempest-Stewart, Marchioness of] Londonderry to the estates of her mother the late [Anne Katherine MacDonnell] Countess of Antrim, on the harbour of Carnlough, 1834.

27 Stewart, *Frances Anne*, p. 228.

28 Angelique Day and Patrick McWilliams (eds), *Ordnance survey memoirs of Ireland, xiii: Parishes of County Antrim, IV: Glens of Antrim* (Belfast: Institute of Irish Studies, Queen's University of Belfast, in association with the Royal Irish Academy, 1992), p. 3.

29 PRONI, Earl of Antrim papers, D/2977/2/4/4/11, copy of case on behalf of Frances Anne Vane-Tempest-Stewart, Lady Londonderry, regarding fisheries, with the opinion of Mr Warren Serjeant, dated 1845.

30 PRONI, Earl of Antrim papers, D/2977/5/1/8/8/25, John Lanktree to Lord Londonderry, 22 May 1847.

31 *Ibid.*

32 PRONI, Earl of Antrim papers, D/2977/2/4/4/9, draft notice from Mr Lanktree to Edmund MacDonnell, dated 21 May 1847.

33 PRONI, Earl of Antrim papers, D/2977/2/4/3/13, the opinions of counsel on the right of [Frances Anne Vane-Tempest-Stewart, Marchioness of] Londonderry to the estates of her mother the late [Anne Katherine MacDonnell] Countess of Antrim, on the harbour of Carnlough, 1834.

34 PRONI, Earl of Antrim papers, D/2977/2/4/4/11, copy of the case on behalf of [Frances Anne Vane-Tempest-Stewart,] Lady Londonderry, with the opinion of Mr Serjeant Warren, 27 March 1845.

35 Lawrence Stone, *Road to divorce: England, 1530–1987* (Oxford: Oxford University Press, 1990), pp. 322–46.

36 PRONI, Abercorn papers, T/3691/1, petition of the Marquess of Abercorn, asking leave to bring a bill to parliament to dissolve his marriage, 1799.

37 Stone, *Road to divorce*, pp. 322–46.

38 Gibb, *The complete peerage*, I, p. 8.

39 Brooke, 'Rights of married women', p. 281; Stone, *Road to divorce*, pp. 192–4.

40 Stone, *Road to divorce*, I, p. 181.

41 PRONI, Clanmorris papers, D/4216/F/1, last will and testament and two codicils and probate of Bernard Ward, will dated 30 August 1779, probate granted 1781.

42 Stone, *Road to divorce*, p. 153.

43 PRONI, Kilmorey papers, D/2638/A/13/1, deed of separation between Francis Jack Needham, Earl of Kilmorey, and his wife Jane Needham, Countess of Kilmorey, 24 February 1835.

44 Stone, *Road to divorce*, p. 169.

45 *Ibid.*, p. 154.

46 *Vestry book of the Parish of Aghalow (Caledon, Co Tyrone) with an account of the family of Hamilton of Caledon 1691–1807* (Dungannon: Tyrone Printing Company, 1935), p. 30.

47 *Ibid.*, p. 29.

48 PRONI, Earl of Antrim papers, D/2977/5/1/6/1a, the state of Lord Antrim's affairs, and of the annual expenditure of his rents by interest of annuities and domestic expenses, undated [1776?].

49 PRONI, Earl of Antrim papers, D/2977/5/1/6/1b, report giving advice to Lord Antrim on how to reduce expenditure, undated [1776?].

50 PRONI, Conolly papers, MIC/435, Castletown household accounts, 1772.

51 Lady Louisa Connolly to Emily Fitzgerald, Countess of Kildare, 28 July [1759], in Fitzgerald (ed.), *Correspondence*, iii, p. 23.

52 Lady Louisa Connolly to Emily Fitzgerald, Duchess of Leinster, 13 September 1775, in Fitzgerald (ed.), *Correspondence*, iii, p. 150.

53 *Ibid.*

54 Lady Louisa Conolly to Emily Fitzgerald, Duchess of Leinster 7 January 1770, in Fitzgerald (ed.), *Correspondence*, iii, pp. 30–1.

55 PRONI, Dufferin and Ava papers, D/1071/F/A3/4, typescript of a letter from Helen Blackwood to Georgiana Sheridan, 15 September 1826.

56 PRONI, Dufferin and Ava papers, D/1071/F/A2/1, typescript of a letter from Helen Blackwood to Price Blackwood, dated 19 February 1833.

57 PRONI, Dufferin and Ava papers, D/1071/F/B2/1/1, typescript of a letter from Helen Blackwood to Price Blackwood, dated 31 January 1834.

58 PRONI, Dufferin and Ava papers, D/1071/F/B2/1/1, typescript of a letter from Price Blackwood to Helen Blackwood, dated 18 March 1834.

59 PRONI, Dufferin and Ava papers, D/1071/A/N2/11a&b, appointment of new trustees to the marriage settlement of Price Blackwood and Helen Blackwood, 9 March 1837.

60 PRONI, Dufferin and Ava papers, D/1071/D/8, typescript of a letter from Price Blackwood to Helen Blackwood, dated 4 July 1841.

61 PRONI, Dufferin and Ava papers, D/1071/F/B4/4, account book and diary of Helen Blackwood, 1837.

62 PRONI, Dufferin and Ava papers, D/1071/F/A3/1, typescript of a letter from Price Blackwood, to Henrietta Sheridan, dated 4 December 1830.

63 PRONI, Dufferin and Ava papers, D/1071/F/A2/2, typescript of a letter from Helen Blackwood to Elizabeth Blackwood, dated 1 June 1830; PRONI, Dufferin and Ava papers, D/1071/F/A2/2, typescript of a letter from Helen Blackwood to Price Blackwood, dated 1832.

64 PRONI, Dufferin and Ava papers, D/1071/F/A2/1, typescript of a letter from Helen Blackwood to Price Blackwood, dated 23 November 1831.

65 PRONI, Dufferin and Ava papers, D/1071/F/B2/1/1, typescript of a letter from Price Blackwood to Helen Blackwood, dated 31 October 1833.

66 PRONI, Dufferin and Ava papers, D/1071/F/B2/1/1, typescript of a letter from Price Blackwood to Helen Blackwood, dated 14 February 1834.

67 PRONI, Dufferin and Ava papers, D/1071/F/A3/3, typescript of a letter from Helen Blackwood to Brinsley Sheridan, dated 30 September 1830.

68 PRONI, Dufferin and Ava papers, D/1071/F/B2/1/1, typescript letter from Price Blackwood to Helen Blackwood, 2 November 1831.

69 PRONI, Dufferin and Ava papers, D/1071/F/A2/1, typescript of a letter from Helen Blackwood to Price Blackwood, dated 19 February 1833.

70 PRONI, Foster/Massereene papers, D/562/2522, Emily Stratton to Harriet Skeffington, Countess of Massereene, 27 August 1821.

71 PRONI, Verner-Wingfield papers, D/2538/E/19, Sarah Devezney to Anne Elizabeth Stratford, Countess of Aldborough, 15 [August] 1783.

72 PRONI, Ward papers, D/2092/1/9, a state of the County of Down infirmary for the year ending 24 June 1772.

73 Lady Louisa Connolly to Emily Fitzgerald, Duchess of Leinster, 31 March 1794, in Fitzgerald (ed.), *Correspondence*, iii, pp. 420–1.

74 PRONI, Earl of Antrim papers, D/2977/5/1/8/8/5, John Lanktree to Frances Anne Vane-Tempest-Stewart, Lady Londonderry, 14 March 1847.

75 John McParland, *Statistical survey of the county of Mayo* (Dublin: Graisberry and Campbell, 1802), p. 98.

76 Samuel Lewis, *A topographical dictionary of Ireland* (London: S. Lewis, 1847), p. 244.

77 *Ibid.*, p. 10.

78 *Ibid.*, p. 4.

79 Oliver MacDonagh, 'The economy and society, 1830–45' in Vaughan (ed.), *A new history of Ireland*, v, p. 233.

80 R. B. McDowell, 'Ireland on the eve of the Famine' in R. Dudley Edwards and T. Desmond Williams, *The Great Famine: studies in Irish history, 1845–52* (Dublin: Browne and Nolan, 1962), p. 36.

81 Innes, 'State, Church and voluntarism', pp. 29–30.

82 James S. Donnelly jr, 'The soup kitchens' in Vaughan (ed.), *A new history of Ireland*, v, p. 307.

83 Kinealy, 'The poor law during the Great Famine, p. 164.

84 James S. Donnelly jr, *The great Irish potato famine* (Stroud: Sutton, 2001), p. 92.

85 PRONI, Earl of Antrim papers, D/2977/5/1/8/25, resolution made by the Drum Crow tenantry to Lord and Lady Londonderry, 28 November 1844.

86 PRONI, Earl of Antrim papers, D/2977/5/1/8/6/1, John Lanktree to Frances Anne Vane-Tempest-Stewart, Lady Londonderry, 1 January 1846; PRONI, Earl of Antrim papers, D/2977/5/1/8/7/1, address from the Antrim tenantry to Frances Anne Vane-Tempest-Stewart, Lady Londonderry, 1846.

87 George Hill, *An historical account of the MacDonnells of Antrim* (Belfast: Glens of Antrim Historical Society, 1873), p. 371.

88 PRONI, Earl of Antrim papers, D/2977/5/1/8/4/2, John Lanktree to Frances Anne Vane-Tempest-Stewart, Lady Londonderry, 1 July 1844.

89 PRONI, Earl of Antrim papers, D/2977/5/1/8/6/2, John Lanktree to Frances Anne Vane-Tempest-Stewart, Lady Londonderry, 8 March 1846.

90 PRONI, Earl of Antrim papers, D/2977/5/1/8/6/5, John Lanktree to Frances Anne Vane-Tempest-Stewart, Lady Londonderry, 23 March 1846.

91 PRONI, Earl of Antrim papers, D/2977/5/1/8/6/7, John Lanktree to Frances Anne Vane-Tempest-Stewart, Lady Londonderry, 29 April 1846.

92 PRONI, Earl of Antrim papers, D/2977/5/1/8/4/8, Antrim estate accounts, compiled by John Lanktree, 1 October 1844.

93 *Ibid.*

94 PRONI, Earl of Antrim papers, D/2977/5/1/8/7/6, petition from Alice MacDonnell to Frances Anne Vane-Tempest-Stewart, Lady Londonderry, undated.

95 PRONI, Earl of Antrim papers, D/2977/5/1/8/8/4, John Lanktree to Frances Anne Vane-Tempest-Stewart, Lady Londonderry, 29 November 1849.

96 PRONI, Earl of Antrim papers, D/2977/5/1/8/6/6, John Lanktree to Frances Anne Vane-Tempest-Stewart, Lady Londonderry, 27 March 1846.

97 PRONI, Earl of Antrim papers, D/2977/5/1/8/5/7, list of persons to whom blankets were distributed, 1844 and 1845, by John Lanktree [1845].

98 PRONI, Earl of Antrim papers, D/2977/5/1/8/5/2, John Lanktree to Frances Anne Vane-Tempest-Stewart, Lady Londonderry, 22 January 1845.

99 PRONI, Earl of Antrim papers, D/2977/5/1/8/8/5, John Lanktree to Frances Anne Vane-Tempest-Stewart, Lady Londonderry, 14 March 1847.

100 PRONI, Earl of Antrim papers, D/2977/5/1/8/6/6, John Lanktree to Frances Anne Vane-Tempest-Stewart, Lady Londonderry, 27 March 1846.

101 PRONI, Earl of Antrim papers, D/2977/5/1/8/6/4, John Lanktree to Frances Anne Vane-Tempest-Stewart, Lady Londonderry, 20 March 1846.

102 PRONI, Earl of Antrim papers, D/2977/5/1/8/4/11, John Lanktree to Frances Anne Vane-Tempest-Stewart, Lady Londonderry, 31 December 1844.

103 James S. Donnelly jr, 'Famine and government response, 1845–6' in Vaughan (ed.), *A new history of Ireland*, v, p. 278.

104 PRONI, Earl of Antrim papers, D/2977/5/1/8/6/7, John Lanktree to Frances Anne Vane-Tempest-Stewart, Lady Londonderry, 25 September 1846.

105 PRONI, Earl of Antrim papers, D/2977/5/1/8/8/38, memorandum of Antrim estate accounts of the year ending 30 September 1847.

106 PRONI, Earl of Antrim papers, D/2977/5/1/8/8/2, John Lanktree to Frances Anne Vane-Tempest-Stewart, Lady Londonderry, 13 January 1847.

107 PRONI, Earl of Antrim papers, D/2977/5/1/8/8/38, memorandum on expenditure on the Antrim estate, compiled by John Lanktree, undated [October 1847].

108 PRONI, Earl of Antrim papers, D/2977/5/1/8/10/6, John Lanktree to Frances Anne Vane-Tempest-Stewart, Lady Londonderry, 16 May 1849.

109 PRONI, Earl of Antrim papers, D/2977/5/1/8/17/3, John Lanktree to Frances Anne Vane-Tempest-Stewart, Lady Londonderry, 29 June 1850.

110 PRONI, Earl of Antrim papers, D/2977/5/1/8/8/44, memorandum on Ballymacaldrick school, undated [1847].

111 PRONI, Earl of Antrim papers, D/2977/5/1/8/8/22, John Lanktree to Frances Anne Vane-Tempest-Stewart, Lady Londonderry, 15 May 1847.

112 PRONI, Earl of Antrim papers, D/2977/5/1/8/8/4, John Lanktree to Frances Anne Vane-Tempest-Stewart, Lady Londonderry, 8 February 1847; PRONI, Earl of Antrim papers, D/2977/5/1/8/8/5, John Lanktree to Frances Anne Vane-Tempest-Stewart, Lady Londonderry, 14 March 1847.

113 PRONI, Earl of Antrim papers, D/2977/5/1/8/8/45, unsigned and undated latter from Lord Londonderry's agent possibly to John Lanktree [October 1847].

114 James S. Donnelly jr, 'The administration of relief, 1847–51' in Vaughan (ed.), *A new history of Ireland*, v, pp. 334–6.

6

Widows and property

Widows were discernably marginalised from family property at this time. Throughout the period, all women in the families in this study received jointure in place of dower, which in most cases was significantly less than the widow would have received as dower. Widows also had no rights to their husbands' personal property, which tended to be treated as an extension of estate property and bequeathed as such to the heir. Family practices, such as the use of trustees, further sidelined widows from family financial business. The stereotypical image of the greedy dowager bleeding dry an already encumbered estate was a common feature in the correspondence of this class. It appears to have been acceptable to consider jointure a burden on the family estate. In 1799, for example, William Fitzgerald, Duke of Leinster, regarded the jointure of his grandmother, Lady Kildare, as something he 'must put up with . . . for some years longer for I think Lady Kildare will turn the hundred'.[1]

However, while it is apparent that the relationship between widows and money in wealthy landed circles was an uncomfortable one, financial business was an integral part of widowhood. Widows were responsible for ensuring the regular payment of their own jointure. Although some widows did very well from arrangements made for them on the deaths of their husbands, the experience that widows had of property in this class varied according to financial situation, circumstances and personality. Jointure was not always paid in accordance with the arrangements in marriage settlements or wills. As William Fitzgerald, Duke of Leinster, told his mother, Emily, Duchess of Leinster, when her jointure was delayed, he 'desired no legal opinion' and would gladly pay Emily's jointure 'as soon as my affairs are settled'.[2] In June 1801, the biennial jointure payment of £500 due to be paid to Amelia Wingfield, Viscountess Powerscourt, every March and September was two months late, prompting Lady Powerscourt to write to the family agent, Henry Stewart, in June 1801: 'When it is convenient to him, will he oblig[e]d [sic] by his letting her have all what is due to her last March . . . Mr

Stewart will be so good to name the day . . . that she may be at home.'[3]
As *feme sole*, the widow was a property owner in her own right, and as
might be expected in the wealthy landed class, some widows were exceptionally wealthy and, through their separate estates, enjoyed financial
independence.

Jointure was secured by settlement and was under the protection of the
Court of Chancery, and there was therefore a degree of security attached
to it. The family estate was legally bound to the payment of jointure, and
furthermore, if a widow's jointure was settled on the family estate it was
usual for her marriage settlement to contain reference to her right, in the
event of non-payment, to redeem what was owed to her by 'powers of
distress and entry'. In 1778, Lady Aldborough threatened to use such
powers when she informed the agent for her son's County Wicklow estate
that 'if [the agent] did not immediately pay of her ladyship's jointure she
would instantly send down to the country [and] drive your lordships
estates'. It appears to have been the case that she had taken similar action
in the past and had succeeded in receiving her payment.[4] Lady
Aldborough's direct approach to the retrieval of her jointure may have
been exceptional, but she was within her legal rights to take such action.

Another possible strategy available to the widow in the event of
repeated non-payment was the threat of Chancery proceedings and the
resettlement of the jointure, so that another trustee handled her affairs.
This course of action was employed by Barbara Chichester, Marchioness
of Donegall (d. 1829), the third wife of Arthur Chichester, first Marquess
of Donegall (1739–99). According to the terms of her marriage settlement, Lady Donegall had the right to demand £1,000 a year, charged on
'certain tenements' in Belfast.[5] The jointure was rarely paid on time, and
Lady Donegall found herself in financial difficulties on numerous occasions. As she noted in 1808, the reality of a widow's experience was
sometimes different from that intended by the arrangements made for her
in her husband's will: 'anyone may see by them how much the last Lord
Donegall had attended to my convenience, and by the conduct of his two
sons, how little his wishes have been fulfilled by either'.[6] Between 1799
and 1810 Lady Donegall threatened Chancery proceedings on several
occasions in an attempt to force Lord Donegall to honour her jointure
payments. By 1804 new trustees were appointed, although payments
were still not forthcoming. In 1810 Lady Donegall requested that one of
her trustees, Lord Massereene, use his power of attorney to ensure that
the part of the Belfast estate on which her jointure was settled was 'dis-
trained for arrears' due to her.[7] Despite the fact that the Court of
Chancery supported Lady Donegall's pursuit of what was owing to her
from the Donegall estate, the outcome of this case was a compromise

between Lord and Lady Donegall, and she therefore only received part of what she was owed.[8] This case demonstrates that although the Court of Chancery was perceived to be sympathetic to the needs of widows, it could not compel full payment from a son who was determined not to honour jointure arrangements.

Not all women were wholly dependent on jointure for survival, as some had access to considerable landed estates. From the families surveyed here, five women for whom separate estate information is available held a separate estate in land. The remaining three held separate estate in investments. In addition, a widow might have additional income from estates as a life interest which took effect after the death of her husband.

In a survey of testamentary bequests made by ten widows in the families surveyed here (see Table 6.1) references to moveable property, which included furniture, jewellery and trinkets, were the most common, and investments remained a more common income-making type of property than land. Last wills and testaments are an unreliable source in some respects, as they do not list all family property transactions, and widows may have possessed freehold land and devised this in separate agreements. However, while acknowledging the limitations of this sample, tentative conclusions can be drawn from it.

The devising of life interests in freehold land to widows indicates the primacy of consolidating estates, and the consequent marginalisation of family members from the main landed estate. However, these widows were undoubtedly wealthy, and this independent income enabled them to raise the money required to purchase other, freehold, property as well as property in stocks. Investments also provided further finance for the expansion of estates. For example, Mary Hill, Marchioness of Downshire, owned a life interest in Ormbersley Court and an estate in Worcester, which she had inherited from her uncle Edwin, Lord Sandys. Lady Downshire also possessed a freehold interest in a mansion and estate at Roehampton, Surrey. Before her death she purchased an additional landed property, Bourne House in Worcestershire, for which she paid £3,300. In order to cover the costs of this purchase, Lady Downshire mortgaged the property as well as her shares in Holt Fleet Bridge, before conveying the property to trustees for the use of Baron Sandys.[9]

Widows also received income from house rentals: Theodosia Meade, Countess of Clanwilliam, rented a house for two years to Robert Ward, the younger son of Bernard, Lord Bangor.[10] Another possible source of income for women at this time was interest from loans. Debts and loans were a prominent part of financial business among these families. Single, married and widowed women were involved in lending money to family

Table 6.1 Types of property noted in widows' wills, 1771–1855

Type of property	Number of wills in which property is mentioned
Freehold land	4
Stocks/investments	6
Moveable property/heirlooms	8
Trinkets	7
Total	25

Sources: PRONI, Abercorn papers, D/623/B/3/14, last will and testament of Ann Hamilton, Countess of Abercorn, extracted from the will registers of the Prerogative Court of Canterbury, will dated 1771, probate granted 10 August 1776; PRONI, Earl of Antrim papers, D/2977/1/2/4, copy of the last will and testament of Letitia MacDonnell, Marchioness of Antrim, extracted from the will registers of the Prerogative Court of Canterbury, will dated 31 July 1799, probate granted 10 February 1802; PRO, PROB/11/1455, last will and testament of Dorcas Blackwood, Baroness Dufferin and Clandeboye, extracted from the will registers of the Prerogative Court of Canterbury, will dated 7 February 1807, probate granted 26 February 1807; PRO, PROB/11/1714, last will and testament of Philadelphia Hannah Dawson, Viscountess Cremorne, extracted from the will registers of the Prerogative Court of Canterbury, will dated 1 October 1824, probate granted 18 March 1824; PRO, PROB/11/1766, last will and testament of Barbara Chichester, Marchioness of Donegall, extracted from the will registers of the Prerogative Court of Canterbury, will dated 9 December 1826, probate granted 11 February 1830; PRONI, Downshire papers, D/671/D14/2/22A&B, last will and testament of Mary Hill, Marchioness of Downshire, 3 May 1832, probate granted September 1836; PRONI , Foster/Massereene papers, D/4084/2/5, last will and testament and probate of Anne Skeffington. Countess of Massereene, will dated 21 January 1800, codicil dated 21 January 1801, probate granted 22 May 1812; PRO, PROB/11/1956, last will and testament of Mary Caroline Creighton, Countess of Erne, extracted from the will registers of the Prerogative Court of Canterbury, will dated 13 September 1841, probate granted 31 January 1842; PRONI, Charity Brownlow Testamentary document, T/26, copy of the last will and testament and probate of Charity Brownlow, dated 1 December 1842, probate granted 16 May 1843; PRONI, Downshire papers, D/671/D14/2/24, last will and testament of Maria Hill, Marchionness of Downshire, 17 December 1846, probate granted 7 April 1855.

friends and outstanding debts could be bequeathed as interests to bene-ficiaries. The informal nature of such transactions may have facilitated the involvement of women, as loans could be arranged without docu-mentation and without payment of interest. The control of insolvent family members by those who lent or gave them financial support was an important aspect of property relations at this time. Financial dependence was an underlying feature in the control fathers exerted over children. However, a wealthy widow would also have wielded such control over financially straitened family members. Financial solvency formed part of a wider moral framework of decent, 'gentlemanly' behaviour that was as influential among the wealthy landed class as it was among their middle-class contemporaries. By lending money to financially straitened family members, women could effect a degree of influence in moral matters. Between 1802 and 1822, John Wingfield-Stratford was involved in a lawsuit with George Powell over their respective claims to the Aldborough estate. In 1802 his mother, Amelia Wingfield, Viscountess Powerscourt, lent him £400 to assist with the costs of the case, while advising him against borrowing money from anyone but a family member, as 'tis a very expensive way, great charges which all fall on the borrower; premium is also expected'.[11] These loans were supplemented by gifts of money. In 1803 Viscountess Powerscourt sent her son a draft for £500,[12] and by 1805 noted that she had in total contributed £700.[13] Viscountess Powerscourt's involvement with her son's financial situation was motivated by her desire that he would take her advice and get his financial affairs into order. When this had not been achieved in the year following the loan she wrote of her disappointment:

> I wish you would exert and settle your affairs, 'tis really shameful to see them so long neglected. I would not wish you know all I hear about it, but I feel it and know it myself. Had I been a man, I wou[l]d have settled all myself before this time . . . I beseech you not to lose your time in indolence, but look to your affairs to some purpose. I have advised you, as is my duty. *I* have never failed in that point; *you* will act as you choose [emphasis in original].[14]

The importance of personal morality in the lending of money is further suggested by the reasons behind the loans that Helen Blackwood, Lady Dufferin, made to family members. Lady Dufferin frequently borrowed money from her mother both during her first marriage to Price Blackwood, Lord Dufferin, and after her husband's death, while in turn lending sums of money to her sisters and brothers. While living in Italy in January 1842, Lady Dufferin was anxious for her brother Frank Sheridan, who was staying with her, to return to England. She lent him money for the 'express purpose of *getting him off to England* (which was such a difficult matter to effect) I thought it well bestowed [emphasis in original]'.[15] In 1846 Lady Dufferin lent money to another brother, Charles Sheridan so that she could exert a degree of influence in the

Table 6.2 Lady Erne's loan network, c.1800

Year of loan	Recipient of loan	Principal sum £	Interest rate %	Amount paid to Lady Erne
1772	Ross Mahon	1,000	5	110
1772	Ross Mahon	1,000	5	110
1789	Joseph Kane	550	6	16.10.0
1789	Arthur French	1,000	6	60
1789	Richard Hill	1,000	5	25
1791	Robert Wallace	500	6	30
1792	Pat Smith	500	6	30
1793	Viscount Gosford	800	6	24
1795	John Kingley	2,000	5	50
1795	John Usher	500	6	15
1798	Reverend Hill	400	6	24
1799	Frank Marsh	600	5	30
Total		9,850		524.10.0

Sources: NLI, Erne papers, MS 15360, outstanding loans of Lady Erne, c.1800.

ending of his relationship with a woman of whom she did not approve: 'by this means . . . I acquire *a right* to demand a sacrifice in return from Charley, which will be the solemn promise to put an end to his present connection with M[ada]m D., an object which I have much at heart [emphasis in original]' .[16]

Loan networks could provide widows with investment opportunities outside the boundaries of the family. Between 1772 and 1799, Jane Creighton, Lady Erne, conducted an extensive loan network (see Table 6.2). Lady Erne was the second wife of Abraham Creighton, first Baron Erne of Crom Castle (c.1770–1772), and Lord Erne was also Lady Erne's second husband. After Lord Erne's death in 1772, her annual income totalled £1,783 from landed estates in counties Armagh and Tyrone, and included jointure from both of her marriages. [17]

The loan network demonstrates an alternative form of investment to public or private stocks. By 1800 it was made up of loans to eleven people, none of whom were related to Lady Erne, and the loans ranged in value from £400 to £2,000, charged at the typical rates during this period of either 5 per cent or 6 per cent. By 1800 Lady Erne had lent a total of £9,850, and her income from these loans for that year was £524.10.0. This amount was equivalent to 29 per cent of Lady Erne's total income, a significant proportion.[18]

The fact that the loans date from after the death of Lord Erne suggests, as would be expected, that Lady Erne had more income at her disposal during those years. However, it does not necessarily follow that it was less acceptable for a married woman to be involved with this type of money lending. There is nothing to suggest that Lady Erne was an isolated example of a wealthy woman who had a substantial list of debtors. Earlier in the eighteenth century, Harriet Boyle (d. 1746), the Countess of Kildare, wife of Henry Boyle (d. 1764), the first Earl of Shannon, also had a list of debts that included three bonds, to different people, dated April 1744, each payable within fifteen months and each loaned at 5 per cent interest, totalling nearly £13,000.[19] The Countess of Kildare was married at this time, and, in fact, her husband outlived her by eighteen years, so it was clearly acceptable for a married woman to lend money in this way.

It is also clear that such transactions did present a viable alternative to banks. As Large notes, in contrast with English banks, which did offer mortgages to landowners, 'the principal dealings of the Irish banking system in the eighteenth century were exchange dealings'. One exception to this was the banking facilities offered by the La Touche bankers, which included rent remittances to absentee landlords.[20] Presumably, privately arranged loans, such as those offered by Lady Erne, were more convenient than the available banking facilities.

Charity

The household and personal expenses of Lady Erne also provide a useful example of how charitable benevolence operated in the daily financial lives of widows. As Rosemary Raughter notes, Lady Erne was possibly more generous than many of her aristocratic and wealthy landed contemporaries, although she was at the same time not as generous as the major benefactors, such as Lady Arabella Denny, who were personally, as well as financially, involved in a range of philanthropic activity.[21] A significant proportion of Lady Erne's income as a widow was given to charitable causes. In her study of Lady Erne's accounts, Raughter has noted that in this period her expenditure on charity was 9 per cent of her total expenditure, 'a proportion not far short of the biblically-ordained tithe'.[22]

Lady Erne's household and personal accounts provide a useful indication of the structure of her charitable activity over the period 1776–99, and these have been listed and divided into six categories in appendix G. The most numerous beneficiaries, as would be expected, were the poor. Named recipients were more numerous than the anonymous poor, and Lady Erne had approximately three regular petitioners at any one time, although in some years there were fewer. 'Poor Anne' and 'old Fleming' appear in the early accounts. 'Poor Anne' received quarterly amounts from Lady Erne until 1786.[23] After this date her place was apparently taken by a new petitioner, Mary Nowlan, who appears in the accounts from 1787 until 1799.[24] 'Blind Hawkins' appears as a regular beneficiary between 1779 and 1783.[25] After 'Blind Hawkins' disappears from the accounts, another beneficiary appears in 1784, 'Casey', who received a quarterly amount for his son's schooling.[26]

Apart from Casey, reasons for the amounts given to named petitioners were not detailed in the accounts, and they can therefore be assumed to have been for the relief of poverty. Occasional donations were made to other named beneficiaries, such as 'poor Sampson' the hairdresser, 'for his wife's lying in'.[27] There is a sense of continuity with the families of these petitioners. 'Old Fleming' received quarterly amounts from Lady Erne from 1776 until his death in 1779. After his death, his widow received the amount in his place until 1783.[28] His place appears to have been taken from 1786 to 1799 by 'Biddy Cash', who had previously worked as a maid for Lady Erne's mother.[29] Similarly, reasons for the benevolence to the unnamed poor were not detailed in the accounts in most cases, although in some cases money was given in response to disasters, such as the donations to the 'poor woman' in 1784 'whose house has blown down' and the 'poor people' in County Tyrone in 1796 'who have been distressed by floods and storms'.[30] On one occasion assistance to disaster victims also reached beyond Ireland: in 1781 a subscription was made to the distressed in the West Indian islands.[31]

Lady Erne's contribution to institutionalised poor relief and reform makes up a smaller, but regular presence in the accounts. The two institutions mentioned most frequently are the Houses of Industry and the Magdalen Asylum. The Houses of Industry were established in 1771 as a response to the perceived problem of the homeless poor.[32] Lady Erne subscribed to the Houses of Industry annually until 1786. After this time she appears to have replaced this subscription with another to a charity which arranged loans to the poor.[33] The Magdalen Asylum, established by Lady Arabella Denny in 1767 for reformed prostitutes, was a focal point for charitable benevolence from women of this class. Emily, Duchess of Leinster, and her sister Louisa Conolly both acted on the female management committee, visiting the asylum and taking part in activities such as overseeing discipline and advising on skills and employment.[34] Lady Erne was an annual subscriber until 1793, a year after Lady Arabella Denny's death, after which there appears to have been a decline in the institution's effectiveness.[35]

Included under the category of charitable institutions were organisations that promoted education and religious instruction in schools and Sunday schools. Lady Erne's donations to Sunday schools date from the beginning of the Sunday school movement in Ireland. The Hibernian Sunday School Society was founded in 1809, and became the Sunday School Society for Ireland in 1815. In 1810, forty schools and over 5,000 pupils had received assistance from the society. [36] The first list of officials was made up of eight women from this class, including Viscountess Powerscourt and the Countess of Meath.[37] The Dublin Sunday schools, supported by Lady Erne, had been promoted by Arthur Guinness and Samuel Bewley, and by 1798 had their own premises in School Street and North Strand.[38]

Donation to charitable causes through third parties was a more sporadic form of benevolence and was absent from the accounts in some years. Owing to the nature of this type of benevolence, the causes also varied: for example, money was relayed to Mrs Graves by a third party for the purpose of assisting her son in the 'cattlers trade'.[39] However, in 1793 Lady Erne recorded five such donations, which included two amounts 'for a poor family', one for 'poor manufacturers', one 'for charity' and one 'to bring a poor girl into this country'.[40] Another method of contributing to the poor was through attendance at charity sermons. Charity sermons were an annual feature in all accounts from 1776 to 1799.

The final category noted in appendix G consists of the miscellaneous causes that do not neatly fit into any of the other categories. Although focused on the lower-class poor, Lady Erne's charity was not wholly confined to it. In 1787, for example, an inflated amount of £144.4.10½ is recorded, the highest amount spent in the period recorded in the accounts. In this year, Lady Erne gave £100 'to a gentleman and his family and home I thought in distress'.[41] Other beneficiaries were a 'poor gentleman' in 1782, a 'poor clergyman' in 1783 and a 'poor French count' in 1794.[42]

Lady Erne's charitable behaviour was therefore a combination of personal, local benevolence to the poor, which included regular petitioners, and contributions by subscription to institutional and church charitable measures, as well as encompassing the unfortunate from the middle and upper classes. Her patterns of benevolence are also a useful indication of how personal, institutional and church approaches to poverty co-existed at this time. The accounts reveal a predominant interest in providing for the local poor. Within this there were distinctions between named, regular petitioners and the anonymous, unnamed poor. Although Lady Erne's benevolence, where it was intended for the relief of poverty, was directed towards local needs, it was occasionally directed to other causes outside Ireland. It was focused on the indigent poor, but it was also occasionally extended to those from the middle and upper classes who were in financial distress. Lady Erne's support of institutional charities aimed to encourage reform and self-help among the poor. Her concerns for education and religious instruction were also directed to the relevant charitable organisations. The concern accorded to children, and to the poor in general, provided a basis for Lady Erne's benevolence that was in keeping with the role of women.

The focus of charity among women in these families was most commonly the local poor; however, alongside this women supported charitable institutions and occasional charitable fund-raising events. Harriet Skeffington, Countess of Massereene (d. 1831), the wife of Chichester Skeffington, Marquess of Massereene, was a supporter of the Belfast Lying-In Hospital.[43] She contributed to the local poor on the Massereene estate in County Antrim, and to petitioners in Dublin, one of whom, for example, received money to keep her daughter at school.[44] Helen, Lady Dufferin, wrote the epilogue for a performance of *The hunchback* at St James's Theatre, in which Fanny Kemble was to act the part of Julia 'for the benefit of the starving Irish'.[45] Lady Dufferin also visited poor tenants on the Dufferin estate, and prayed with them; for example, in 1849 she prayed with the wife of Willie Flanaghan, who was dying after giving birth to a dead child.[46] Additionally, a widow might have the task of administering their late husband's wishes regarding charitable bequests from his estate. William Brownlow bequeathed £50 to the Free School of Lurgan, £50 to the poor of the parish of Shankhill and £400 to be laid out 'in such manner as Mrs Brownlow my wife may consider useful'.[47]

There were also occasions when women in this class adopted poor foreign children. Caroline Norton, writing to her sister Helen, Lady Dufferin, from Rome in 1849 noted the recent death of a Lady Strachan, who had not seen her family much in the years preceding her death, but had adopted an Italian child, 'a poor little girl, to whom she has left £150 a year, an Italian fortune!'[48] Five years later, in 1854, Helen, Lady Dufferin, attempted to adopt a child saved from a shipwreck off the coast of Dublin. By the time she had written to the clergyman in Dublin who had charge of the orphan, there had been '*fifteen* other offers to provide for, and adopt it, one of which is from a gentleman near Liverpool, who desires to be allowed to settle a *landed estate* upon it! [emphasis in original]'.[49]

Bequests made by widows in last wills and testaments

Last wills and testaments provide a useful source for the study of women's experience of property, recording in each case the type of property owned and the testator's views on disposition. In a sample of twenty wills, ten written by the head of the family estate and ten written by the widows of such men, a wider range of property was bequeathed by male testators. As indicated by Table 6.3, women did bequeath capital interests in land, although on a lesser scale than men within this sample. The range of other property bequeathed is also similar. Both male and female testators bequeathed annuities, legacies and moveable property. The most numerous bequests made by male testators were of annuities in land and life interests in family houses, a pattern which reflects the usual provision for family members made by the male head of the family.

In several instances, when a widow owned both entailed and freehold property, the freehold property was bequeathed to younger sons. This practice is in accordance with practice in some landed families to keep some of a widow's separate estate as a 'cadet' estate, apart from the main estate, usually in accordance with the wishes of her father.[50] By the death of her brother, Lord Viscount Mount Morres, Letitia MacDonnell, Marchioness of Antrim, had become entitled as one of his co-heiresses at law to 'a moiety of all his freehold and copyhold' lands in Ireland, which she devised to her son from her previous marriage, Lord Dungannon.[51]

The bequest of cadet estates can be interpreted as the representation of a family interest, even if the family in question was that of the widow's father. However, it may also have been motivated by personal preference. Theodosia Meade, Countess of Clanwilliam, took possession of her family estates at Gill Hall and Rathfriland during her marriage.[52] The Gill Hall estate was entailed on her eldest son, Lord Gilford, while Theodosia was free to bequeath the Rathfriland estate, which she did, to her second son, Captain Robert Meade. Her house in Stephens Green was also not entailed, and when she bequeathed it to Robert, she was free to do so: 'On arranging the title, I found it is not entailed; but that to you should make no difference, more than being obliged to the old lady's memory for it or what you may sell it for.'[53]

The influence that the particular type of property owned had on disposition is considered in Table 6.4. Both men and women in this sample bequeathed mostly to their immediate family, eldest sons, daughters and younger sons, as well as to wider kin. However, a significant number of widows' bequests were made to non-relatives and servants, while men made no bequests to non-relatives, and only one to a servant.

Most bequests made by widows were legacies settled upon personal estate and capital interests on moveable goods, and this reflects the different perspective on disposition held by the male head of a family and a widow. Such bequests carried no continuity across generations, and did not revert to the family estate. It is probable that the different type of property owned by widows encouraged more careful disposition, so

Table 6.3 **Range of property bequeathed by husbands and widows, 1768–1836**[a]

Type of property	Bequeathed by husbands	Bequeathed by widows
Gross sum to widow	4	N/A
Capital interest in freehold land	5	3
Life interest in freehold land	3	0
Annuities charged on land	7	1
Annuities charged on stock	2	4
Legacies charged on land	6	3
Legacies charged on personal estate	2	7
Capital interest in moveable property	5	8
Life interest in moveable property	3	1
Paraphernalia to widow	5	N/A
House interest for life	7	0
Capital interest in house	0	1
Total	59	27

Note: [a] Entailed estates and jointure have not been noted, as the concern here is with choices regarding bequests. All male testators inherited their family's landed estate and all female testators were the widows of men who inherited the family estate.

Sources: PRONI, Downshire papers, D/671/D14/2/17, copy of the last will and testament of James Fitzgerald, Duke of Leinster, 9 February 1768; PRONI, Dufferin and Ava papers, D/1071/A/N3/3b, copy last will and testament of John Blackwood, 31 December 1781; PRONI, Enniskillen papers, D/1702/1/27/7a, last will and testament and probate of William Willoughby, Earl of Enniskillen, 21 June 1793, probate granted 25 July 1805; PRONI, Brownlow papers, D/1928/T/3/5, solicitor's copy of the last will and testament and two codicils of William Brownlow, will dated 19 April 1791, probate granted 1794; PRONI, Downshire papers, D/671/D14/2/20a, copy of the last will and testament of Arthur Hill, Marquess of Downshire extracted from the Registry of the Prerogative Court of Canterbury, 24 November 1797, probate granted 1801; PRONI, Foster/Massereene papers, D/4084/2/8a, copy last will and testament and probate of Chichester Skeffington, Earl of Massereene, will dated 20 February 1816, probate granted 17 October 1816; PRONI, Abercorn papers, D/623/B/3/25, last will and testament and probate of John James Hamilton, Marquess of Abercorn, 18 March 1809, probate granted 9 May 1818; PRONI, Galway, McIlwaine and Seeds papers, D/665/4, copy of the last will and testament and probate of Robert Stewart, Marquess of Londonderry, will dated 14 August 1818, codicils dated 17 August 1818, probate granted 10 May 1823; PRONI, Erne papers, D/1939/25/1/12, last will and testament and probate of John Creighton, Earl of Erne, will dated 11 November 1828, probate granted 1829; PRONI, Powerscourt papers, D/1957/1/17, solicitor's copy of the last will and testament of Richard Wingfield, Viscount Powerscourt, 3 February 1836. See Table 6.1 for sources for widows' wills.

Table 6.4 **Numbers of bequests to family members in wills
of husbands and widows, 1768–1855**

Range of beneficiaries	Husbands' wills	Widows' wills
Wife	10	N/A
Eldest son	4	6
Daughters	8	7
Younger sons	6	4
Wider female kin	5	9
Wider male kin	2	5
Non-relatives	0	2
Servants	1	5
Charity	0	2
Total	36	40

Sources: See Tables 6.1 and 6.3.

widows were likely to bequeath more legacies to more people. There are more instances of the bequest of small items such as ornaments, books and jewellery, as well as relatively small sums of money, in the wills of widows than in those of husbands. Anne Skeffington, Countess of Massereene, bequeathed £100 each to her daughter, Lady Leitrim, and her daughter's husband 'for a ring' as well as bequeathing china, picture frames, a money box and all her clothes.[54] Maria Hill, Marchioness of Downshire, included seven separate bequests of mementoes to her children. This will also included the one bequest in this sample of a life interest in estate jewellery, vested in trustees for the use of the Marchioness's daughter during her life. On her daughter's death, ownership of the jewellery was to revert to the Downshire estate.[55]

There is no extant record of the last will and testament of Helen, Lady Dufferin, although an apparent rough draft of her 'latest instructions' regarding the disposal of her personal property after her death suggests that her personal property consisted of her linens, clothes and jewels. Her jewels were 'to be delivered' to her daughter-in-law, Harriet Blackwood, Marchioness of Dufferin and Ava. Helen instructed that her maid 'Rumble' was 'to have all my linens and any part of my wardrobe which Lady Dufferin pleases to give her'. She also wished that 'some little things to be given to each of my sisters, and to [her niece] Maria Sheridan in remembrance of me. My little travelling clock is for Lizzie Ward [her sister-in-law] and the work basket, which my dear Harriet [Blackwood] brought me from Paris to be given to Mrs Nugent'.[56]

It is also possible that there was a tendency in last wills and testaments to bequeath according to the perceived need of the beneficiary. As noted

in chapter 2, the concept of bequeathing according to the need of the beneficiary was also present in husbands' wills, although it was limited to
immediate family and younger children in particular. That the idea had
common currency is suggested by the practice of noting, when not
bequeathing anything to a particular family member, that they have been
provided for elsewhere. Therefore, when Mary, Marchioness of
Downshire, did not bequeath anything to her eldest son, the Marquess
of Downshire, it was due to the fact that he was 'amply provided for by
the large estate of which he is in possession'.[57] Similarly, the separate
estate bequeathed by Letitia, Countess of Antrim, to her daughter Lady
Charlotte Kerr, noted in chapter 5, consisted of a life interest in £10,000
invested in government securities, arrears of jointure owing to her at her
time of death and a further gross sum of £3,000. This contrasts with the
token amount bequeathed to Charlotte's sister Anne Katherine, Countess
of Antrim, who, Lady Antrim noted, 'cannot be supposed to be in want
of money'. Lady Antrim bequeathed £500 to Anne Katherine 'to buy her
a mourning ring' and, significantly, added 'as I wish to prove I am per-
fectly reconciled and also bless her and trust she may always continue
happy'.[58]

Another feature of these wills consists of the bequests and recommen-
dations made for servants. Ann Hamilton, Countess of Abercorn,
bequeathed various legacies to servants who had been with the family for
three or more years.[59] Letitia MacDonnell, Lady Antrim bequeathed one
year's wages to servants who had been in her service for five years or
more, in addition to what they were owed as wages at the time of her
death. She also 'begs' that her son, Lord Dungannon, recommend the servants as 'they have lived a long time with me and are attentive and
careful'. Lady Antrim also made particular reference to a maid, Clebert,
to whom she bequeathed, on the condition that Clebert was still her maid
at her time of death, 12 guineas and an additional 50 guineas, later
increased to 100 guineas, 'as a small acknowledgement of her having
been extremely attentive'.[60] The disparity between the wills of male and
female testators regarding bequests to servants may have been due to the
fact that a widow would have had her own establishment, which might
not pass on to another family member on her death, unlike the family
mansion, which was entailed on the heir to the estate. Servants of widows
in landed families were therefore more likely to be made unemployed, as
the example of Lady Erne's mother's maid, Biddy Cash, who was the
recipient of charity from Lady Erne, demonstrates.

It is therefore a feature of widows' wills that they bequeathed more
moveable property than land, that their bequests tended to be detailed,
and that they acknowledged a wider kin and non-kin network. This is

Table 6.5 **Residuary legatees in husbands' and widows' wills, 1768–1855**

Residuary legatee	Husbands' wills	Widows' wills
Widow	3	N/A
Eldest/only son	6	4
Daughter	0	0
Younger son	0	1
Wider male kin	0	2
Wider female kin	0	2
Trustees	1	1
Total	10	10

Sources: See Tables 6.1 and 6.3.

further illustrated by the choices of residuary legatees, shown in Table 6.5. As with the husbands' wills, the detailed bequests of a widow's will might mean that the residuary legatee did not receive much, although none of the wills in the sample was as detailed as that of Ellinor, Countess of Blessington, who recorded forty-three separate and detailed bequests.[61] As Table 6.5 indicates, both husbands and widows were more likely to appoint their eldest, or only, son as residuary legatee than a daughter, younger son or wider kin. Trustees were mentioned on one occasion by both male and female testators, and therefore clearly played a visible role in the affairs of both men and women in these families. Daughters were not mentioned in any of the sample wills, although daughters do feature as residuary legatees in last wills and testaments outside this sample. Catherine, Countess of Charleville, for example, appointed her daughter residuary legatee and joint executor of her last will and testament.[62] However, widows in this sample named younger sons, nephews and grandchildren as residuary legatees, thereby recognising a wider range of appointees from their extended kin network. Although these were a minority, they indicate the greater importance of kin and wider kin in the financial affairs of widows than in those of their husbands.

In the sample wills there were no bequests to charity by husbands, and only two by widows. Each of these was a legacy to be distributed to the poor of the parish. Anne Skeffington, Countess of Massereene, bequeathed £200 to parishes in Antrim, and Charity Brownlow bequeathed £25 to the parish of Shankhill and £15 to the parish of Kilhoney in County Armagh.[63] There is no reason to suppose that in their focus on the local poor, these two wills were unrepresentative of women's charitable bequests. As noted above, locally based philanthropy was a significant element in the charitable behaviour of women from this class. Furthermore, Raughter, in her analysis of legacies reproduced in the

Abstracts of wills, argues that the majority of female testators 'directed their largesse towards the poor of their own locality, or of an area with which they had some connection, through birth or land ownership'.[64] However, the fact that only two out of the ten wills make any reference to charity is significant, and it may be that bequests to charity though last wills and testaments were not as widely practised by women from the wealthy landed class as by their middle-class contemporaries. A survey of the Charitable Bequests Index between 1800 and 1825 reveals only seven titled women. The average total number of bequests in 1801 and 1821 was fifty-six, eighteen of them from women, these represented a very small proportion of all bequests, especially when the women in question were among the wealthiest in Ireland.[65]

Bequests in the wills of Anne Skeffington, Countess of Massereene, and Charity Brownlow also indicate that their benevolence was much lower in value than that of their middle-class contemporaries. Women from the wealthy landed class were perhaps more restricted in the scope of their charitable benevolence, possibly because of the particular intersection of gender and class which led to their focus on the local poor. An admittedly unrepresentative example of another will that included charitable dona- tions is the last will and testament of Dame Elizabeth Hutchinson, sister of Peter La Touche, from the wealthy Dublin banking family, and a member of a family renowned for its involvement in charitable causes.[66] Dame Hutchinson bequeathed £6,000 in Consolidated and Joint Government Irish Stock at 4 per cent interest to the Commissioners of Charitable Donations and Bequests to thirteen separate charitable causes, covering both institutional charities, such as the House of Refuge in Baggot Street 'founded by the late Mrs Blackford for young women looking for services', and the Magdalen Asylum, as well as the Sunday School Society in the city of Dublin. A further bequest of £1,000 consolidated 3½ per cent stock to the Archbishop of Tuam was intended to help the widows and sons of curates, while another bequest of £1,000 consolidated 3½ per cent stock to Bishop Killale was intended to assist clergymen's widows and sons. Finally, after arranging for an annuity of £5 to be paid to the minister of the parish of Killashee, in order to have railings around her late husband's grave painted, she directed that any left-over money was go to to the poor people of Killashee.[67] The La Touche family were exceptionally prominent in Irish charity and the extent of Dame Hutchinson's charitable bequests was there- fore uncommon. However, her will is a useful indication of the wider pos- sibilities of women's involvement in charity.

The evident concerns in the last wills and testaments of widows in this sample are in accordance with those of female testators in England. Richard Vann, in his study on will-making in the English town of

Banbury, which covers part of this period, has noted that women were beginning to take up the role of 'kinship expert', becoming increasingly likely to make bequests to kinsmen, to friends and to servants.[68] Amy Erickson also notes that female testators bequeathed to a wider range of kin and non-kin than men in early modern England.[69]

The marginal place that widows occupied in relation to the main family estate also determined their testamentary behaviour. If a widow died intestate, there was no obvious pattern of descent for her property. The detailed bequest of moveable property and cash, as is evident in some last wills and testaments, was a response to this situation. The different requirements of a widow's will from those of a husband are also illustrated by the more numerous bequests made to servants. Servants were more likely to become unemployed on the death of a widow, whereas on the death of a husband the house in which they worked was part of the estate and would therefore continue in the family. As in the case of single women, noted in chapter 4, widows' bequests to non-kin may also reflect the types of significant relations in their lives of widows.

Remarriage

Among the sample families it was more common for men than for women to remarry. Out of the seventy-six marriages within the sample families in this period, eighteen men married more than once (24 per cent). In six cases men married widows (8 per cent), and in five cases the widows of these men remarried (6 per cent).[70] These figures are in keeping with the wider experience of widows and remarriage. In early modern England, fewer widows than men ever remarried. Of all widows, wealthy widows 'from medieval England to nineteenth-century Virginia' were least likely of all to remarry.[71]

The reasons for the low rate of remarriage among widows were a combination of social and financial factors. The remarrying widow was in a socially anomalous position. As a woman heading her own household she contradicted the patriarchal structure of landed society that was defined by male heads of family. However, a widow who remarried further challenged the supremacy of her late husband by replacing him. This contradictory situation was personified by comic images of widows which presented enduring stereotypes of 'foolish, pathetic creatures . . . who anxiously sought a husband at any cost'.[72] The loss of independence that marriage involved was another possible factor. By remarrying, a widow would be forced to relinquish her legal identity once again and, despite her ability to arrange separate estate for herself on this marriage, may have been unwilling to do so.

It is likely that financial considerations were equally important. Widows who did not remarry possibly could not afford to. In this period, the concentration of family property in the hands of the heir and the tendency to limit the widow's interest to moveable property and residence rights to life, as long as she remained unmarried, was a principal financial barrier. Such restrictions in some cases also extended to the guardianship of children. On deciding to remarry, the widow would have to assess the implications of this regarding losses from the family estate and the impact on her social position. The advantages of a second, later marriage were that the widow would be able to arrange her own separate estate, having possibly more money and more experience than she had at the time of her first marriage.[73] A widow of independent financial means may have been more likely to marry for love than a single woman in straitened circumstances.

Just as some widows who did not marry could not afford to do so, a widow with an adequate separate estate alongside generous jointure provision from her first husband may have been economically positioned to act independently of the wishes of her family and society. The payment of jointure was independent of a late husband's wishes and therefore could not be conditional upon a widow remaining unmarried. As already noted, Jane Creighton, Lady Erne's income on the death of her second husband in 1772, which totalled £1,783 a year, included £566 from the jointure settled on her first marriage to Arthur Acheson.[74] A widow was also able to arrange for part of her jointure to be paid to her new husband. Anne Dawson, Lady Cremorne, arranged for her £1,107 jointure to be divided between herself and her new husband, settling £600 on Colonel John Rawdon and retaining the remainder for herself.[75]

When Emily Fitzgerald, Duchess of Leinster, married William Ogilvie, her children's tutor, a year after her first husband's death in 1774, her actions divided the Fitzgerald family and scandalised aristocratic society. The financial independence that the Duchess was ensured by her jointure from the Leinster estate may have provided the basis for her independence of action in the face of such hostility. The marriage was clearly a marriage for love from her perspective, and was portrayed as a choice between happiness and social approval. As the Duchess's sister, Louisa Conolly, noted: '[y]ou hurt your rank in the world, in my opinion; that is all you do; and if you gain happiness by it, I am sure you make a good exchange, and it would be hard indeed if your friends were not satisfied with that'.[76] The luxury of personal happiness could therefore be costly to the widow. By the terms of her husband's will, the Duchess of Leinster would have lost her life interest in the Fitzgerald houses in Carton and Blackrock, as well as her right to be guardian to any of the children from her marriage to the late Duke of Leinster. Her relationship with her son, the second Duke of Leinster, ameliorated the severity of these conditions. However, her remarriage did lead to her losing authority over the management of the landed property of her sons.

The experience of the Duchess of Leinster can be compared with that of Helen Blackwood, Lady Dufferin, who was in a less advantageous financial situation after the death of her first husband in 1841. Lady Dufferin appears to have conducted a private, intimate friendship with George Hay, Lord Gifford, for twenty years before they married in 1862, over two decades after her first husband's death. The frustration felt by Helen at the clandestine nature of their relationship is clear from her correspondence: '[h]ow I wish you were in a dungeon of your own!' she wrote in 1842, 'for then I would come and read, and chat with you, in the face of all the proper-ties in the world!'[77] Lord Gifford was ten years younger than Lady Dufferin, which may have provided an obstacle to their earlier marriage. The problems their relationship would cause for her social standing were recognised by Lady Dufferin, who noted on another occasion that she could not visit Lord Gifford because of 'that thin thing, my reputation'.[78]

Although he had proposed marriage on numerous occasions, Lady Dufferin consented only after Lord Gifford was involved in a fatal accident, the injuries from which led to his death one month later. The marriage was considered shocking among some members of London society. Reported comments were that the marriage to a dying man was considered 'wicked'. Lord Gifford's parents, Lord and Lady Tweedale, alluded to the property that Lord Gifford was heir to, and condemned the marriage as motivated on Lady Dufferin's part by 'the basest motives'.[79]

Lady Dufferin noted a number of reasons for her previous decision not to marry Lord Gifford, such as the fact that he was ten years younger than her and her duty to her son, Frederick, Lord Dufferin: 'the difference in our ages, the great and rational dread I entertain of confliction duties, the deep affection I bear towards my son, and the fear of diminishing (by an unsuitable union) the respect he owed me; lastly, and not least, the consideration of what was best and wisest for Gifford's own prospects and position'.[80] The sense of obligation to her son was alleviated when he married Harriet Rowan-Hamilton the previous year; however, there were also financial obstacles to the earlier marriage of Lady Dufferin and Lord Gifford. Lord Gifford had a stormy relationship with his family, which appears to have made his financial situation unstable, and Lady Dufferin's income consisted largely of her jointure from the Dufferin estate, which, although secure, was not a large sum.

It is significant that the main criticism levelled at Lady Dufferin was not the difference in age between herself and Lord Gifford, but his potential financial situation as the heir to his father. Lord Gifford had an acrimonious relationship with his father, Lord Tweedale, on whom he was financially dependent. Lord Tweedale condemned the marriage and refused to assist with the cost of his son's medical bills, despite his reported wealth.[81] Lady Dufferin asserted the respectability of the union in two ways: by making it known to her social circle that Lord Gifford had embraced religion before his death by taking the sacrament, and by attempting to pay all her late husband's medical bills and funeral costs, a financial burden that she regarded as a 'sacred duty' which 'few people will understand'.[82]

The remarrying widow therefore had to consider a variety of factors, such as social reputation and family duty, as well as finances. The economic position of a widow, however, provided the basis on which other factors could be balanced. A widow could act according to her own wishes in social matters only if she was not facing the threat of financial ruin by her choice to remarry. The trend in landed families to concentrate family property in the hands of the heir, limiting the widow's interest to life, and the further trend of specifying conditions of continued widowhood to life interests, were therefore important factors in constraining the financial independence of widows to make such decisions.

Conclusion

The relationship that widows had to property in these families is complex. In family settlements, widows were increasingly marginalised from family financial business as well as from income from the estate, as provisions were often life interests conditional upon the widow not remarrying. Settled jointure was also not guaranteed in practice, as the experience of Lady Donegall illustrates. At the same time, it was acceptable in family correspondence to resent the payment of jointure.

The amount and type of property owned by widows varied. Some widows were very wealthy, in terms of both jointure and possession of separate estate in land. Some widows were dependent upon the good will of family members for the payment of jointure and any additions to this income. The power enjoyed by widows in family affairs consequently differed between those who exercised formal authority and those who used more indirect means. A widow who was dependent upon the good will of her family for financial support could also find herself bound by the wishes of her late husband in her future life choices, such as remarriage.

Prevailing notions of appropriate roles for women in the family did impact on women in this sample. Informal advice and loan networks represented the basis of widows' financial authority in families. The lending of money raised the issue of moral control of financially straitened family members. However, loan networks were an integral part of the financial management of this class, and these extended outside the family, providing significant sources of income. Charity was another area of activity that accorded with contemporary views on acceptable public roles for women. In the absence of government intervention, for much of this period, poor relief, in terms of the private, localised charity practised by women in this class, provided the only form of assistance to the indigent poor in many areas.

Some widows did own land, and they demonstrated the same dynastic considerations as their male contemporaries by bequeathing it to immediate family members. However, the testamentary bequests made by widows also indicate a concern to provide for wider kin and non-kin. This factor reflects the different type of property generally owned by widows in the families surveyed here, which was, in most cases, moveable, cash property. A widows also occupied a different place in the family from a male heir. If a widow died intestate, there was no obvious pattern of descent for her property, and after her death her servants were likely to be unemployed.

Notes

1 NLI, Brian Fitzgerald papers, MS 13,022, William Fitzgerald, Duke of Leinster, to Emily Fitzgerald, Duchess of Leinster, 13 May 1779.
2 NLI, Brian Fitzgerald papers, MS 13,022, William Fitzgerald, Duke of Leinster, to Emily Fitzgerald, Duchess of Leinster, 17 December 1775.
3 PRONI, Verner-Wingfield papers, D/2538/C/14, Amelia Wingfield, Viscountess Powerscourt, to Henry Stewart, 19 June 1801.
4 PRONI, Verner-Wingfield papers, D/2538/E/19, Annesley Devenzy to Edward Stratford, Lord Aldborough, 12 December 1778.
5 PRONI, Foster/Massereene papers, D/562/2819, Barbara Chichester, Lady Donegall, to Chichester Skeffington, Earl of Massereene, 28 November 1808.
6 PRONI, Foster/Massereene papers, D/562/2821, Barbara Chichester, Lady Donegall, to Chichester Skeffington, Earl of Massereene, 2 October 1808.
7 PRONI, Foster/Massereene papers, D/562/2826, Barbara Chichester, Lady Donegall, to Chichester Skeffington, Earl of Massereene, 22 June 1810.
8 Maguire, *Living like a lord*, pp. 42–3.
9 PRONI, Downshire papers, D/671/D14/2/221&b, last will and testament of Mary Hill, Marchioness of Downshire, 3 May 1832, probate granted September 1836.

10 PRONI, Ward papers, D/2092/1/9/71, Reverend Hugh Montgomery to Arabella Ward, 1 August 1802.

11 PRONI, Verner-Wingfield papers, D/2538/E/37, Amelia Wingfield, Viscountess Powerscourt, to John Wingfield-Stratford, 19 March 1802.

12 PRONI, Verner-Wingfield papers, D/2538/E/37, Amelia Wingfield, Viscountess Powerscourt, to John Wingfield-Stratford, 20 January 1803.

13 PRONI, Verner-Wingfield papers, D/2538/E/37, Amelia Wingfield, Viscountess Powerscourt, to John Wingfield-Stratford, 19 November 1805.

14 PRONI, Verner-Wingfield papers, D/2538/E/37, Amelia Wingfield, Viscountess Powerscourt, to John Wingfield-Stratford, 16 August [1802/03].

15 PRONI, Dufferin and Ava papers, D/1071/F/A3/2, Helen Blackwood, Lady Dufferin, to Henrietta Sheridan, 2 January [1842].

16 PRONI, Dufferin and Ava papers, D/1071/F/A1/8/1, Helen Blackwood, Lady Dufferin, to Henrietta Sheridan, 21 June 1846.

17 NLI, Erne papers, MS 2178, household and personal expenses of Jane Creighton, Lady Erne, 1776–99 (hereafter Erne accounts).

18 Erne accounts, 1776–99.

19 PRONI, Shannon papers, D/2707/B13/1-34, Boyle family bonds and related papers, 1726–88.

20 Large, 'The wealth of the greater Irish landowners', p. 22.

21 Raughter, 'A natural tenderness', p. 69.

22 *Ibid.*, p. 68.

23 Erne accounts, 1777–86.

24 *Ibid.*, 1777–99.

25 *Ibid.*, 1779–83.

26 *Ibid.*, 1784–99.

27 *Ibid.*, 1789.

28 *Ibid.*, 1779–83.

29 *Ibid.*, 1786–99.

30 *Ibid.*, 1784 and 1796.

31 *Ibid.*, 1781.

32 Joseph O'Carroll, 'Contemporary attitudes towards the homeless poor 1725–1775' in David Dickson (ed.), *The gorgeous mask* (Dublin: Trinity History Workshop, 1987), pp. 64–85.

33 Erne accounts, 1787–89.

34 Raughter, 'A natural tenderness', pp. 131–2.

35 *Ibid.*, pp. 128–61.

36 Helen Clayton, *To school without shoes: a brief history of the Sunday School Society for Ireland 1809–1979* (Dublin?, 1979?), pp. 10–11.

37 *Ibid.*, *To school without shoes*, p. 35.

38 *Ibid.*, pp. 8–10.

39 Erne accounts, 1781.

40 *Ibid.*, 1793.

41 *Ibid.*, 1777 and 1787.

42 *Ibid.*, 1782, 1783 and 1794.

43 PRONI, Foster/Massereene papers, D/562/289, Mary Isabella Joy to Harriet Skeffington, Countess of Massereene, 20 September 1826.

44 PRONI, Foster/Massereene papers, D/562/305, Mrs S. Hughes to Harriet Skeffington, Countess of Massereene, 5 August 1816.

45 PRONI, Dufferin and Ava papers, D/1071/F/A1/8/1, Helen Blackwood, Lady Dufferin, to Frederick Blackwood, Lord Dufferin, 2 March [1847].

46 PRONI, Dufferin and Ava papers, D/1071/F/A1/8/1, Helen Blackwood, Lady Dufferin, to Frederick Blackwood, Lord Dufferin [1849].

47 National Archives of Ireland, Dublin (hereafter NAI), MFS 49, '*A return of all charitable donations and bequests contained in the wills registered in the prerogative and consistorial offices of Dublin, from the 1st January 1814 to the 1st January 1815* (Dublin, 1815), detail of the last will and testament of William Brownlow, will dated 10 May 1814, probate granted 13 December 1815.

48 PRONI, Dufferin and Ava papers, D/1071/F/E1/5, Caroline Norton to Helen Blackwood, Lady Dufferin [1849].

49 PRONI, Dufferin and Ava papers, D/1071/F/A1/7/1, Helen Blackwood, Lady Dufferin, to Frederick Blackwood, Lord Dufferin [31 May 1843].

50 Malcomson, *The pursuit of the heiress*, p. 30.

51 PRONI, Earl of Antrim papers, D/2977/1/2/4, copy of the last will and testament of Letitia Macdonnell, Marchioness of Antrim, 31 July 1799, extracted from the will registers of the Prerogative Court of Canterbury.

52 Malcomson, 'A woman scorned?', p. 3.

53 PRONI, Clanwilliam/Meade papers, D/3044/D/1/51, photocopy of a letter from Theodosia, Countess of Clanwilliam, to Robert Meade, 21 October 1808.

54 PRONI, Foster/Massereene papers, D/4084/2/5, last will and testament and probate of Anne Skeffington, Countess of Massereene, will dated 21 January 1800, probate granted 22 May 1812.

55 PRONI, Downshire papers, D/671/D14/2/24, last will and testament of Maria Hill, Marchionness of Downshire, 17 December 1846, probate granted 7 April 1855.

56 PRONI, Dufferin and Ava papers, D/1071/F/A4/17, the 'latest instructions' of Helen Hay, Lady Gifford [1866].

57 PRONI, Downshire papers, D/671/D14/2/221&b, last will and testament of Mary Hill, Marchioness of Downshire, 3 May 1832, probate granted September 1836.

58 PRONI, Eari of Antrim papers, D/2977/1/2/4, copy of the last will and testament of Letitia Macdonnell, Marchioness of Antrim, 31 July 1799, extracted from the will registers of the Prerogative Court of Canterbury.

59 PRONI, Abercorn papers, D/623/B/3/14, last will and testament of Ann Hamilton, Countess of Abercorn, dated 1771, administration granted 10 August 1776, extracted from the Court of Probate in the Prerogative Court of Canterbury.

60 PRONI, Earl of Antrim papers, D/2977/1/2/4, copy of the last will and testament of Letitia MacDonnell, Marchioness of Antrim, 31 July 1799, extracted from the will registers of the Prerogative Court of Canterbury.

61 PRONI, Downshire papers, D/671/17a&b, copy of the last will and testament of Ellinor Stewart, Countess of Blessington, dated 7 February 1774.

62 PRONI, Howard–Bury papers, T/3069/B/96, last will and testament of Catherine Maria, Countess of Charleville, extracted from the will registers of the Prerogative Court of Canterbury, probate granted 20 March 1851.

63 PRONI, Foster/Massereene papers, D/4084/2/5, last will and testament and probate of Anne Skeffington, Countess of Massereene, will dated 21 January 1800, codicil dated 21 January 1801, probate granted 22 May 1812; PRONI, Charity Brownlow Testamentary document, T/26, copy of the last will and testament and probate of Charity Brownlow, dated 1 December 1842, probate granted 16 May 1843.

64 Raughter, 'A natural tenderness', p. 60.

65 NAI, MFS 49, *A return of all charitable donations and bequests contained in the wills registered in the prerogative and consistorial offices of Dublin, January 1801 – January 1826* (Dublin, 1826).

66 David Dickson and Richard English, 'The La Touche dynasty', in Dickson (ed.), *The gorgeous mask*, pp. 17–29.

67 NAI, MFS 49, *A return of all charitable donations and bequests contained in the wills registered in the prerogative and consistorial offices of Dublin, from the 1st January 1827 to the 1st January 1828* (Dublin, 1828), detail of the last will and testament of Dame Elizabeth Hutchinson, dated 1827.

68 Richard T. Vann, 'Wills and the family in an English town: Banbury, 1550–1800', *Journal of Family History*, 4 (winter 1979), p. 347.

69 Erickson, *Women and property*, p. 207.

70 These figures are derived from a survey of marriages within the twenty families surveyed here, between 1750 and 1850, as listed in Gibb, *The complete peerage*.

71 Erickson, *Women and property*, p. 196.

72 Barbara J. Todd, 'The remarrying widow: a stereotype reconsidered' in Mary Prior (ed.), *Women in English society 1500–1800* (London: Methuen, 1985).

73 Staves, *Married women's separate property*, p. 50.

74 Erne accounts, 1776–99.

75 PRONI, Dartrey papers, D/3053/1/8/7, instructions for counsel to settle the draft deed of settlement on the marriage of Lord Baron Cremore with Augusta Stanley [1841].

76 Fitzgerald (ed.), *Correspondence of Emily Duchess of Leinster*, iii p. 94, Louisa Connolly to Emily Fitzgerald, 22 October 1774.

77 PRONI, Dufferin and Ava papers, D/1071/F/A2/4, copy of a letter from Helen Blackwood, Lady Dufferin to George Hay, Lord Gifford, dated 31 August/1 September 1842.

78 PRONI, Dufferin and Ava papers, D/1071/F/A2/4, copy of a letter from Helen, Countess of Gifford, to George Hay, Lord Tweedale [1862].
79 PRONI, Dufferin and Ava papers, D/1071/F/A1/10/1, Helen, Countess of Gifford, to Frederick Blackwood, Lord Dufferin [1863].
80 Letter from Helen, Countess of Gifford, to Lord Tweedale, dated 13 October 1862, quoted in Blackwood (ed.) *Songs*, p. 90.
81 PRONI, Dufferin and Ava papers, D/1071/F/A4/14, Helen, Countess of Gifford, to Mrs Nugent, 2 February 1863.
82 PRONI, Dufferin and Ava papers, D/1071/F/A4/4, copy of a letter from Helen, Countess of Gifford, to Antony Fonblanque, dated 26 December 1862.

Conclusion

In Ireland in the period covered here, elite women's experience of property was influenced both by public, statutory developments and by the concurrent evolution of private, family practice in the control and distribution of property. Such settlements formed the basis of the economic survival of all women – single, married and widowed – and also could override the impact that the common law fiction of coverture had on a married woman's ability to control her own property.

The experience that elite women had of property in Ireland had much in common with that of their English contemporaries. In practice, family property relations in Irish wealthy landed families were organised along similar foundations to those in England. The families surveyed here were among the wealthiest landowners in Ireland and had strong English connections. Many of the women in the sample families were English, and some families owned substantial estates in England as well as Ireland. All would have lived in England, and possibly abroad, at least part of every year. Coupled with this was the influence of English settlement practice, as it seems to have been the case that landowners on both sides of the Irish Sea were at least consulting the same conveyancing manuals.[1]

However, there were also important differences. Although property and marriage in Ireland was governed by English common law, statute law in Ireland developed along different lines. Irish statutory intervention in the marriage act predated similar developments in England, and the debate that accompanied the introduction of Hardwicke's Marriage Act in England was apparently absent in Ireland, in parliament and in public. Irish marriage law ensured that Irish fathers wielded greater authority over their children in the area of marriage and family property. However, as other historians have noted, the development of Irish marriage law reflected the main, and sometimes conflicting, concerns of the protestant parliamentary elite. Concern over clandestine marriages and the problem of the abduction of heiresses led to the introduction of legislation that increased the authority of fathers over their children and therefore bolstered the patriarchal family structure. At the same time, legislation overturned the patriarchal family structure in the case of protestant–catholic intermarriage.[2]

Although Irish families used similar methods to provide for the wives and children of a marriage, the experience that women had of property varied significantly between families, and also within families. Again, it is likely that there were more similarities between English and Irish families than there were differences. There were significant differences in the type and amount of provision made for women in the sample families. Although this reflects the differences in wealth between the families, it also suggests that much depended on individual personalities within them. For example, there was a wide variation in the ratio of portion to jointure, from 10 per cent to 40 per cent. Practice concerning the necessity of portion also varied. In many cases portion represented an essential element in the marriage negotiation process. However, this was not uniformly the case, and in some cases, such as on the marriage of Helen Sheridan and Price Blackwood, investments arranged after the marriage took the place of a portion brought by the bride.

Family settlements provide some insight into the structure of family property relations. In the families surveyed here the male head of the family, the husband or the father, exercised increasing power over the distribution of family property. The interests of women and younger sons were in most cases removed from the estate interest. This was most obvious in the case of jointure. All of the married women in this study expected to receive jointure instead of dower. Although in some cases this payment was equivalent to dower, the percentage of jointure to family estates was, in most cases, much less than what the equivalent in dower would have been.

The desire to consolidate landed and other estate property, such as houses and heirlooms, and the practice of bequeathing life interests in estate property effectively marginalised the interests of wives, daughters and younger sons from the family estate. The practice of settling minimum jointure on marriage added to the control exercised by the head of the family over his wife's share of the family property after his decease. Although some women were in fact well provided for, such generous provision depended upon the good will of their husbands.

The structure of Irish family property relations and the corresponding power balance within families is further apparent if we consider the provisions made for children of these marriages. Children had an equitable right to a share in the family estate, and all family settlements uniformly made provision for future children. Although there are examples among the sample families of daughters inheriting family estates in default of male heirs, for most daughters and sons provision was limited to settlements made on their parents' marriage, with additional interests being added by the last will and testament of their fathers. The dependence of children on their fathers' wills further suggests the patriarchal nature of Irish landed families. Contrary to the argument made by Lawrence Stone in his study of families in England, it is questionable that such provision was an indication that parental affection was the basis of property relations in eighteenth-century families.[3] As Susan Staves has noted: '[e]xtreme testamentary freedom violates the principle that parents, by nature, love all their children, and that they have a moral duty to provide for them'.[4]

The conclusions reached here regarding the patriarchal structure of Irish landed families are in accordance with patterns identified by recent histories of women and property in England. In her study on women in English landed families, Spring argues that women were increasingly marginalised from landed estates, and that this was facilitated by the use of settlements.[5] Staves's study of legal developments in married women's separate property in England also considers how settlements were instrumental in the marginalisation of women from family property in the eighteenth century.[6]

The roles taken by women in family property matters were, to a certain degree, influenced by acceptable boundaries of female behaviour, family relationships and circumstances. The position of married women was determined by their individual wealth and the type of property they owned. There was a variety of wealth, and therefore a variety of experience, among women in this sample. Some women among these families were very wealthy as a result of separate property arrangements, as well as being the recipients of substantial incomes from the main landed estates. The countesses of Antrim and the marchionesses of Downshire and Londonderry all received substantial incomes from separate estates, and all inherited landed property in default of male heirs. Although all families practised strict settlement, and therefore entailed the main family estates on male heirs, such life interests did accord these women increased authority within the family. As property owners in their own right during, as well as after, marriage, some women exercised a degree of influence on their estates and in local politics. However, this was not uniformly the case among the sample families. Income levels varied widely, with some women, such as Helen, Lady Dufferin, mainly dependent on jointure throughout their lives.

As *femes soles*, single women and widows legally exercised complete control over their property. However, spinsters and widows had a different relationship with the family estate. An unmarried daughter's provision was limited to the provision made for her in her father's will. Widows received regular jointure payments and possible additional interests based on estate property. The importance of non-kin in the testamentary bequests of single women suggests that they occupied a place outside the boundaries of the family. As in the case of wives, the status of widows within the family depended upon their independent wealth. A wealthy widow occupied a powerful position. However, the structure of the landed family increasingly excluded widows. In this period a widow could play a significant role as executor of her husband's last will and testament, and as guardian of the estate and persons of heirs to the family estate. However, sons and trustees increasingly took the place of widows as executors and as joint guardians of landed heirs in this period. The exclusion of widows from these roles is further evidence that women were being excluded from family estate business, and this suggests a diminishing of their power within the family.

There were common factors that applied to all women in relation to property. The roles that women took in relation to family financial matters were influenced by perceptions of acceptable female behaviour. Wives and widows acted as intermediaries for their husbands and sons in matters of finance and career, as well as politics. Wives negotiated family business and managed estates and households in their husbands' absence. Some widows managed estates on behalf of minor heirs. Single, married and widowed women all took part in informal and formal lending to family and friends. The loan of money to financially straitened family members also provided possibilities for the promotion of moral values and the control of family members. At the same time, loan networks were an important aspect of financial management within this class generally. It appears to have been acceptable for women with spare financial resources to lend substantial sums of money and receive significant amounts of money in interest payments, thus providing themselves with additional sources of income. As the example of Lady Erne's loan network suggests, such arrangements provided a viable alternative to banks in this period.

Charity was an important element in the property experience of women, whatever their marital status, and was in accordance with their elite status and prevailing notions of ideal feminine behaviour. This charity mainly took the form of private and localised poor relief, although landowners such as Frances Anne, Lady Londonderry, also interacted with the increased government involvement during the Great Famine, thus demonstrating the shifting boundaries at this time between public and private poor relief.

The place of women in the family structure is also indicated by the different testamentary behaviour displayed by men and women. When women bequeathed land, they did so to elder or younger sons, a practice that was in accordance with family interest in this survey. Also, apart from the main family estate, both men and women bequeathed according to the perceived need of the beneficiary. However, women tended to bequeath to a wider family and non-kin network. This trend is more pronounced in the wills of single women, possibly reflecting the distance of the testators from family affairs. The care that some women took over bequeathing their personal property also highlights the fact that on a woman's death, especially if she was single, there were no obvious beneficiaries.

The varied experience that women in the families surveyed here had of property is significant as it indicates the range of factors that influenced family property relations. Legal, familial and social factors, as well as the individual wealth of women determined the type of property owned and controlled by women, and their place in the power structures of Irish landed families. Although estate matters were undoubtedly important in such property relations, this was only part of the picture. If we consider the role of marriage settlements, last wills and testaments and separate property arrangements alongside evidence of practice, such as informal loan arrangements, guardianship and the vagaries of family relations, a more complex picture emerges.

Notes

1 Orlando Bridgeman's *Conveyances* was not published in Ireland, yet it is listed in an inventory of the library at Castle Ward, County Down, in 1813.
2 O'Dowd, 'Women and the law', p. 96.
3 Stone, *The family, sex and marriage*, pp. 243–4.
4 Susan Staves, 'Resentment or resignation? Dividing the spoils among daughters and younger sons' in John Brewer and Susan Staves (eds.), *Early modern conceptions of property* (London: Routledge, 1995), p. 199.
5 Spring, *Law, land and family*.
6 Staves, *Married women's separate property*.

Appendix A

Family biographies[1]

Note: * = see Appendix B for details.

Alexander (Caledon)

After a career in the East India Company's civil service, James Alexander (1730–1802), the future first Lord Caledon, returned to Ireland in 1772 when he purchased the Caledon estates. In 1790 he was created Baron Caledon, in 1797 Viscount Caledon, and in 1800 Earl of Caledon. In 1774 he married Anne Crawford (d. 1777). The first Earl was succeeded by his only son, Du Pre Alexander, Earl of Caledon (1777–1839). In 1811 the second Earl married Catherine Freeman (1786–1863).* He was succeeded by his only son, James Du Pre Alexander, Earl of Caledon (1812–55). In 1845 the third Earl married Jane Grimston (1825–88).

Landed estate: counties Tyrone and Armagh

Main Irish residence: Castle Caledon, County Tyrone

Blackwood (Dufferin)

The Blackwood family was of Scottish origin, and settled in County Down in the early seventeenth century. In 1751 John Blackwood (d. 1799) married Dorcas Stevenson (1726–1807),* the eldest daughter and, the heiress of James Stevenson of County Down. In 1800 Dorcas was created Baroness Dufferin and Clandeboye; she was succeeded by her eldest son, James Stevenson Blackwood, Lord Dufferin (1755–1836). In 1801 Lord Dufferin married Anna Dorothea Foster (d. 1865),* the daughter of Margaretta, Viscountess Ferrard, and John Foster, Baron Oriel of Ferrard. In 1836 he was succeeded by his brother, Hans Blackwood, Lord Dufferin (1758–1839), who had married first Mehetable Temple (d. 1798) and second Elizabeth Finlay (d. 1843). He was succeeded by his eldest surviving son of his first marriage, Price Blackwood, Lord Dufferin (1794–1841). In 1825 the fourth Lord

Dufferin married Helen Selina Sheridan (1807–67).* Price Blackwood was succeeded by his only son, Frederick Blackwood, first Marquess of Dufferin and Ava, as a minor, in 1847.

Landed estate: County Down

Main Irish residence: Clandeboye, Bangor, County Down

Boyle (Shannon)

Francis Boyle (1623–1680), the first Viscount Shannon, was a younger son of Richard Boyle, Earl of Cork, and was granted land by Charles II. The Boyles were created Earls of Shannon in 1756. In 1715 Henry Boyle (d. 1764), first Earl of Shannon, married firstly Catherine Coote, daughter of Catherine Sandys. He married secondly, in 1726, Henrietta Boyle, daughter of the third Earl of Cork. The fifth son of the first Earl was Robert Boyle-Walsingham, who married Charlotte Hanbury* in 1760, the daughter and co-heir of Sir Charles Hanbury Williams, and eventually inherited the barony of de Ros, which passed on her death to her daughter Charlotte, Lady Fitzgerald. In 1763 Richard Boyle, second Earl of Shannon (1727–1807), married Catherine Ponsonby (1746–1827), daughter of Sir John Ponsonby, speaker of the Irish House of Commons, and Elizabeth (Cavendish). He was succeeded by his eldest surviving son, Henry Boyle (1771–1842). The third Earl of Shannon married Sarah Hyde (d. 1820), fourth daughter of John Hyde of County Cork and Sarah (Burton) in 1798. Along with two sons, six daughters were born of the marriage: Charlotte (d. 1880s?), Sarah (d. 1884), Louisa Grace (d. 1856), Jane (d. 1876), Elizabeth (d. 1886) and Katherine Boyle (d. 1867). Henry, Lord Shannon, was succeeded by his eldest surviving son, Richard Boyle (1809–68). In 1832 the fourth Earl of Shannon married Emily Henrietta Seymour (d. 1887), daughter of Lord George Seymour and Isabella (Hamilton).

Landed estate: County Cork

Main Irish residence: Castlemartyr, County Cork

Browne (Kenmare)

The Brownes were a prominent catholic landowning family from the late sixteenth century, and were created Viscounts Kenmare in 1798 and Earls of Kenmare in 1801. Valentine Browne, Earl of Kenmare (1754–1812), married firstly Charlotte Dillon (1755–82)* in 1777 and secondly Mary Aylmer (d. 1806) in 1785. He was succeeded by his eldest son by his second marriage, also Valentine Browne (1788–1853). The second

Earl of Kenmare married Augusta Anne Wilmot (d. 1873) in 1816, and was created Baron Kenmare of Castlerosse in the UK peerage.

Landed estate: counties Kerry and Cork, Limerick

Main Irish residence: Killarney House, County Kerry

Brownlow (Lurgan)

The Brownlow family's connection with Ireland dates from the sixteenth-century plantation of Ulster. William Brownlow of Lurgan (d. 1794) married firstly, in 1754 Judith Letitia Meredyth (d. 1763), and secondly, in 1765, Catherine Hall (d. 1843),* the daughter of Roger Hall of Mount Hall, County Down. He was succeeded by his eldest son, William Brownlow (1755–95), who in 1795 married Charity Forde,* daughter of Matthew Forde of Seaforde, County Down. William Brownlow died without issue and was succeeded by his brother, Charles Brownlow (1757–1822). Charles Brownlow married Caroline Ashe (d. 1838), of Bath, in 1785. He was succeeded by his eldest surviving son, Charles Brownlow (1795–1847), who was created first Baron Lurgan in 1839. Lord Lurgan married firstly Lady Mary Bligh (1796–1823),* daughter of the Earl and Countess of Darnley, and secondly Jane MacNeill (d. 1878),* daughter of Roderick MacNeill of Barra, Inverness.

Landed estate: counties Armagh, Down and Monaghan

Main Irish residence: Brownlow House, Lurgan, County Armagh

Chichester (Donegall)

The Chichesters were created Earls of Donegall in 1647. Arthur Chichester (1739–99) was created Marquess of Donegall in 1791. He married firstly Anne Hamilton (1738–80), the daughter of the Duke of Hamilton; secondly Charlotte Moore (d. 1789), widow of Thomas Moore; and thirdly Barbara Godfrey (d. 1829),* daughter of the Reverend Luke Godfrey. The first Marquess was succeeded in 1799 by his eldest son, George Augustus Chichester (1769–1844). The second Marquess married Anna May (d. 1849) in 1795, although the marriage was afterwards declared void owing to her illegitimacy. The Donegall landed estate was one of the largest in Ireland, estimated at a quarter of a million acres. In the period of the second Marquess it was also one of the most heavily indebted.

Landed estate: counties Donegal, Antrim, Londonderry

Main Irish residence: Belfast Castle, Belfast, County Antrim

Cole (Enniskillen)

The Cole family estate was based on seventeenth-century plantation grants. In 1760 the Coles were created Lords Enniskillen, in 1776 Viscounts Enniskillen and in 1789 Earls of Enniskillen. In 1763 William Willoughby Cole, the first Earl of Enniskillen (1736–1803), married Anne Lowry-Corry (1742–1802),* the sister of the Earl of Belmore and daughter of Galbraith Lowry and Sarah (Corry). The first Earl was succeeded by his eldest son, John Willoughby Cole, Earl of Enniskillen (1768–1840). In 1805 the second Earl married Charlotte Paget (1781–1817), sister of the Marquess of Anglesby and daughter of the Earl of Uxbridge. The second Earl of Enniskillen was succeeded by his eldest son, William Willoughby Cole, Earl of Enniskillen (1807–86).

Landed estate: County Fermanagh and Wiltshire, England

Main Irish residence: Florence Court, Enniskillen

Conolly

The Conolly family was first established at Castletown in 1709 by William Conolly (1662–1729), speaker of the Irish House of Commons, 1715–29. The estate was inherited in 1729 by Speaker Conolly's nephew, William Conolly (d. 1754). William Conolly's son Thomas Conolly (1734–1803) inherited the estate on his father's death in 1754. In 1758 Thomas Conolly married Lady Louisa Lennox (1743–1821),* daughter of the Duke and Duchess of Richmond and sister of Emily Fitzgerald, Duchess of Leinster.* The Conollys are the only example of a non-peerage family in this study, but in 1758 Thomas Conolly was regarded as one of the wealthiest landowners in Ireland.

Landed estate: counties Donegal, Londonderry, Leitrim, Fermanagh, Roscommon, Westmeath, Meath, Kildare, King's County

Main Irish residence: Castletown, Celbridge, County Kildare

Creighton (Erne)

The Creighton family's connection with Ireland dates from the seventeenth century. In 1768 Abraham Creighton was created Baron Erne of Crom Castle (c.1700–1772). Lord Erne married firstly in 1729, Elizabeth Rogerson (d. 1760) and secondly, in 1762, Jane Acheson (d. 1800),* widow of Arthur Acheson. The first Lord Erne was succeed by his eldest surviving son, John Creighton (c.1738–1828), who was created Viscount Erne in 1781 and Earl Erne of Crom Castle in 1789. The first Earl Erne married firstly Catherine Howard (d. 1775), daughter of the Bishop of Elphin, in 1761, and secondly, in 1776, Mary Caroline Hervey (d. 1842),* daughter of the Bishop of Derry. He was succeeded by his eldest son, Abraham Creighton (d. 1842), who died unmarried. He was succeeded by his nephew, John Creighton, Earl Erne of Crom Castle (1802–85). The third Earl married Selina Griselda Beresforde (1804–84) in 1837.

Landed estate: counties Fermanagh, Donegal, Mayo and Sligo

Main Irish residence: Crom Castle, County Fermanagh

Dawson (Dartrey)

The Dawsons were created Barons Cremorne of Castle Dawson in 1797. The family estates in County Monaghan date from the seventeenth century. Thomas Dawson, Lord Cremorne (1725–1813), married firstly Anne Fermor (1733–69) and secondly Philadelphia Hannah (d. 1826). His great-nephew, Richard Thomas Dawson, Lord Cremorne (1788–1827), inherited the family title and estates and married Anne Whaley (d. 1885) in 1815. His second but only surviving son, Richard Dawson, (1817–97), married Augusta Stanley (1823–87) in 1841. This Richard Dawson was created Lord Dartrey in 1847.

Landed estate: counties Armagh, Monaghan, Waterford, Louth as well as English estates in Devon

Main Irish residence: Dartrey House, County Monaghan

Fitzgerald (Leinster)

The Fitzgerald family's connection with Ireland dates from the eleventh century. Known as the Geraldines, the Fitzgeralds, Earls of Kildare, were among the first peers of Ireland, and one of the oldest surviving families of the Irish aristocracy. James Fitzgerald, twentieth Earl of Kildare (1722–73), was created Duke of Leinster in 1766. In 1746/47 he married Emilia (Emily) Mary Lennox (1731–1814),* daughter of the Duke and Duchess of Richmond and sister of Louisa Conolly.* James Duke of Leinster was succeeded by his eldest son, William Robert Fitzgerald, Duke of Leinster (1748–1804), in 1773. William, Duke of Leinster, married Emilia Olivia Usher St George (d. 1798) in 1775.

Landed estate: counties Kildare and Meath

Main Irish residences: Carton, Maynooth, County Kildare; Leinster House, Dublin

Hamilton (Abercorn)

The Hamilton family's connection to Ireland dates from the grant of land made to James Hamilton, first Earl of Abercorn (d. 1618), in the early seventeenth century. The Hamiltons were created Lords Abercorn in 1603 and Earls of Abercorn in 1606, both in the Scottish peerage. John James Hamilton (1756–1818) was created Marquess of Abercorn in the Irish peerage in 1794. John James Hamilton, Marquess of Abercorn, married three times. His first wife, Catherine Copely (d. 1791), predeceased him, and he divorced his second wife, Cecil Hamilton, by private Act of Parliament on the grounds of adultery in 1799. His third wife, Lady Ann Hatton (1763–1827), was a widow. John James survived his only son and heir by his first marriage, James, Viscount Hamilton (1786–1814). In 1809 Viscount Hamilton married Harriet Douglas (Gordon) (d. 1833),* daughter of John Douglas and Frances Lascelles. The eldest son of this marriage, James Hamilton (1811–85), succeeded to the Abercorn estate and title on the death of the first Marquess in 1818.

Landed estates: counties Tyrone and Donegal, and Scotland

Main Irish residence: Barons Court, County Tyrone

Hill (Downshire)

The Hill family's connection with Ireland dates from the sixteenth century when Moseys Hill acquired a grant of land in County Antrim. In 1751 the Hills were created Viscounts Kilwarlin; in 1772 Viscounts Fairford and Earls of Hillsborough; and in 1789 Marquesses of Downshire. Wills Hill, the first Marquess of Downshire (1718–93), married firstly Margaretta Fitzgerald (1729–66), and secondly Mary Bilson-Legge (1726–1780). He was succeeded by his son Arthur Hill, Lord Fairford (1753–1801). In 1786 the second Marquess married Mary Sandys (d. 1836),* only daughter and heiress of Martin Sandys and Mary (Blundell). He was succeeded by his eldest son, Arthur Blundell Sandys Hill (1788–1845), while he was still a minor. The Downshire estates were managed by Mary, Marchioness of Downshire, during the minority. In 1811, the third Marquess married Maria Hickman (1790–1855),* first daughter of the fifth Earl of Plymouth and Sarah (Archer).

Landed estates: counties Down, Wicklow, King's County, Antrim and Kildare

Main Irish residence: Hillsborough Castle, County Down

MacDonnell (Antrim)

The MacDonnells were created Earls of Antrim in 1620 when Randal MacSorley MacDonnell received a grant of land from James I. Randall William MacDonnell, sixth Earl of Antrim (1794–91), married Letitia Trevor (d. 1801)* in 1774. He died without male issue, and devised the Antrim estate to his three daughters, Anne Katherine,* Letitia* and Charlotte MacDonnell,* as well as arranging for the special creation of the Earldom of Antrim to pass to daughters.

Landed estates: counties Antrim and Londonderry

Main Irish residence: Glenarm Castle, County Antrim

Meade (Clanwilliam)

The Meades were of Gaelic descent, and were established in County Cork from the fourteenth century. In 1765 John Meade (1744–1800) married Theodosia Hawkins-Magill (1743–1817),* and in 1766 he was created Viscount Clanwilliam, advancing to Earl of Clanwilliam in 1776. The Meades were created Barons Clanwilliam in the UK peerage in 1828. In 1799 the Clanwilliam estates were estimated at £14,000 per annum, but their fortune was dissipated in the following years, and in 1805 the entail of the Tipperary estates was broken and sold.

Landed estate: counties Tipperary and Down

Main Irish residence: Gill Hall, Dromore, County Down

Skeffington (Massereene)

The Skeffington family's connection with Ireland dates from the seventeenth century and Sir Hugh Clotworthy's involvement with the nine years' war in Ulster. In 1660 his son and heir, Sir John Clotworthy (d. 1665), was created Viscount Massereene. Clotworthy Skeffington (d. 1757), fifth Viscount, was created Earl of Massereene in 1756. He married firstly Anne Daniel, daughter of the Reverend Richard Daniel, and secondly, in 1741, Anne Eyre (c.1716–1805),* daughter of Henry Eyre, of Derbyshire. He was succeeded by his eldest son from his second marriage, Clotworthy Skeffington (c.1742–1805). The second Earl of Massereene married Marie Anne Barcier (d. 1838) while imprisoned in Paris. After her death he married Elizabeth Lane (d. 1838). After the second Earl's death in 1805, the Massereene title and estates passed to his brother Henry Skeffngton (c.1744–1811), who died unmarried. He was succeeded by his brother, Chichester Skeffington (c.1746–1816). The fourth Earl married Harriet Jocelyn (d. 1831),* daughter of the Earl of Roden, in 1780. The only daughter and heir of the marriage was Harriet Skeffington (d. 1831).* In 1810 she married Thomas Foster (d. 1843), the future Viscount Ferrard. On the death of the fourth Earl, Harriet inherited the Massereene title and estate.

Landed estates: counties Antrim, Louth, Meath and Monaghan

Main Irish residence: Antrim Castle; Oriel Temple, County Louth

Stewart (Londonderry)

The Stewarts settled in Ireland in the seventeenth century. They were created Marquesses of Londonderry in 1816. Robert Stewart, first Marquess of Londonderry (1739–1821), married firstly Sarah Francis Seymour Conway (1747–70) in 1766 and secondly Frances Pratt (d. 1833) in 1775. He was succeeded by his eldest surviving son, Robert Stewart (1769–1822), who married Amelia Anne Hobart (1772–1829),* the daughter of the Earl and Countess of Buckinghamshire, in 1794. The second Marquess committed suicide in 1822 and was succeeded by his half-brother, Charles Stewart (1778–1854). The third Marquess married firstly Catherine Bligh (1774–1812) in 1804. In 1819 he married secondly Frances Anne Emily Vane-Tempest (1800–65),* the only daughter, and heiress, of Henry Vane-Tempest and Anne Catherine, Countess of Antrim.

Landed estate: counties Down, Londonderry and Donegal, English estate in County Durham

Main Irish residence: Mount Stewart, Newtownards, County Down

Ward (Bangor)

The Wards of Castle Ward, County Down, were created Viscounts Bangor in 1781. In 1747 the first Lord Bangor, Bernard Ward (1719–81), married Ann Hawkins-Magill (1728–89),* widow of Robert Hawkins-Magill of Gill Hall, County Down, and mother of Theodosia Meade, Countess of Clanwilliam.* There were seven children of the marriage, three sons, Nicholas, Edward and Colonel Robert Ward, and four daughters: Anne Catherine,* Sophia,* Sarah and Emilia.* Lord and Lady Bangor separated in 1766, and Lady Bangor left Ireland to live in Bath, where she died in 1789. Bernard, Lord Bangor, died in 1789 and was succeeded by his eldest son, Nicholas. Nicholas, Lord Bangor, was decared insane in 1781 and died unmarried and without issue in 1827. He was succeeded by Edward Southwell Ward, the eldest son of Edward Ward and his wife Arabella.*

Landed estate: County Down

Main Irish residence: Castle Ward, Strangford, County Down

Westenra (Rossmore)

The landed estate of the Westenra family, Barons Rossmore, came into the possession of the family by the marriage of Robert Cunninghame (d. 1801) of Mount Kennedy, County Wicklow, to Elizabeth Murray (d. 1824), second daughter of Colonel John Murray and Elizabeth Blayney, widow of the seventh Lord Blayney; Cunninghame was created Baron Rossmore of Monaghan in 1796. After his death in 1801 he was succeeded by Warner William Westenra (1765–1842), the nephew of his late wife. In 1791 the second Lord Rossmore married firstly Mary Anne (Mariane) Walsh (d. 1807), daughter of Charles and Sarah Walsh of Tipperary. In 1819 he married secondly Lady Augusta Charteris (d. 1840),* youngest daughter of Sarah and Francis Charteris-Wemyss, Lord Elcho. Warner, Lord Rossmore, was succeeded by his eldest son, Henry Robert Westenra (1792–1860). In 1820 the third Lord Rossmore married firstly Anne Douglas-Hamilton (d. 1844), the illegitimate daughter of the Duke of Hamilton. After her death, he married in 1846 his cousin Josephine Julia Helen Lloyd (d. 1912), daughter of Henry Lloyd of County Tipperary.

Landed estate: County Monaghan

Main residence: Rossmore Park, County Monaghan

Wingfield (Powerscourt)

The Wingfield family's connection to Ireland dated from the sixteenth century. In 1609 Richard Wingfield (d. 1634) was granted land for service as Marshal of Ireland, and in 1617 he was created Viscount Powerscourt. Richard Wingfield (1730–88), the fifth Viscount Powerscourt, married Amelia Stratford (d. 1831),* daughter of John Stratford, Earl of Aldborough, and Martha O'Neale, in 1760. He was succeeded by his eldest son, Richard Wingfield (1762–1809). In 1789 the sixth Viscount Powerscourt married firstly Catherine Meade (1770–93), daughter of John Meade, Earl of Clanwilliam, and Theodosia, Countess of Clanwilliam.* After her death, he married in 1796 Isabella Brownlow (d. 1848), daughter of William Brownlow and his second wife Catherine (Hall). The sixth Viscount was succeeded by his eldest son by his first marriage, Richard Wingfield (1790–1823). In 1813 the seventh Viscount Powerscourt married firstly Francis Theodosia Jocelyn (1795–1820), daughter of Robert Jocelyn, Earl of Roden, and Frances Theodosia (Bligh), Countess of Roden. In 1822 he married secondly Theodosia Howard (d. 1836), daughter of Hugh Howard and Alice, Countess of Wicklow.

Landed estate: counties Wicklow, Wexford and Dublin

Main Irish residence: Powerscourt, Enniskerry, County Wicklow

Notes

1 The biographical information in this appendix was compiled from Gibb (ed.), *The complete peerage* and from family papers. All peerage details refer to the Irish peerage unless stated otherwise.

Appendix B

Select biographical index of women

Anna Blackwood, Lady Dufferin (d. 1865)
Born Anna Foster, she was the daughter of Margaretta, Viscountess Ferrard, and John Foster, Baron Oriel of Ferrard. In 1801 she married James Stevenson Blackwood, Lord Dufferin (1755–1836).

Dorcas Stevenson Blackwood, Baroness Dufferin and Clandeboye (1726–1807)
Born Dorcas Stevenson, she was the eldest daughter and the heiress of James Stevenson of County Down. In 1751 she married John Blackwood (d. 1799). In 1800 Dorcas was created Baroness Dufferin and Clandeboye, and she was succeeded by her eldest son, James Stevenson Blackwood, Lord Dufferin (1755–1836).

Helen Blackwood, Lady Dufferin (Countess of Gifford) (1807–67)
Born Helen Selina Sheridan, she was the daughter of Thomas Sheridan and Caroline Henrietta (Callendar), granddaughter of Richard Brinsley Sheridan, playwright and politician, and the sister of Carline Norton and Georgiana Seymour, Duchess of Somerset. In 1825 she married Price Blackwood (1794–1841), the future fourth Lord Dufferin. On Lord Dufferin's death in 1841 she became guardian of the person of the only child of the marriage, Frederick Blackwood, the fifth Lord Dufferin. In 1862 she married secondly George Hay, Lord Gifford.

Lady Charlotte Boyle (d. 1880s?)
Eldest unmarried daughter of Henry Boyle, third Earl of Shannon, and Sarah Hyde.

Lady Elizabeth Boyle (d. 1886)
Younger unmarried daughter of Henry Boyle, third Earl of Shannon, and Sarah Hyde.

Lady Jane Boyle (d. 1876)
Younger unmarried daughter of Henry Boyle, third Earl of Shannon, and Sarah Hyde.

Lady Katherine Boyle (d. 1867)
Youngest unmarried daughter of Henry Boyle, third Earl of Shannon, and Sarah Hyde.

Lady Louisa Grace Boyle (d. 1856)
Younger unmarried daughter of Henry Boyle, third Earl of Shannon, and Sarah Hyde.

Lady Sarah Boyle (d. 1884)
Younger unmarried daughter of Henry Boyle, third Earl of Shannon, and Sarah Hyde.

Charlotte Boyle-Walsingham
Born Charlotte Hanbury, she was the daughter, and co-heir of Sir Charles Hanbury Williams and eventually inherited the barony of de Ros, which passed on her death to her daughter Charlotte, Lady Henry Fitzgerald. In 1760 she married Robert Boyle-Walsingham, the fifth son of Henry Boyle, first Earl of Shannon.

Charlotte Browne, Countess of Kenmare (1755–82)
Born Charlotte Dillon, she was the fourth daughter of Henry Dillon, Viscount Dillon of Costello-Galen. In 1777 she married, as his first wife, Valentine Browne, Earl of Kenmare (1754–1812).

Catherine Brownlow (d. 1843)
Born Catherine Hall, she was the daughter of Roger Hall of Mount Hall, County Down. In 1765 she married, as his second wife, William Brownlow of Lurgan (d. 1794).

Charity Brownlow
Born Charity Forde, she was the daughter of Matthew Forde of Seaforde, County Down. She married in 1795 William Brownlow (1755–1815), uncle of the future first Lord Lurgan.

Mary Brownlow (1796–1823)
Born Lady Mary Bligh, she was the daughter of the Earl and Countess of Darnley. In 1822 she married her cousin, Charles Brownlow (1795–1847), the future first Lord Lurgan. She predeceased her husband.

Jane Brownlow, Lady Lurgan (d. 1878)
Born Jane MacNeill, she was the daughter of Roderick MacNeill of
Barra, Inverness. In 1828 she married, as his second wife, Charles
Brownlow (1795–1847), the future first Lord Lurgan. After the death of
her husband in 1847, she was guardian of the persons and estates of her
children, including the heir to the estate, Charles Brownlow, second Lord
Lurgan (1831–82).

Louisa Conolly (1743–1821)
Born Louisa Lennox, she was the daughter of the Duke and Duchess of
Richmond and sister of Emily Fitzgerald, Duchess of Leinster. In 1758
she married Thomas Conolly (1734–1803), nephew of Speaker Conolly
and heir to the Conolly estates.

Barbara Chichester, Marchioness of Donegall (d. 1829)
Born Barbara Godfrey, she was the daughter of the Reverend Luke
Godfrey and Mary (Cope). In 1790 she married, as his third wife, Arthur
Chichester, Marquess of Donegall.

Jane Creighton, Countess of Erne (d. 1800)
Born Jane King, she was the daughter of John and Rebecca King, of
Charlestown, County Roscommon, She married firstly Arthur Acheson
(d. 1758), and secondly, in 1762, Abraham Creighton, Baron Erne of
Crom Castle (c.1700–1772), as his second wife.

Mary Creighton, Countess of Erne (d. 1842)
Born Mary Caroline Hervey, she was the first daughter of Frederick
Hervey, Earl of Bristol and Bishop of Derry. In 1776 she married, as
his second wife, John Creighton (c.1738–1828), Earl Erne of Crom
Castle.

Anne Eyre (Skeffington) (c.1716–1805)
She was the daughter and heiress of Henry Eyre of Derbyshire, the second
wife of Clotworthy Skeffington, Earl of Massereene, and the mother of
the second Earl of Massereene, Clotworthy Skeffington.

Emily Fitzgerald, Duchess of Leinster (1731–1814)
Born Emilia Mary Lennox, she was the second surviving daughter of the
Duke and Duchess of Richmond, and sister of Louisa Conolly. In
1746/47 she married James Fitzgerald, Earl of Kildare (1722–73) and
later second Duke of Leinster. After her husband's death she married secondly William Ogilvie, her children's tutor (1740–1832).

Harriet Gordon, Countess of Aberdeen (d. 1833)

Born Harriet Douglas, she was the daughter of John Douglas and Frances Lascelles. In 1809 she married James, Viscount Hamilton (1786–1814), son of John James Hamilton, Marquess of Abercorn. Her husband's father survived him, and Harriet's eldest son of her marriage to Viscount Hamilton, James Hamilton (1811–85), Marquess of Abercorn, succeeded his grandfather to the Abercorn title and estates. In 1815 Harriet married secondly George Gordon, fourth Earl of Aberdeen, with whom she acted as joint guardian to the children of her first marriage.

Theodosia Meade, Countess of Clanwilliam (1743–1817)

The daughter and heiress of Robert Hawkins-Magill and Anne Bligh, his second wife (see Ann Ward). In August 1765 she married John Meade (1744–1800), who was created Earl of Clanwilliam in 1776.

Maria Hill, Marchioness of Downshire (1790–1855)

Born Maria Hickman, she was the first daughter of Other Hickman Windsor, the fifth Earl of Plymouth, and Sarah Archer. In 1811 she married Arthur Blundell Sandys Hill (1788–1845), the third Marquess of Downshire.

Mary Hill, Marchioness of Downshire (d. 1836)

Born Mary Sandys, she was the only daughter and heiress of Martin Sandys and Mary (Blundell). She was the heiress of her mother, her father and her uncle, Edwin Sandys, Baron Oombersley. In 1786 she married Arthur Hill, Lord Fairford (1753–1801), the future second Marquess of Downshire. On her husband's death in 1801 she managed the Downshire estates during the minority of her eldest son, Arthur Blundell Sandys Hill (1788–1845), the third Marquess of Downshire.

Anne Lowry, Viscountess of Enniskillen (1742–1802)

Born Anne Lowry, she was the daughter of Galbraith Lowry and Sarah Corry and the sister of Armar Lowry-Corry, Earl of Belmore. In 1763 she married WilliamWilloughby Cole, the first Earl of Enniskillen (1736–1803).

Anne Katherine MacDonnell, Countess of Antrim (1778–1834)

She was the eldest surviving daughter Randall MacDonnell, Earl of Antrim, and inherited a portion of the Antrim estate, and title, on her father's death in 1791. Lady Antrim married firstly, in 1799, Henry Vane-Tempest, and secondly, in 1817, Edmund Phelps (d. 1852), who took the name MacDonnell. She was the mother of Frances Ann Vane-Tempest, Marchioness of Londonderry.

Letitia Mary MacDonnell (b. 1778)
She was the twin sister of Anne Katherine MacDonnell and the unmarried daughter of Randall MacDonnell, Earl of Antrim.

Charlotte MacDonnell (Kerr) (1779–1835)
She was the youngest daughter of Randall MacDonnell, Earl of Antrim. Along with her sister, Anne Katherine MacDonnell, she inherited a portion of the Antrim estate, on the death of her father. She inherited the Antrim title on the death of her sister in 1834. She married Lord Mark Kerr (1776–1840) in 1799.

Emily Montgomery
Born Emilia Ward, she was the youngest daughter of Bernard Ward, the first Lord Bangor, and Ann Hawkins-Magill. She married the Reverend Hugh Montgomery, one of the committee of the estate of Nicholas Ward, Lord Bangor.

Harriet Skeffington, Countess of Massereene (d. 1831)
Born Harriet Skeffington, she was the daughter of Robert Jocelyn, Earl of Roden. In 1780 she married Chichester Skeffington, Earl of Massereene (c.1746–1816). The only daughter of their marriage Harriet Skeffington, inherited the Massereene title and estate.

Harriet Skeffington, Countess of Massereene (d. 1831)
Born Harriet Skeffington, she was the daughter of Chichester Skeffington, Earl of Massereene (c.1746–1816), and Harriet (née Jocelyn), Countess of Massereene (d. 1831). In 1810 she married Thomas Foster (d. 1843), the future Viscount Ferrard. On the death of the fourth Earl, Harriet inherited the Massereene title and estate.

Amelia Stewart, Marchioness of Londonderry (1772–1829)
Born Amelia Anne Hobart, she was the daughter of the Earl and Countess of Buckinghamshire. In 1794 she married Robert Stewart, Viscount Castlereagh and the furture second Marquess of Londonderry. Her husband committed suicide in 1822.

Letitia Trevor (MacDonnell) (d. 1801)
Daughter of Harvey Morres, Viscount Mountmorres, and widow of Arthur Trevor, she married Randall MacDonnell, Earl of Antrim, in 1774.

Frances Anne Vane-Tempest Stewart, Marchioness of Londonderry (1800–65)
Born Frances Anne Emily Vane-Tempest, she was the only daughter, and

the heiress, of Henry Vane-Tempest and Anne Catherine MacDonnell, Countess of Antrim. In 1819 she married Charles Stewart (1778–1854), Lord Stewart and the future third Marquess of Londonderry, as his second wife. She owned estates in counties Antrim and Durham, and was prominent in local politics, as well as being regarded as a leading Tory hostess in London.

Ann Catherine Ward
Unmarried eldest daughter of Bernard Ward, Lord Bangor, and Ann Hawkins-Magill.

Anne Ward, Lady Bangor (1728–89)
Born Anne Bligh, she was the daughter of John Bligh, first Earl of Darnley, and Theodosia Hyde, daughter of Edward Hyde, third Earl of Clarendon. She was the second wife of Robert Hawkins-Magill of Gill Hall, County Down (d. 1745). She married Bernard Ward in 1747. They separated in 1766.

Arabella Ward (d. 1813)
Born Arabella Crosbie, she was the daughter of William Crosbie, first Earl of Glandore. Some time in the 1780s she married Edward Ward (d. 1812), second son of Bernard Ward, Lord Bangor, and heir to his brother, Nicholas Ward, Lord Bangor. After Nicholas, Lord Bangor, was declared insane, Edward Ward acted as committee of the demesne at Castle Ward until his death in 1812, after which time Arabella acted in his place until her death in 1813. The eldest surviving son of her marriage, Edward Southwell Ward (1790–1837), became the third Lord Bangor on the death of Nicholas Lord Bangor, in 1827.

Sophia Ward
Unmarried younger daughter of Bernard Ward, Lord Bangor, and Anne Hawkins-Magill.

Amelia Wingfield, Viscountess Powerscourt (d. 1831)
Born Amelia Stratford, she was a daughter of John Stratford, Earl of Aldborough, and Martha O'Neale. In 1760 she married Richard Wingfield (1730–88), the fifth Viscount Powerscourt.

Augusta (Charteris) Westenra, Lady Rossmore (d. 1840)
Born Augusta Charteris, she was the youngest daughter of Sarah and Francis Charteris-Wemyss, Lord Elcho. In 1819 she married, as his second wife, William Westenra (1765–1842), the second Lord Rossmore.

Appendix C

Provisions made for women on marriage, 1747–1845[1]

Name	Date	Portion	Jointure settled	Actual jointure in will	Pin money	Additional income interests settled at marriage	Additional income interests settled by will	Family estate rental[2]
James Fitzgerald, Earl of Kildare, m. Emily Lennox[3]	1747		£3,000	£4,000				£12,000[4]
Sir John Blackwood m. Dorcas Stevenson[5]	1751	Land 5,400 acres	£500	£600		Life interest in entailed land		£10,000[6]
Alexander McDonnell, Earl of Antrim, m. Catherine Taylor[7]	1755	£5,000	£1,000	Died				£9,774[8]
Thomas Conolly m. Louisa Lennox[9]	1758	£10,000	£2,500	£2,500 +			Life interest in £25,000[10] entailed land	
William Willoughby Cole, Earl of Enniskillen, m. Anne Lowry[11]	1763		£1,200	Died			Interest in investment with power of appointment + capital interest in land	£6,430[12]

Name	Year					One half share of principal sum and dividends of investment	
Richard Boyle, Earl of Shannon, m. Catherine Ponsonby[13]	1765						
William Brownlow m. Catherine Hall[14]	1765	£1,000	£500	£2,500		One half share of principal sum and dividends of investment	£9,000[15]
Robert Stewart, Marquess of Londonderry, m. Sarah Conway[16]	1766	£6,500	£1,500	died	£300		£7,500[17]
Thomas Dawson, Lord Cremorne, m. Philadelphia Hannah[18]	1770		£1,200	Life interest in land			£12,000[19]
Robert Stewart, Marquess of Londonderry, m. Frances Pratt[20]	1773	£5,000	£1,000	£3,200	£300		£7,500[21]
Randall McDonnell, Earl of Antrim, m. Letitia Trevor[22]	1774	£10,000	£1,000	£1,500			£9,774[23]
John Creighton, Earl of Erne of Crom Castle, m. Mary Caroline Hervey[24]	1776			£600+		Life interest in freehold land	£8,246[25]
Valentine Browne, Earl of Kenmare, m. Charlotte Dillon[26]	1777	£5,000	£1,000	Died	£300		£10,096[27]
John James Hamilton m. Catherine Copely[28]	1779	£17,020	£12,000	Died		Life interest in investment	£19,709[29]
Valentine Browne, Earl of Kenmare, m. Mary Aylmer[30]	1783		£1,000	£1,300	£300		£10,096[31]

Appendix C (cont.)

Name	Date	Portion	Jointure settled	Actual jointure in will	Pin money	Additional income interests settled at marriage	Additional income interests settled by will	Family estate rental[2]
Arthur Hill, Lord Fairfax, m. Mary Sandys[32]	1786	£4,504 rental and £41,486 in stock	£5000	£5,000	£1,200			£17,104[33]
Arthur Chichester, Earl of Donegall, m. Barbara Godfrey[34]	1790		£2,000	£2,000				£35,622[35]
Robert Stewart, Marquess of Londonderry, m. Amelia Hobart[36]	1794	£20,000	£2,500		£1,600	Life interest in freehold land		£12,000[37]
William Brownlow m. Charity Forde[38]	1765	£6,000	£700					£9,000[39]
John James Hamilton, Marquess of Abercorn, m. Lady Anne Jane Hatton[40]	1800		£2,000	£3,000				£19,709[41]
James Stevenson Blackwood, Baron Dufferin and Clandeboye, m. Anna Foster[42]	1801	£10,000	£1,000	£3,000	£500		Investment with power of appointment	£18,000[43]
James Hamilton, Viscount Hamilton, m. Harriet Douglas[44]	1809	£10	£2,000	£2,000				£19,709[45]
Dupre Alexander, Earl of	1811	£10,000	£2,500	£2,500	£500			£16,000[47]

Caledon, m. Lady Catherine Freeman[46]							£17,100[49]
Valentine Brown, Earl of Kenmare, m. Augusta Ann Wilmot[48]	1816		£3,000				
Charles Stewart, Baron Stewart of Stewart's Court and Ballylawn, m. Frances Anne Vane-Tempest[50]	1819	£10,000	£1,000		£2,000	Real and personal estate of her husband	£8,000 (heir to £31,500)[51]
Warner William Westenra, Baron Rossmore of Monaghan, m. Lady Augusta Charteris[52]	1819		£1,000	£1,000	£500		£11,000[53]
Charles Brownlow m. Mary Bligh[54]	1822	£10,000	£800 or £1,200	Died	£400		£9,000[55]
Price Blackwood m. Helen Sheridan[56]	1825	N/A	£1,000	£1,000	£133		£18,000[57]
Charles Brownlow, Baron Lurgan, m. Jane MacNeill[58]	1828	£10 nominal sum	£1,200	£2,289	£1,000 for house and gardens	Capital interest in land	£9,000[59]
James Hamilton, Marquess of Abercorn, m. Louisa Russell[60]	1832	£12,000	£5,000	£1,000	£1,000		£26,916[61]
Richard Dawson, Baron Dartrey, m. Augusta Stanley[62]	1841	£5,000	£2,500	Died	£500		£11,577[63]
James Du Pre Alexander, Earl of Caledon, m. Jane Grimston[64]	1845	£10,000	£2,000	£2,000	£400	Life interest in investment	£16,000[65]

Appendix C (cont.)

Notes

1 For the purposes of providing the basis upon which meaningful comparisons could be made between families, this table is based only on details of arrangements made on the marriage of eldest sons who had already inherited estate, or eldest sons who were heirs at law to family estates.

2 See Appendix D for further information on how rental was calculated for this table.

3 PRONI, Downshire papers, D/671/D14/2/17, copy of the last will and testament of James Fitzgerald, Duke of Leinster, 9 February 1768.

4 Malcomson, *The pursuit of the heiress*, p. 10.

5 PRONI, Dufferin and Ava papers, D/1071/A/N1/17a, copy of the marriage settlement of Sir John Blackwood and Dorcas Stevenson, dated 1751; PRONI, Dufferin and Ava papers, D/1071/A/N3/3b, copy of the last will and testament of John Blackwood, 31 December 1781.

6 It has been estimated that by 1800 John Blackwood's estate received an annual rental of £10,000. Harrison, 'The First Marquess of Dufferin and Ava', p. 10.

7 PRONI, Earl of Antrim papers, D/2977/1/1/20, marriage settlement of Alexander McDonnell and Catherine Taylor, 16 July 1755.

8 Roebuck, 'Rent movement proprietorial incomes and agricultural development', p. 97.

9 PRO, PROB/11/1482, last will and testament of Thomas Conolly, extracted from the will registers of the Prerogative Court of Canterbury, probate granted 15 July 1808.

10 Gibb (ed.), *The complete peerage*, iv, p. 575.

11 PRONI, Enniskillen papers, D/1702/1/9/3, settlement referring to the 1763 marriage settlement of William Willoughby Cole, Earl of Enniskillen, and Anne Willoughby, Countess Enniskillen [1793?]; PRONI, Enniskillen papers, D/1702/1/27/7a, last will and testament and probate of William Willoughby, Earl of Enniskillen, will dated 21 June 1793, probate granted 28 March 1809.

12 The rental of the Enniskillen estates, as recorded by Bateman, was £19,290. In the absence of adequate rental accounts upon which to base a figure for rental in 1763, the 1876 figure was reduced by two-thirds. Bateman, *The great landowners*, p. 152.

13 PRO, PROB/11/1465, last will and testament of Richard Boyle, Earl of Shannon, extracted from the will registers of the Prerogative Court of Canterbury, will dated 3 March 1801, probate granted 11 July 1807.

14 PRONI, Brownlow papers, D/1928/T/2/10, marriage settlement of William Brownlow and Catherine Hall, 4 November 1765; PRONI, Brownlow papers, D/1928/T/2/15, deed of revocation and new appointment by Charles Brownlow the elder on the intended marriage of Charles Brownlow the younger and Mary Bligh, undated.

15 The Brownlow estate consisted of lands in County Armagh and County Monaghan. In the last will and testament of William Brownlow (d. 1794) the estate was divided between his first and second son: William Brownlow, his eldest son, inherited the estate in County Armagh, and his second son, Charles, inherited the estate in County Monaghan. In 1799, Vicary Gibb noted, the estate of 'Mr Brownlow' took an annual rental of £9,000. This almost certainly refers to the County Armagh estate, which was the main family estate. PRONI, Brownlow papers, D/1928/T/3/5, certified copy of the last will and testament of William Brownlow, dated 1791.

16 PRONI, Londonderry Estate Office papers, D/654/F1/10, marriage settlement of Robert Stewart and Lady Sarah Conway, 3 June 1766.

17 PRONI, Londonderry Estate Office papers, D/654/H/1/13, account book of Lord Londonderry, 1791–1803; H. Montgomery Hyde, *The Londonderrys: a family portrait* (London: H. Hamilton, 1979), p. 1; Malcomson, *The pursuit of the heiress*, p. 13.

18 PRO, PROB/11/1542, last will and testament of Thomas Dawson, Viscount Cremorne, extracted from the will registers of the Prerogative Court of Canterbury, will dated 29 May 1812, probate granted 31 March 1813.

19 Gibb (ed.), *The complete peerage*, iv, p. 575.

20 PRONI, Londonderry Estate Office papers, D/654/F1/11, marriage settlement of Robert Stewart and Frances Anne Pratt, 6 June 1773; PRO, PROB/11/1813, last will and testament of Frances Anne Stewart, Marchioness of Londonderry, extracted from the will registers of the Prerogative Court of Canterbury, will dated 13 January 1828, probate granted 19 March 1833.

21 See note 19.

22 PRONI, Earl of Antrim papers, D/2977/1/1/27, deed to secure jointure for Letitia McDonnell, Countess of Antrim, 25 June 1776; PRONI, Earl of Antrim papers, D/2977/1/2/4, copy of the will of Letitia McDonnell, Countess of Antrim, will dated

31 July 1799, probate granted 10 February 1802, extracted from the Prerogative Court of Canterbury; PRONI, Earl of Antrim papers, D/2977/1/2/1a, deed to secure portions for the daughters of Randall McDonnell, Earl of Antrim [undated]; PRONI, Earl of Antrim papers, D/2977/1/2/2, last will and testament and probate of Randall MacDonnell, Marquess of Antrim, 14 August 1790, probate granted 15 August 1791.

23 See note 8.

24 PRONI, Erne papers, D/1939/25/1/2, last will and testament and probate of John Creighton, Earl of Erne, probate granted 11 November 1828.

25 PRONI, Erne papers, D/1939/21/7/3, memorandum of rentals and family accounts of the Earl of Erne, 1828–75.

26 PRONI, Kenmare papers, D/4151/A/13, marriage settlement of Valentine Browne, Earl of Kenmare, and Charlotte Dillon, 5 July 1777.

27 James S. Donnelly has estimated that rental from the Kenmare estate in Kerry was £3,600 in 1756 and the hospital estate was £2,300 in 1768. The rental of both these estates increased significantly by 1814, with a rental of £12,800 and £4,300 respectively. To estimate the rentals for the Kenmare family for the purpose of this table I have increased the 1756 and 1768 rentals in proportion to the increase recorded in 1814. James S. Donnelly jr, 'The Kenmare estates during the nineteenth century: part 1', *Kerry Archaeological and Historical Society Journal*, 21 (1988), p. 23.

28 PRONI, Abercorn papers, D/623/B/3/25, last will and testament and probate of John James Hamilton, Marquess of Abercorn, 18 March 1809, probate granted 9 May 1818.

29 PRONI, Abercorn papers, D/623/C/4/1, rental account book for the manor of Strabane, County Tyrone, 1794–1810; PRONI, Abercorn papers, D/623/C/4/3, rental account book for the manor of Donelong, County Tyrone, 1794–1810; PRONI, Abercorn papers, D/623/C/4/5, rental account book for the manor of Cloghogel, County Tyrone, 1794–1810; PRONI, Abercorn papers, D/623/C/4/8, rental account book for the Donegal estate, 1794–1810.

30 PRONI, Kenmare papers, D/4151/A/17, abstract of title referring to settlements made in 1783 and 1806, undated; PRONI, Kenmare papers, D/4157/D/3, copy of the last will and testament of Valentine Browne, Earl of Kenmare, dated 1806, probate granted 1812.

31 See note 29.

32 PRONI, Downshire papers, D/671/D14/1/3a, marriage settlement of Arthur Hill, Viscount Fairford, and Mary Sandys, 20 June 1786; PRONI, Downshire papers, D/671/D14/2/20a, last will and testament of Arthur Hill, Marquess of Downshire,

extracted from the will registers of the Prerogative Court of Canterbury, 24 November 1797, probate granted 7 October 1801.

33 PRONI, Downshire papers, D/671/D14/1/3a, marriage settlement of Arthur Hill, Viscount Fairford, and Mary Sandys 20 June 1786.

34 PRONI, Rose Cleland papers, T/761/18, copy of the last will and testament of Arthur Chichester, Marquess of Donegall, and two codicils, will dated 7 August 1795; Maguire, *Living like a lord*, pp. 33–4.

35 See note 12.

36 PRONI, The Londonderry Estate Office papers, D/654/F1/14a, marriage settlement of Robert Stewart and Lady Amelia Hobart, 7 June 1794; PRONI, Galway, McIlwaine and Seeds papers, D/665/40, copy of the last will and testament of Robert Stewart, Marquess of Londonderry, will dated 14 August 1818, codicils dated 17 August 1818, probate granted 10 May 1823.

37 Gibb (ed.), *The complete peerage*, iv, p. 575; Malcomson, *The pursuit of the heiress*, p. 13.

38 PRONI, Brownlow papers, D/1928/T/2/13, marriage settlement of William Brownlow and Charity Forde, 23 February 1765; PRONI, Brownlow papers, D/1928/T/3/5, copy of the last will and testament, and two codicils of William Brownlow, will dated 19 April 1791.

39 See note 17.

40 PRONI, Abercorn papers, D/623/B/2/23, marriage settlement of John James Hamilton, Marquess of Abercorn, and Lady Ann Jane Hatton, April 1800; PRONI's Abercorn papers, D/623/B/3/25, last will and testament and probate of John James Hamilton, Marquess of Abercorn, October 1818.

41 See note 31.

42 PRONI, Dufferin and Ava papers, D/1071/A/N2/1, copy of the marriage settlement of James Blackwood, Baron Dufferin and Clandeboye, dated November 1801; PRONI, Dufferin and Ava papers, D/1071/A/N/3/1, copy of the will and probate of James Stevenson Blackwood, Lord Dufferin, dated 5 March 1836.

43 This figure is preferable to the previous Blackwood rental (see note 6) as after the death of Dorcas Blackwood, Baroness Dufferin, the rental from her estate passed to James Blackwood, Lord Dufferin. PRONI, Dufferin and Ava papers, D/1071/A/B6/3, rent schedules for the minority of Frederick Blackwood, 1841–47.

44 PRONI, Abercorn papers, D/623/B/3/25, last will and testament and probate of John James Hamilton, Marquess of Abercorn, October 1818; PRONI, Abercorn papers, D/623/B/2/29, settlement of annuity of Harriet Douglas on her

marriage to John James, Viscount Hamilton, 1809; PRONI, Abercorn papers, D/623/B/2/30, appointment by the Marquess of Abercorn to Viscountess Hamilton of a further rent charge of £1,200, 14 May 1811; PRONI, Abercorn papers, D/623/B/2/31, appointment by the Marquess of Abercorn to Viscountess Hamilton of a further rent charge of £800, 14 May 1811.

45 See note 31.

46 PRONI, Caledon papers, D/2433/A/1/371/1, marriage settlement of Dupre Alexander, Earl of Caledon, and Catherine Freeman, 15 October 1811; PRONI, Caledon papers, D/2433/B/11/2, solicitor's copy of the last will and testament of Dupre Alexander, Earl of Caledon, probate granted 23 August 1839.

47 PRONI, Caledon papers, D/2433/A/7/5, report of the Caledon estate, 1855, not including Caledon town or demesne.

48 PRONI, Kenmare papers, D/4151/A/17, abstract of title referring to settlements made in 1783 and 1806, undated.

49 See note 29.

50 PRONI, Londonderry Estate Office papers, D/654/F1/25a–c, marriage settlement of Charles Stewart, Baron Stewart of Stewart's Court and Ballylawn, and Frances Anne Vane-Tempest, 27 March 1819; PRONI, Earl of Antrim papers, D/2977/2/4/2/4, legal opinion regarding a claim on Lady Londonderry's Antrim estate by Mr McDonnell, undated; PRO, PROB/11/2189, last will and testament of Charles William Vane, Marquess of Londonderry, extracted from the will registers of the Prerogative Court of Canterbury, will dated 20 May 1852, probate granted 11 April 1854.

51 In 1804 the first Marquess of Londonderry settled the Londonderry estates in County Donegal and County Londonderry on Charles Stewart, while the County Down estates were settled on his elder brother, Robert Stewart, Lord Castlereagh. On his marriage to Frances Anne Vane-Tempest, therefore, his estate was only part of Londonderry estate, and worth a rental of £8,000. Copies of affadavit in the Chancery case concerning the marriage of Frances Anne Vane-Tempest to Charles Stewart, 1818, PRONI, Londonderry Estate Office papers, D/654/G1/3; Malcomson, *The pursuit of the heiress*, p. 30.

52 PRONI, Rossmore papers, T/2929/37/8/3, marriage settlement of Warner William Westenra, Baron Rossmore of Monaghan, and Lady Augusta Charteris, 2 June 1819; PRO, PROB/11/1981, last will and testament of Warner William Westenra, Baron Rossmore, extracted from the will registers of the Prerogative Court of Canterbury, will dated 9 October 1841, probate granted 19 June 1843.

53 The figure used here is A. P. W. Malcomson's estimate of the rental of the Earl of Clermont's County Monaghan estate, which passed into the possession of Lord Rossmore in 1827, and the rental of an estate in King's County (County Offaly)

and Queen's County (County Laois) inherited by Lord Rossmore from his father in 1822. A. P. W. Malcomson, 'The Earl of Clermont: a forgotten Co. Monaghan magnate of the late eighteenth century', *Clogher Record*, 8 (1973), pp. 46, 66.

54 PRONI, Brownlow papers, D/1928/T/2/15, marriage settlement of Charles Brownlow and Lady Mary Bligh, 29 May 1822.

55 See note 17.

56 PRONI, Dufferin and Ava papers, D/1071/A/N2/11a, copy of the appointment of new trustees to the marriage settlement of Price Blackwood and Helen Blackwood; PRONI, Dufferin and Ava papers, D/1071/F/B4/4, diary and account book of Helen Blackwood, 1837; PRO, PROB/11/1951, last will and testament of Price Blackwood, Lord Dufferin, extracted from the will registers of the Prerogative Court of Canterbury, will dated 7 September 1834, probate granted 22 November 1841.

57 See note 45.

58 PRONI, Brownlow papers, D/1928/T/2/17, marriage settlement of Charles Brownlow and Jane MacNeill, 27 June 1828; PRONI, Brownlow papers, D/1928/T/3/8, last will and testament and probate of Charles Brownlow, Lord Baron Lurgan, will dated 8 June 1832, probate granted 18 June 1849.

59 See note 17.

60 PRONI, Abercorn papers, D/623/B/2/44, marriage settlement of James Hamilton, Earl of Abercorn and Louisa Jane Russell, 5 October 1832.

61 PRONI, Abercorn papers, D/623/C/4/2, rental account book for the manor of Strabane, County Tyrone, 1809–33; PRONI, Abercorn papers, D/623/C/4/4, rental account book for the manor of Donelong, County Tyrone, 1809–33; PRONI, Abercorn papers, D/623/C/4/6, rental account book for the manor of Cloghogel, County Tyrone, 1809–33; PRONI, Abercorn papers, D/623/C/4/9, rental account book for the Donegal estate, 1810–33.

62 PRONI, Dartrey papers, D/3053/1/8/14, marriage settlement of Richard Dawson, Lord Cremorne, and Augusta Stanley, 10 July 1841; PRONI, Dartrey papers, D/3053/1/8/10, appointment by Edward Stanley and his wife Mary Stanley of £5,000 and £2,500 in favour of Miss Augusta Stanley in contemplation of her marriage with Lord Cremorne, 10 July [1841].

63 PRONI, Dartrey papers, D/3053/1/8/14, instructions for counsel to settle the draft deed of settlement on the marriage of Lord Baron Cremorne with Miss Augusta Stanley a minor [1841].

64 PRONI, Caledon papers, D/2433/A/1/566/1, marriage settlement of James Dupre, Earl of Caledon, and Jane Grimston, 4 September 1845; PRO, PROB/11/2217, last will and testament of James Dupre, Earl of Caledon, and two codicils, extracted from the will registers of the Prerogative Court of Canterbury, will dated 21 June 1855, probate granted 23 August 1855.

65 See note 49.

Appendix D

Guardians and executors, 1767–1855

Appointee	Guardian	Executor of will
Widow	6	5
Widow and heir	2	3
Widow and trustee	4	4
Heir	0	7
Heir and trustees	1	1
Younger son and trustees	0	1
Trustee	1	4
Widow and sister-in-law	1	0
Sister-in-law and heir	0	1
N/A or no details	13	2
Total	28	28

Sources: PRONI, Enniskillen papers, D/1702/1/27/4a, last will and testament and one codicil of John Cole, Lord Mountflorence, 7 April 1767; PRONI, Downshire papers, D/671/D14/2/17, copy of the last will and testament of James Fitzgerald, Duke of Leinster, 9 February 1768; PRONI, Dufferin and Ava papers, D/1071/A/N3/3b, copy of the last will and testament of John Blackwood, dated 31 December 1781; abstract of the last will and testament of Richard Wingfield, Viscount Powerscourt, 1788, in E. Ellis and P. B Eustace, *Registry of Deeds Dublin: abstracts of wills, iii: 1785–1832* (Dublin: Stationery Office for the Irish Manuscripts Commission, 1984), p. 36; PRONI, Brownlow papers, D/1928/T/3/5, solicitor's copy of the last will and testament `and two codicils of William Brownlow, will dated 19 April 1791, probate granted 1794; PRONI, Earl of Antrim papers, D/2977/1/2/2, last will and testament and probate of Randall MacDonnell, Marquess of Antrim, 14 August 1790, probate granted 15 August 1791; PRONI, Enniskillen papers, D/1702/1/27/7a, last will and testament and probate of William Willoughby, Earl of Enniskillen, 21 June 1793, probate granted 25 July 1805; PRONI, Rose Cleland papers, T/761/18, copy of the last will and testament of Arthur Chichester, Marquess of Donegall, and two codicils, will dated 7 August 1795; PRONI, Downshire papers, D/671/D14/2/20a, last will and testament of Arthur Hill, Marquess of Downshire, extracted from the will registers of the Prerogative Court of Canterbury, 24 November 1797, probate granted 7 October 1801; PRO, PROB/11/1482, last will and testament of Thomas Conolly, extracted from the will registers of the Prerogative Court of Canterbury, probate granted 15 July 1808; PRONI, Kenmare papers, D/4151/D/3, copy of the last will and testament of Valentine Browne, Earl of Kenmare, dated 1806, probate granted 1812; PRO, PROB/11/1465, last will and testament of Richard Boyle, Earl of Shannon, extracted from the will registers of the Prerogative Court of Canterbury, will dated 3 March 1801, probate granted 11 July 1807; PRONI, Enniskillen papers, D/1702/1/27/7a, last will and testament of John Cole, Lord Baron Mount Florence, 7 April 1767, probate granted 1811; PRONI, Earl of Antrim papers, D/2977/1/2/15, solicitor's copy of the will of Sir Henry Vane Tempest Bart, will dated 4 August 1811, probate granted 1813; PRO, PROB/11/1542, last will and testament of Thomas Dawson, Viscount Cremorne, extracted from the will registers of the Prerogative Court of Canterbury, will dated 29 May 1812, probate granted 31 March 1813; PRONI, Foster/Massereene papers, D/4084/2/8a, copy of the last will and testament and probate of Chichester Skeffington, Earl of Massereene, will dated 20 February 1816, probate granted 17 October 1816; PRONI, Abercorn papers, D/623/B/3/25, last will and testament and probate of John James Hamilton, Marquess of Abercorn, 18 March 1809, probate granted 9 May 1818; PRONI, Brownlow papers, D/1928/T/3/6, last will and testament and one codicil and probate of Charles Brownlow, will dated 20 December 1821, probate granted 22 October 1822; PRONI, Galway, McIlwaine and Seeds papers, D/665/40, copy of the last will and testament and probate of Robert Stewart, Marquess of Londonderry, will dated 14 August 1818, codicils dated 17 August 1818, probate granted 10 May 1823; PRONI, Erne papers, D/1939/25/1/12, last will and testament and probate of John Creighton, Earl of Erne, will dated 11 November 1828, probate granted 1829; PRONI, Farrer and Co. Solicitors papers D/585/55, last will and testament with codicils and probate of Robert Ward, will dated 30 March 1829, codicils dated 1831, probate granted 6 June 1831; PRONI, Powerscourt Lord (Benburb) estate papers, D/1957/1/17, solicitor's copy of the last will and testament of Richard Wingfield, Viscount Powerscourt, 3 February 1836; PRONI, Caledon papers, D/2433/B/11/2, solicitor's copy of the last will and testament of Dupre Alexander, Earl of Caledon, probate granted 1840; PRO, PROB/11/1951, last will and testament of Price Blackwood, Lord Dufferin, extracted from the will registers of the Prerogative Court of Canterbury, will dated 7 September 1834, probate granted 22 November 1841; PRO, PROB/11/1981, last will and testament of Warner William Westenra, Lord Rossmore, extracted from the will registers of the Prerogative Court of Canterbury, will dated 9 October 1841, probate granted 19 June 1843; PRONI, Brownlow papers, D/1928/T/3/8, last will and testament and probate of Charles Brownlow, Lord Lurgan, will dated 8 June 1832, probate granted 1 July 1847; PRO, PROB/11/2189, last will and testament of Charles William Vane, Marquess of Londonderry, extracted from the will registers of the Prerogative Court of Canterbury, will dated 20 May 1852, probate granted 11 April 1854; PRO, PROB/11/2217, last will and testament of James Dupre, Earl of Caledon, and two codicils, extracted from the will registers of the Prerogative Court of Canterbury, will dated 21 June 1855, probate granted 23 August 1855.

Appendix E

Provision for daughters and younger sons, 1767–1855

Name	Date of will	Provision settled on marriage	Provision in will[1]	Type of bequests to daughters	Type of bequests to sons
John Cole, Lord Mountflorence[2]	1767	£8,000	£8,000	Legacies	Land
James Fitzgerald, Earl of Kildare[3]	1768	£20,000	£50,000+	Legacies	Land
Bernard Ward, Lord Bangor[4]	1779	£8,000	£29,000+	Legacies	Legacies
Sir John Blackwood[5]	1781	£12,000	£34,940	Legacies	
Alexander McDonnell, Earl of Antrim[6]		£6,000	£6,000+	Land	
Randall McDonnell, Earl of Antrim[7]	1791	£36,000	£36,000	Land	
Arthur Chichester, Earl of Donegall[8]	1795	£15,000	£45,000+		Land
William Brownlow[9]	1799	£4,000	£37,000	Legacies	Legacies
Arthur Hill, Marquess of Downshire[10]	1801	£40,000	£40,000	Legacy	Legacy
James Alexander, Earl of Caledon[11]	1802	£10,000	£30,000	Legacy	
William Willoughby Cole, Earl of Enniskillen[12]	1805	£10,000	£24,000	Legacies	Land, legacies
Richard Boyle, Earl of Shannon[13]	1807		£20,000+	Land, legacies	Land, legacies
Valentine Brown, Earl of Kenmare[14]	1812	£20,000	£20,000+	Legacies	Legacies
John James Hamilton, Marquess of Abercorn[15]	1818	£20,000	£20,000	Legacies	Legacies
Charles Brownlow[16]	1821	£12,000	£14,000	Legacy	Legacy

John Creighton, Earl of Erne of Crom Castle[17]	1828	£5,000	£5,000+	Legacy, investment	Land
Warner William Westenra, Baron Rossmore[18]	1843	£20,000	£20,300+	Legacies	Land
Charles Brownlow, Lord Lurgan[19]	1847	£20,000	£20,000	Legacies	Legacies
James Du Pre Alexander, Earl of Caledon[20]	1855	£35,000	£35,000	Legacies	Legacies

Notes

1 When the actual amount bequeathed is unclear from last wills and testaments, but when an increase in the settled amount is indicated, the amount that can be ascertained is marked with a +.

2 PRONI, Enniskillen papers, D/1702/1/27/4a, last will and testament and one codicil of John Cole, Lord Mountflorence, 7 April 1767.

3 PRONI, Downshire papers, D/671/D14/2/17, copy of the last will and testament of James Fitzgerald, Duke of Leinster, 9 February 1768.

4 PRONI, Ward papers, D/4216/F/1, copy of the last will and testament and probate of Bernard Ward, Lord Bangor, probate granted 30 August 1779.

5 PRONI, Dufferin and Ava papers, D/1071/A/N1/17a, copy of the marriage settlement of Sir John Blackwood and Dorcas Stevenson, dated 1751; PRONI, Dufferin and Ava papers, D/1071/A/N3/3b, copy of the last will and testament of John Blackwood, 31 December 1781.

6 PRONI, Earl of Antrim papers, D/2977/1/1/20, marriage settlement of Alexander McDonnell and Catherine Taylor, 16 July 1755.

7 PRONI, Earl of Antrim papers, D/2977/1/1/2/1a, deed to secure portions for the daughters of Randall McDonnell, Earl of Antrim [undated]; PRONI, Earl of Antrim papers, D/2977/1/2/2, last will and testament and probate of Randall MacDonnell, Marquess of Antrim, 14 August 1790, probate granted 15 August 1791.

8 PRONI, Rose Cleland papers, T/761/18, copy of the last will and testament of Arthur Chichester, Marquess of Donegall, and two codicils, will dated 7 August 1795, probate granted 11 January 1799; Maguire, Living like a lord, pp. 33–4.

9 PRONI, Brownlow papers, D/1928/T/2/13, marriage settlement of William Brownlow and Charity Forde, 23 February 1765; PRONI, Brownlow papers, D/1928/T/3/5, copy of the last will and testament and two codicils of William Brownlow, dated 11 October 1794, probate granted 1799.

10 PRO, PROB/11/1363, last will and testament of Arthur Hill, Marquess of Downshire, extracted from the will registers of the Prerogative Court of Canterbury, will dated 30 September 1801, probate granted 7 October 1801.

11 PRONI, Caledon papers, D/2433/A/1/127/5, last will and testament and one codicil and probate of James Alexander, Earl of Caledon, will dated 30 January 1799, probate granted 29 March 1802.

12 PRONI, Enniskillen papers, D/1702/1/9/3, settlement referring to the 1763 marriage settlement of William Willoughby Cole, Earl of Enniskillen, and Anne Willoughby, Countess Enniskillen [1793?]; PRONI, Enniskillen papers, D/1702/1/27/7a, last will and testament and probate of William Willoughby, Earl of Enniskillen, will dated 21 June 1793, probate granted 28 March 1809.

13 PRO, PROB/11/1465, last will and testament of Richard Boyle, Earl of Shannon, extracted from the will registers of the Prerogative Court of Canterbury, will dated 3 March 1801, probate granted 11 July 1807.

14 PRONI, Kenmare papers, D/4151/D/3, copy of the last will and testament and two codicils of Valentine Browne, Lord Kenmare, will dated 17 November 1806, probate granted 15 September 1812; PRONI, Kenmare papers, D/4151/A/17, abstract of title referring to settlements made in 1783 and 1806, undated.

15 PRONI, Abercorn papers, D/623/B/2/23, marriage settlement of John James, Marquess of Abercorn, and Lady Ann Jane Hatton; PRONI, Abercorn papers, D/623/B/3/25, last will and testament and probate of John James Hamilton, Marquess of Abercorn, October 1818.

16 PRONI, Brownlow papers, D/1928/T/3/6, last will and testament and probate of Charles Brownlow, will dated 20 December 1821, probate granted 22 October 1822.

17 PRONI, Erne papers, D/1939/25/1/2, last will and testament and probate of John Creighton, Earl of Erne, probate granted 11 November 1828.

18 PRO, PROB/11/1981, last will and testament of Warner William Westenra, Baron Rossmore, extracted from the will registers of the Prerogative Court of Canterbury, will dated 9 October 1841, probate granted 19 June 1843.

19 PRONI, Brownlow papers, D/1928/T/2/15, marriage settlement of Charles Brownlow and Lady Mary Bligh, 29 May 1822;

PRONI, Brownlow papers, D/1928/T/2/17, marriage settlement of Charles Brownlow and Jane MacNeill, 27 June 1828; PRONI, Brownlow papers, D/1928/T/3/8, last will and testament and probate of Charles Brownlow, Lord Lurgan, will dated 8 June 1832, probate granted 18 June 1847.

20 PRONI, Caledon papers, D/2433/A/1/566/1, marriage settlement of James Dupre, Earl of Caledon, and Jane Grimston, 4 September 1845; PRO, PROB/11/2217, last will and testament of James Dupre Alexander, Earl of Caledon, and two codicils, extracted from the will registers of the Prerogative Court of Canterbury, will dated 21 June 1855, probate granted.

Appendix F

Types of property bequeathed to daughters and younger sons, 1771–1836

Table 1 Bequests to daughters

Type of property	Women's wills	Men's wills
Land–capital		
Land–life	1	
Chattel–capital	4	
Chattel–life		
Annuity–land		3
Annuity–investments		1
Legacy	5	5
House		
Total	10	9

Table 2 Bequests to younger sons

Type of property	Women's wills	Men's wills
Land–capital	3	3
Land–life		1
Chattel–capital	2	
Chattel–life		
Annuity–land	1	3
Annuity–investments		
Legacy	1	4
House	1	
Total	9	11

Sources: Tables 1 and 2 have been compiled from bequests noted in the following twenty last wills and testaments, ten for female testators and ten for male testators, among the core families: PRONI, Abercorn papers, D/623/B/3/14, last will and testament of Ann Hamilton, Countess of Abercorn, extracted from the will registers of the Prerogative Court of Canterbury, will dated 1771, probate granted 10 August 1776; PRONI, Earl of Antrim papers, D/2977/1/2/4, copy of the last will and testament of Letitia MacDonnell, Marchioness of Antrim, extracted from the will registers of the Prerogative Court of Canterbury, will dated 31 July 1799, probate granted 10 February 1802; PRO, PROB/11/1455, last will and testament of Dorcas Blackwood, Baroness Dufferin and Clandeboye, extracted from the will registers of the Prerogative Court of Canterbury, will dated 7 February 1807, probate granted 26 February 1807; PRO, PROB/11/1714, last will and testament of Philadelphia Hannah Dawson, Viscountess Cremorne, extracted from the will registers of the Prerogative Court of Canterbury, will dated 1 October 1824, probate granted 18 March 1824; PRO, PROB/11/1766, last will and testament of Barbara Chichester, Marchioness of Donegall, extracted from the will registers of the Prerogative Court of Canterbury, will dated 9 December 1826, probate granted 11 February 1830; PRONI, Downshire papers, D/671/D14/2/22a&b, last will and testament of Mary Hill, Marchioness of Downshire, 3 May 1832, probate granted September 1836; PRONI, Foster/Massereene papers, D/4084/2/5, last will and testament and probate of Anne Skeffington, Countess of Massereene, will dated 21 January 1800, codicil dated 21 January 1801, probate granted 22 May 1812; PRO, PROB/11/1956, last will and testament of Mary Caroline Creighton, Countess of Erne, extracted from the will registers of the Prerogative Court of Canterbury, will dated 13 September 1841, probate granted 31 January 1842; PRONI, Charity Brownlow testamentary document, T/26, copy of the last will and testament and probate of Charity Brownlow, dated 1 December 1842, probate granted 16 May 1843; PRONI, Downshire papers, D/671/D14/2/24, last will and testament of Maria Hill, Marchioness of Downshire, 17 December 1846, probate granted 7 April 1855; PRONI, Downshire papers, D/671/D14/2/17, copy of the last will and testament of James Fitzgerald, Duke of Leinster, 9 February 1768; PRONI, Dufferin and Ava papers, D/1071/A/N3/3b, copy of the last will and testament of John Blackwood, 31 December 1781; PRONI, Enniskillen papers, D/1702/1/27/7a, last will and testament and probate of William Willoughby, Earl of Enniskillen, 21 June 1793, probate granted 25 July 1805; PRONI, Brownlow papers, D/1928/T/3/5, solicitor's copy of the last will and testament and two codicils of William Brownlow, will dated 19 April 1791, probate granted 1794; PRONI, Downshire papers, D/671/D14/2/20a, copy of the last will and testament of Arthur Hill, Marquess of Downshire, extracted from the registers of the Prerogative Court of Canterbury, 24 November 1797, probate granted 1801; PRONI, Foster/Massereene papers, D/4084/2/8a, copy of the last will and testament and probate of Chichester Skeffington, Earl of Massereene, will dated 20 February 1816, probate granted 17 October 1816; PRONI, Abercorn papers, D/623/B/3/25, last will and testament and probate of John James Hamilton, Marquess of Abercorn, 18 March 1809, probate granted 9 May 1818; PRONI, Galway, McIlwaine and Seeds papers, D/665/40, copy of the last will and testament and probate of Robert Stewart, Marquess of Londonderry, will dated 14 August 1818, codicils dated 17 August 1818, probate granted 10 May 1823; PRONI, Erne papers, D/1939/25/1/12, last will and testament and probate of John Creighton, Earl of Erne, will dated 11 November 1828, probate granted 1829; PRONI, Powerscourt Lord (Benburb) papers, D/1957/1/17, solicitor's copy of the last will and testament of Richard Wingfield, Viscount Powerscourt, 3 February 1836.

Appendix G

Lady Erne's accounts 1776–99: charitable donations

Year	Total expenditure (£)	Unnamed poor	Named poor	Charitable institution	Third party	Charity sermon	Other charitable cause
1776	25.18.6	1	1	2	1	1	0
1777	18.9.5	3	2	2	0	1	0
1778	24.9.9	3	4	3	0	1	0
1779	26.11.5	3	3	3	0	1	0
1780	64.14.10	8	4	2	0	1	0
1781	41.17.0	5	5	3	0	1	0
1782	85.1.1 ½	4	4	2	3	1	1
1783	48.18.3	4	5	3	0	1	1
1784	70.15.9 ½	6	5	2	1	1	0
1785	49.18.10	2	5	3	4	0	0
1786	52.6.6	3	8	4	4	1	1
1787	144.4.10 ½	2	5	3	2	1	1
1788	44.13.10 ½	4	2	5	1	1	0
1789	44.19.1 ½	4	5	4	2	1	0
1790	44.14.4 ½	3	4	1	1	5	0
1791	46.18.8 ½	5	4	3	2	3	0
1792	36.13.5	2	4	2	2	4	0
1793	42.13.1 ½	2	3	3	5	3	1
1794	52.6.6	1	3	4	2	4	2

Year							
1795	113.14.0	0	3	4	1	3	1
1796	79.0.3	1	4	6	0	3	0
1797	72.8.4 ½	2	3	4	1	1	0
1798	39.19.11 ½	3	3	5	1	3	1
1799	143.14.0	4	4	4	1	2	1
Total	1419.2.0	75	93	77	34	9	9

Sources: NLI, Erne papers, MS 2178, Erne accounts, 1776–99; Raughter, 'A natural tenderness', p. 68, Table 1.

Select bibliography

Manuscript sources

Public Record Office of Northern Ireland, Belfast

Abercorn papers, D/623.
Aldborough papers, T/3300/13.
Anglesey papers, D/610.
Belmore papers, D/3007.
Blackwood papers, D/1231.
Brownlow papers, D/1928.
Caledon papers, D/2431–2433.
Clanmorris papers, D/421.
Clanwilliam/Meade papers, D/3044.
Conolly papers, D/2094; D/663; MIC/435.
Dartrey papers, D/3053.
De Ros papers, D/638; MIC/573.
Downshire papers, D/607; D/671.
Dufferin and Ava papers, D/1071.
Earl of Antrim papers, D/2977.
Enniskillen papers, D/1702.
Erne papers, D/1939.
Farrer and Co. Solicitors papers, D/585.
Foster/Massereene papers, D/207; D/562; D/4084.
Galway, McIlwaine and Seeds papers, D/665.
Howard-Bury papers, T/3069.
Kenmare papers, D/4151.
Kilmorey papers, D/2638.
Leinster papers, D/3078.
Londonderry Estate Office papers, D/654.
Nugent of Portaferry papers, D/552.
Perceval–Price papers, D/993.
Powerscourt Lord (Benburb) estate papers, D/1957.
Rose Cleland papers, T/761/18.
Rossmore papers, T/2929.
Shannon papers, D/2707.
Verner-Wingfield papers, D/2538.
Ward papers, D/2092; D/3735; D/4216.

National Library of Ireland, Dublin
Brian Fitzgerald papers, MS 13,022.
Erne papers, MS 15360; MS2178.
Leinster papers, MS 606–635.
Wicklow papers, MS 4811.

National Archives of Ireland, Dublin
'A return of all charitable donations and bequests contained in the wills registered in the prerogative and consistorial offices of Dublin', 1801–28, MFS 49.

Public Record Office (National Archives), London
Will registers of the Prerogative Court of Canterbury, PROB/11.

Queen's University Belfast, Northern Ireland, Special Collections
Catalogue of books in Castle Ward library, July 1813.

Printed primary sources

Chapone, Sarah, *The hardships of the English laws in relation to wives with an explanation of the original curse of subjection passed upon the woman. In an humble address to the legislature* (Dublin, 1735).

Day, Angelique, and McWilliams, Patrick (eds), *Ordnance survey memoirs of Ireland*, xiii: *Parishes of County Antrim, IV: Glens of Antrim* (Belfast: Institute of Irish Studies, Queen's University of Belfast, in association with the Royal Irish Academy, 1992).

Debrett, John, *Debrett's complete peerage of the United Kingdom of Great Britain and Ireland* (London: J. G. and F. Rivington, 1836).

Ellis, E., and Eustace, P. B., *Registry of Deeds Dublin: abstracts of wills*, iii: *1785–1832* (Dublin: Stationery Office for the Irish Manuscripts Commission, 1984).

Eustace, P. Beryl, *Registry of deeds Dublin, abstracts of wills*, ii: *1746–85* (Dublin: Stationery Office for the Irish Manuscripts Commission, 1954).

Fitzgerald, Brian (ed.), *Correspondence of Emily Duchess of Leinster (1731–1814)*, i:, *Letters of Emily Duchess of Leinster; James first Duke of Leinster; Caroline Fox, Lady Holland* (Dublin: Stationery Office, 1949).

—— *Correspondence of Emily Duchess of Leinster, (1731–1814)*, ii: *Letters of Lord Edward Fitzgerald and Lady Sarah Napier (nee Lennox)* (Dublin: Stationery Office, 1953).

—— *Correspondence of Emily Duchess of Leinster (1731–1814)*, iii: *Letters of Lady Louisa Connolly and William Marquis of Kildare* (Dublin: Stationery Office, 1957).

Gibb, Vickery (ed.), *The complete peerage of England, Scotland and Ireland, Great Britain and the United Kingdom*, 12 volumes (London: St Catherine's Press, 1916).

Herbert, Dorothea, *Retrospections of Dorothea Herbert 1770–1806* (Dublin: Town House, 1988).

Horseman, Gilbert, *Precedents in conveyancing, settled and approved by Gilbert*

Horseman . . . and other eminent counsel, in three volumes (Dublin: Knapton, 1764).

Lewis, Samuel, *A topographical dictionary of Ireland* (London: S. Lewis, 1847).

Stevenson, Pearce [Caroline Norton], *A plain letter to the Lord Chancellor on the Infant Custody Bill* (London, 1839).

Vestry book of the Parish of Aghalow (Caledon, Co Tyrone) with an account of the family of Hamilton of Caledon 1691–1807 (Dungannon: Tyrone Printing Company, 1935).

Secondary sources

Andrew, Donna T., '*Nobless oblige*: female charity in an age of sentiment' in John Brewer and Susan Staves (eds.), *Early modern conceptions of property* (London: Routledge, 1995), pp. 275–300.

Atherton, Rosalind, 'The concept of moral duty in the law of family provision: a gloss or critical understanding?', *Australian Journal of Legal History*, 5:1 (1999), pp. 5–27.

Baker, J. H., *An introduction to English legal history* (London: Butterworths, 1990).

Barnard, Toby, *A new anatomy of Ireland: the Irish protestants 1649–1770* (London and New Haven: Yale University Press, 2003).

—— *Irish protestant ascents and descents, 1641–1779* (Dublin: Four Courts Press, 2002).

—— *The abduction of a Limerick heiress: social and political relations in mid-eighteenth century Ireland* (Dublin: Irish Academic Press, 1998).

Basch, Norma, *In the eyes of the law: women, marriage, and property in nineteenth-century New York* (London: Cornell University Press, 1982).

Bateman, John, *The great landowners of Great Britain and Ireland* (Leicester: Leicester University Press, 1971).

Beckett, J. V., *The aristocracy in England, 1660–1914* (Oxford: Basil Blackwell, 1986).

Bell, G. H. (ed.), *The Hamwood papers of the Ladies of Llangollen and Caroline Hamilton* (London: Macmillan, 1930).

Blackstone, William, *Commentaries on the laws of England*, i (London: Clarendon Press, 1809).

Blackwood, Frederick, Marquess of Dufferin and Ava (ed.), *Songs, poems and verses by Helen, Lady Dufferin (Countess of Gifford)* (London: J. Murray, 1894).

Bolton, G. C., *The passing of the Irish Act of Union: a study in parliamentary politics* (Oxford: Oxford University Press, 1966).

Bonfield, Lloyd, 'Strict settlement and the family: a differing view', *Economic History Review*, 41:3 (1988), pp. 461–6.

—— 'Affective families, open elites and strict family settlements in early modern England', *Economic History Review*, 38:3 (1986), pp. 341–54.

—— 'Normative rules and property transmission: reflections on the link between marriage and inheritance in early modern England' in Lloyd Bonfield et al (eds), *The world we have gained: histories of population and social structure* (Oxford: Blackwell, 1986), pp. 155–76.

—— 'Marriage, property and the "affective" family', *Law and history review*, 1:1 (spring 1983), pp. 297–312.

—— *Marriage settlements 1601–1740: the adoption of the strict settlement* (Cambridge: Cambridge University Press, 1983).

—— 'Marriage settlements, 1660–1740: the adoption of the strict settlement in Kent and Northhamptonshire' in R. B. Outhwaite (ed.), *Marriage and society: studies in the social history of marriage* (London: Europa, 1981), pp. 101–16.

—— 'Marriage settlements and the "rise of the great estates": a rejoiner', *Economic History Review*, 33:4 (1980), pp. 559–63.

Brooke, W. G., 'Rights of married women in England and Ireland', *Irish Law Times and Solicitors Journal*, 7 (1873), pp. 280–82.

Buck, A. R., 'Property, aristocracy and the reform of the land law in early nineteenth century England', *Journal of Legal History*, 16:1 (1995), pp. 63–93.

Byrne, W. J., *A dictionary of English law* (London: Sweet and Maxwell, 1923).

Chalus, Elaine, *Elite women in English political life c. 1754–1790* (Oxford: Clarendon Press, 2005).

—— ' "That epidemical madness": women and electoral politics in the late eighteenth century' in Hannah Barker and Elaine Chalus (eds.), *Gender in eighteenth-century England: roles, representations, and responsibilities* (Harlow: Longman, 1997), pp. 151–77.

Chambers, Lori, *Married women and property law in Victorian Ontario* (London and Toronto: University of Toronto Press, 1996).

Clay, Christopher, 'Marriage, inheritance and the rise of the large estates in England, 1660–1815', *Economic History Review*, second series, 31 (1968), pp. 503–18.

Clayton, Helen, *To school without shoes: a brief history of the Sunday School Society for Ireland 1809–1979* (Dublin?, 1979?).

Colley, Linda, *Britons: forging the nation, 1707–1837* (London: Pimlico, 1994).

Connolly, Sean J., 'A woman's life in eighteenth-century Ireland: the case of Letitia Bushe', *Historical Journal*, 43:2 (2000), pp. 433–51.

—— *Religion, law and power: the making of protestant Ireland 1660–1760* (Oxford: Clarendon Press, 1992).

Corish, Patrick J., 'The Cromwellian regime, 1650–60', in T. W. Moody et al (eds.), *A new history of Ireland, iii: Early modern Ireland, 1534–1691* (Oxford: Oxford University Press, 1991), pp. 353–386.

—— 'Catholic marriage under the penal code' in Art Cosgrove (ed.), *Marriage in Ireland* (Dublin: College Press, 1985), pp. 67–77.

Cosgrove, Art, 'Marriage in medieval Ireland' in Art Cosgrove (ed.), *Marriage in Ireland* (Dublin: College Press, 1985), pp. 25–50.

Crawford, W. H., 'Economy and society in south Ulster in the eighteenth century', *Clogher Record*, 8 (1975), pp. 241–258.

—— 'Landlord–tenant relations in Ulster, 1609–1820', *Irish Economic and Social History*, 2 (1975), pp. 5–21.

Davidoff, Leonore, 'Regarding some "old husband's tales": public and private in feminist history' in L. Davidoff, *Worlds between: historical perspectives on gender and class* (Cambridge: Polity Press, 1995), pp. 227–76.

Davidoff, Leonore and Catherine Hall, *Family fortunes: men and women of the English middle class 1780–1850* (London: Routledge, 1987).

Dickson, David, 'An economic history of the Cork region in the eighteenth century' (Ph.D. thesis, Trinity College Dublin, 1977).

—— and English, Richard, 'The La Touche dynasty', in David Dickson (ed.), *The gorgeous mask* (Dublin: Trinity History Workshop, 1987), pp. 17–29.

Diefendorf, Barbara B., 'Women and property in ancien regime France: theory and practice in Dauphine and Paris' in John Brewer and Susan Staves (eds.), *Early modern conceptions of property* (London: Routledge, 1995), pp. 170–93.

Donnelly, James S. jr, *The great Irish potato famine* (Stroud: Sutton, 2001).

——'Famine and government response, 1845–6' in W. E. Vaughan (ed.), *A new history of Ireland*, v: *Ireland under the Union, I: 1801–70* (Oxford: Clarendon Press, 1989), pp. 272–85.

—— 'The administration of relief, 1846–7' in W. E. Vaughan (ed.), *A new history of Ireland*, v: *Ireland under the Union, I: 1801–70* (Oxford: Clarendon Press, 1989), pp. 294–306.

——'The soup kitchens' in W. E. Vaughan (ed.), *A new history of Ireland*, v: *Ireland under the Union, I: 1801–70* (Oxford: Clarendon Press, 1989), pp. 307–15.

——'The administration of relief, 1847–51' in W. E. Vaughan (ed.), *A new history of Ireland*, v: *Ireland under the Union, I: 1801–70* (Oxford: Clarendon Press, 1989), pp. 316–25.

—— 'Landlord and tenants' in W. E. Vaughan (ed.), *A new history of Ireland*, v: *Ireland under the Union, I: 1801–70* (Oxford: Clarendon Press, 1989), pp. 332–49.

—— 'The Kenmare estates during the nineteenth century: part 1', *Kerry Archaeological and Historical Society Journal*, 21 (1988), pp. 5–41.

Duncan, William R., and Paula E. Scully, *Marriage breakdown in Ireland: law and practice* (Dublin: Butterworths, 1990)

Edwards, Ruth Dudley, and T. Desmond Williams (eds.), *The great famine: studies in Irish history, 1845–52* (Dublin: Browne and Nolan, 1956).

English, Barbara, and John Saville, 'Family settlements and the "rise of the great estates" ', *Economic History Review*, 33:4 (1980), pp. 556–8.

Erickson, Amy Louise, 'Property and widowhood in England 1660–1840' in Sandra Cavallo and Lyndan Warner (eds.), *Widowhood in medieval and early modern Europe* (Harlow: Longman, 1999), pp. 145–63.

—— *Women and property in early modern England* (London: Routledge, 1993).

——'Common law versus common practice: the use of marriage settlements in early modern England', *Economic History Review*, second series, 53:1 (1990) pp. 21–39.

Faloon, W. Harris, *The marriage law of Ireland* (Dublin: Hodges and Figgis, 1881).

Finch, Janet, et al, *Wills inheritance and families* (Oxford: Oxford University Press, 1996).

Fitzgerald, Brian, *Lady Louisa Conolly, 1743–1821: an Anglo-Irish biography* (London: Staples Press, 1950).

—— *Emily Duchess of Leinster 1731–1814: a study of her life and times* (London: Staples Press, 1949).

Froide, Amy, 'Marital status as a category of difference: singlewomen and widows in early modern England' in Judith M. Bennett and Amy M. Froide (eds),

Singlewomen in the European past, 1250–1800 (Philadelphia: University of Pennsylvania Press, 1999), pp. 236–69.

Goldsmith, Elizabeth C. (ed.), *Writing the female voice: essays on epistolary literature* (London: Pinter, 1989).

Goody, Jack, 'Inheritance, property and women: some comparative considerations' in Jack Goody et al (eds.), *Family and inheritance: rural society in Western Europe, 1200–1800* (Cambridge: Cambridge University Press, 1976), pp. 10–36.

Gordon, Mary, *Chase of the wild goose* (New York: Arno Press, 1975).

Grattan, Sheena, 'Of pin money and paraphernalia, the widows shilling and a free ride to mass: one hundred and fifty years of property for the Irish wife' in Norma Dawson et al (eds.) *One hundred and fifty years of Irish law* (Belfast: SLS Legal Publications, 1996), pp. 213–38.

Green, E. R. R., *The industrial archaeology of County Down* (Belfast: Her Majesty's Stationery Office, 1965).

Habakkuk, H. J., 'Marriage settlements in the eighteenth century', *Transactions of the Royal Historical Society*, fourth series, 32 (1950), pp. 15–30.

Hamilton, C. J., *Notable Irishwomen* (Dublin: Sealey, Bryers and Company, 1904).

Harrison, A. T., 'The first Marquis of Dufferin and Ava: whig, Ulster landlord and imperial statesman' (D.Phil. thesis, University of Ulster, 1983).

Hayton, David W., 'Exclusion, conformity, and parliamentary representation: the impact of the sacramental test on Irish dissenting politics' in Kevin Herlihy (ed.), *The politics of Irish dissent, 1650–1800* (Dublin: Four Courts Press, 1997), pp. 52–73.

Hill, Bridget, *Women alone: spinsters in England 1660–1850* (New Haven and London: Yale University Press, 2001).

Hill, George, *An historical account of the MacDonnells of Antrim* (Belfast: Glens of Antrim Historical Society, 1873).

Holcombe, L., *Wives and property: reform of the married women's property law in nineteenth-century England* (Toronto: University of Toronto Press, 1983).

Hufton, Olwen, *The prospect before her: a history of women in Western Europe*, i: *1500–1800* (London: Harper Collins, 1995).

Hughes, T. Jones, 'Historical geography of Ireland from c. 1700' in G. L. H. Davies (ed.), *Irish geography* (Dublin: Geographical Society of Ireland, 1984), pp. 149–66

Hyde, H. Montgomery, *The Londonderrys: a family portrait*, (London: H. Hamilton, 1979).

Ingram, Martin, *Church courts, sex and marriage in England, 1570–1640* (Cambridge: Cambridge University Press, 1987).

Innes, Joanna, 'State, Church and voluntarism in European welfare, 1690–1850' in Hugh Cunningham and Joanna Innes (eds.), *Charity, philanthropy and reform from the 1690s to 1850* (Basingstoke: Macmillan, 1998), pp. 15–65.

Jalland, P., *Women, marriage and politics 1860–1914* (Oxford: Oxford University Press, 1988).

Jephson, Henry, 'Irish statute reform', *Journal of the Statistical and Social Inquiry Society of Ireland*, 25 (July 1879), pp. 375–85.

Jupp, Peter, 'County Down elections 1783–1831', *Irish Historical Studies*, 18 (1972–73), pp. 177–206.

Kelly, James, 'The abduction of women of fortune in eighteenth-century Ireland', *Eighteenth-Century Ireland*, 9 (1994), pp. 7–43.

Kinealy, Christine, 'The poor law during the Great Famine: an administration in crisis' in Margaret E. Crawford (ed.), *Famine: the Irish experience 900–1900* (Edinburgh: J. Donald, 1989), pp. 157–75.

Lanser, Susan S., 'Singular politics: the rise of the British nation and the production of the old maid' in Judith M. Bennett and Amy M. Froide (eds.), *Singlewomen in the European past, 1250–1800* (Philadelphia: University of Pennsylvania Press, 1999), pp. 297–323.

Large, David, 'The wealth of the greater Irish landowners, 1750–1815', *Irish Historical Studies*, 15 (1966–67), pp. 21–47.

Laurence, Anne, *Women in England, 1500–1760: a social history* (London: Weidenfeld and Nicolson, 1994).

Lebstock, Suzanne, *The free women of Petersburg: status and culture in a southern town, 1764–1800* (New York: W. W. Norton and Company, 1984).

Lemmings, David, 'Marriage and the law in the eighteenth century: Hardwicke's Marriage Act of 1753', *Historical Journal*, 39:2 (1996), pp. 339–60.

Leneman, Leah, 'Wives and mistresses in eighteenth-century Scotland', *Women's History Review*, 8:4 (1999), pp. 671–92.

——'English marriages and Scottish divorces in the early nineteenth-century', *Journal of Legal History*, 17:3 (December 1996), pp. 225–43.

Lewins, Frederick Albert, *A practical treatise on the law of trusts* (London: Sweets and Maxwell, 1879).

Liddington, Jill, *Female fortune, land gender and authority: the Anne Lister diaries and other writings, 1833–36* (London: Rivers Oram, 1998).

Lindsay, Deirdre, 'The sick and indigent roomkeeper's society' in David Dickson (ed.), *The gorgeous mask: Dublin 1700–1850* (Dublin: Trinity History Workshop, 1987), pp. 132–56.

Luddy, Maria, 'Religion, philanthropy and the state in late eighteenth and early nineteenth-century Ireland' in Hugh Cunningham and Joanna Innes (eds.), *Charity, philanthropy and reform from the 1690s to 1850* (Basingstoke: Macmillan Press, 1998), pp. 148–67.

—— 'Women and charitable organisations in nineteenth century Ireland', *Women's Studies International Forum*, 11:4 (1988), pp. 301–5.

Lyall, Andrew, 'The Irish House of Lords as a judicial body, 1783–1800', *The Irish Jurist*, new series, 28–30 (1993–95), pp. 314–60.

Lyall, Sir, Alfred Comyn, *The life of the Marquis of Dufferin and Ava* (London: J. Murray, 1905).

MacCurtain, Margaret, 'Marriage in Tudor Ireland' in Art Cosgrove (ed.), *Marriage in Ireland* (Dublin: College Press, 1985), pp. 51–66.

MacDonagh, Oliver, 'Ireland and the Union, 1801–70' in W. E. Vaughan (ed.), *A new history of Ireland, v: Ireland under the Union, I: 1801–70,* (Oxford: Clarendon Press, 1989), pp. xlvii–lxv.

—— 'The economy and society, 1830–45' in W. E. Vaughan (ed.), *A new history of Ireland, v: Ireland under the Union, I: 1801–70* (Oxford: Clarendon Press, 1989), pp. 218–41.

Maguire, W.A., *Living like a lord: the second Marquis of Donegall, 1769–1844*

(Belfast: Appletree Press and the Ulster Society for Irish Historical Studies, 1984).

—— 'The 1822 settlement of the Donegall estates', *Irish Economic and Social History*, 3 (1976), pp. 17–32.

—— *The Downshire estates in Ireland 1801–1845: the management of Irish landed estates in the nineteenth century* (Oxford: Clarendon Press, 1972).

Malcomson, A. P. W., *The pursuit of the heiress: aristocratic marriage in Ireland 1740–1840* (Belfast: Ulster Historical Foundation, 2006).

—— 'A woman scorned? Theodosia, Countess of Clanwilliam (1743–1817)', *Familia*, 15 (1999), pp. 1–25.

—— 'The gentle leviathan: Arthur Hill, second Marquess of Downshire, 1753–1801' in Peter Roebuck (ed.), *Plantation to partition: essays in Ulster history in honour of J.L.McCracken* (Belfast: Blackstaff Press, 1981), pp. 102–18.

—— *John Foster: the politics of the Anglo-Irish ascendancy* (Oxford: Oxford University Press, 1978).

—— 'Absenteeism in eighteenth century Ireland', *Irish Economic and Social History*, 1 (1974), pp. 15–35.

—— 'The Earl of Clermont: a forgotten Co. Monaghan magnate of the late eighteenth century', *Clogher Record*, 8 (1973), pp. 19–72.

—— *The extraordinary career of the second Earl of Massereene, 1743–1805* (Belfast: Her Majesty's Stationery Office, 1972).

MacQueen, John Fraser, *The rights and liabilities of husband and wife* (Dublin: Hodges and Smith, 1848).

Elizabeth Mavor, *The ladies of Llangollen: a study in romantic friendship* (London: Penguin, 2001).

McDowell, R. B., *The Irish administration, 1801–1914* (London: Routledge, 1964).

—— 'Ireland on the eve of the Famine' in R. Dudley Edwards and T. Desmond Williams (eds.), *The Great Famine: studies in Irish history, 1845–52* (Dublin: Browne and Nolan, 1962), pp. 3–86.

Newark, F. H., *Notes on Irish legal history* (Belfast: M. Boyd, 1960).

Nicholson, Harold, *Helen's Tower* (London: Constable and Company, 1937).

O'Carroll, Joseph, 'Contemporary attitudes towards the homeless poor 1725–1775' in David Dickson (ed.), *The gorgeous mask* (Dublin: Trinity History Workshop, 1987), pp. 64–85.

O'Dowd, Mary, *A history of women in Ireland 1500–1800* (Harlow: Longman, 2005).

—— 'Women and the law in early modern Ireland' in Christine Meek (ed.) *Women in renaissance and early modern Ireland* (Dublin: Four Courts Press, 2000), pp. 95–108.

—— 'Women and the Irish chancery court in the late sixteenth and early seventeenth centuries', *Irish Historical Studies*, 31 (November 1999), pp. 470–87.

Ollard, S. L., Cross, Gordon, and Bond, Maurice F. (eds.), *A dictionary of English church history* (London: Mowbray, 1948).

Osbourough, W. N., 'The legislation of the pre-Union Irish parliament' in W. N. Osborough (ed.), *Studies in Irish legal history* (Dublin: Four Courts Press, 1999), pp. 81–100.

Phair, P. H., 'Guide to the Registry of Deeds', *Analecta Hibernica*, 23 (1966), pp. 259–76.

Poovey, Mary, *Uneven developments: the ideological work of gender in mid-Victorian England* (London: Virago, 1989).

Proudfoot, L., 'Landownership and improvement c 1700–1845' in L. Proudfoot (ed.), *Down: history and society: interdisciplinary essays on the history of an Irish county* (Dublin: Geography Publications, 1997), pp. 203–38.

Raughter, Rosemary, 'A natural tenderness: women and philanthropy in eighteenth-century Ireland' (MA thesis, University College Dublin, 1985).

Rendall, Jane, *The origins of modern feminism: women in Britain, France and the United States, 1780–1860* (Basingstoke: Macmillan, 1985).

Reynolds, K. D., *Aristocratic women and political society in Victorian Britain* (Oxford: Clarendon Press, 1998).

Roebuck, Peter, 'Rent movement, proprietorial incomes and agricultural development, 1730–1830' in Peter Roebuck (ed.), *Plantation to partition: essays in Ulster history in honour of J. L. McCracken* (Belfast: Blackstaff Press, 1981), pp. 82–101.

Salmon, Marylynn, *Women and the law of property in Early America* (Chapel Hill and London: University of North Carolina Press, 1986)

Scott, Sarah, *Millenium Hall* (Ontario: Broadview Press, 1995).

Shanley, Mary Lyndon, *Feminism, marriage and the law in Victorian England, 1850–1895* (London: Tauris, 1989).

Shoemaker, R. B., *Gender in English society 1650–1850: the emergence of separate spheres?* (London: Longman, 1998).

Simms, J. G., 'The restoration, 1660–85' in T. W. Moody, F. X. Martin and F. J. Byrne (eds.), *A new history of Ireland*, iii: *Early modern Ireland 1534–1691* (Oxford: Clarendon Press, 1991), pp. 420–53.

Smith, Bonnie, *Ladies of the leisure class: the bourgeoise of northern France in the nineteenth century* (Princeton: Princeton University Press, 1981).

Spring, Eileen, *Law, land and family: aristocratic inheritance in England, 1300–1800* (London: Chapel Hill, 1993).

—— 'The strict settlement: its role in family history', *Economic History Review*, 41:3 (1988), pp. 454–60.

—— 'Law and the theory of the effective family', *Albion*, 16 (1984), pp. 1–20.

—— 'The family, strict settlement and historians', *Canadian Journal of History* 18 (December 1983), pp. 379–98.

Staves, Susan, 'Resentment or resignation? Dividing the spoils among daughters and younger sons' in John Brewer and Susan Staves (eds.), *Early modern conceptions of property* (London: Routledge, 1995), pp. 194–218.

——*Married women's separate property in England, 1660–1833* (London and Cambridge, Massachusetts: Harvard University Press, 1990).

—— 'Separate maintenance contracts', *Eighteenth-Century Life*, 11 (1987), pp. 78–101.

—— 'Pin money', *Studies in Eighteenth-Century Culture*, 14 (1985), pp. 47–77.

Stewart, Edith, Marchioness of Londonderry, *Frances Anne: the life and times of Frances Anne Marchioness of Londonderry and her husband Charles, third Marquess of Londonderry* (London: Macmillan, 1958).

Stone, Lawrence, *Broken lives: separation and divorce in England 1660–1857* (Oxford: Oxford University Press, 1993).

—— *Road to divorce: England, 1530–1987* (Oxford: Oxford University Press, 1990).

——*An open elite? England 1540–1880* (Oxford: Clarendon Press, 1984).

——*The family, sex and marriage in England, 1500–1800* (London: Weidenfeld and Nicolson, 1977).

——*The crisis of the aristocracy, 1558–1641* (Oxford: Clarendon Press, 1965).

Stretton, Tim, *Women waging law in Elizabethan England* (Cambridge: Cambridge University Press, 1998).

Sweet, Katherine Warner, 'Widowhood, custom and property in early modern north Wales', *Welsh History Review,* 18:2 (December 1996), pp. 189–227.

Tillyard, Stella, *Aristocrats: Caroline, Emily, Louisa and Sarah Lennox, 1740–1832* (London: Vintage, 1995).

Todd, Barbara J., 'The remarrying widow: a stereotype reconsidered' in Mary Prior (ed.), *Women in English society 1500–1800* (London: Methuen, 1985), pp. 54–92.

Twigger, Robert, 'Inflation: the value of the pound, 1750–1998'. House of Commons Library Research Paper 99/20, 23 February 1999, p. 10; online at www.parliament.uk/commons/lib/research/rp99/rp99–020.pdf. (accessed 12 November 2007).

Vann, Richard T., 'Wills and the family in an English town: Banbury, 1550–1800', *Journal of Family History,* 4 (winter 1979), pp. 346–67.

Vaughan, W. E., *Landlords and tenants in Ireland, 1848–1904* (Dublin: Economic and Social History Society of Ireland, 1984).

Vickery, A., *The gentleman's daughter: women's lives in Georgian England* (London and New Haven: Yale University Press, 1998).

Waugh, Scott L., *The lordship of England: royal wardships and marriages in English society and politics 1217–1327* (Princeton, New Jersey: Princeton University Press, 1988).

Weiner, Margaret, *Matters of felony: a reconstruction* (London: Heinemann, 1967).

Wood, Henry, *A guide to the records deposited in the Public Records Office of Ireland* (Dublin: His Majesty's Stationery Office, 1919).

Wylie, J. C. W., *Irish land law* (Abingdon: Professional, 1986).

Index